Writing a Translation Com

This essential textbook is a step-by-step guide to how to write a self-reflective translation commentary, a key requirement of most courses on translation.

Starting with the source text analysis, it guides students in how to set out a translation strategy and goes through the most common challenging issues encountered, thus enabling them to set out their translation priorities in an informed manner. Throughout each chapter, there are boxes summarising key concepts and suggestions of tasks and activities, as well as recommendations for further reading. The book is supplemented by online resources for students and teachers on the translation studies portal (www.routledgetranslationstudiesportal.com). There are nine PowerPoints based on the chapters of the book that could be used for teaching or self-study. There are also downloadable versions of sample assessment rubrics, tables for example selection, and checklists. Based on real life examples of students' work in different language combinations, drawing on the author's years of experience of teaching commentary writing, this book focuses on several types of language mediation that go beyond the written word, such as interpreting, audiovisual translation, localisation, and transcreation.

This is a vital textbook for students writing commentaries on translation and interpreting courses, a useful resource for supervisors providing students with guidance on how to write a balanced, articulate, and convincing commentary, and a handy reference for professional translators and interpreters needing to explain their translation decisions to clients.

Penélope Johnson is an Associate Professor in the School of Modern Languages and Cultures at Durham University. She is currently the co-director of the MA in Translation Studies at Durham University. She has published articles on poetry translation, translating multilingual texts, and translator training. She has recently translated into Spanish the fact-based novel by Kim Kupperman (2018), *Five Thousand Miles to Home*.

Routledge Introductions to Translation and Interpreting

Series Editor:
Sergey Tyulenev is the Director of the MA in Translation and Russian Studies at the School of Modern Languages and Cultures, Durham University, UK.
Advisory Board
Luise von Flotow, University of Ottawa, Canada
Ricardo Munoz Martin, University of Bologna, Italy
Kobus Marais, University of the Free State, South Africa
Nike K. Pokorn, University of Ljubljana, Slovenia
James St André, Chinese University of Hong Kong, China
Michaela Wolf, University of Graz, Austria

Routledge Introductions to Translation and Interpreting is a series of textbooks, designed to meet the need for teaching materials for translator/interpreter training. Accessible and aimed at beginning students but also useful for instructors designing and teaching courses, the series covers a broad range of topics, many of which are already core courses while others cover new directions of translator/interpreter teaching.

The series reflects the standards of the translator/interpreter training and professional practice set out by national and international competence frameworks and codes of translation/language service provision and are aimed at a global readership.

All topics combine both practical and theoretical aspects so as to ensure a bridging of the gap between the academic and professional world and all titles include a range of pedagogical support: activities, case studies etc.

Most recent titles in the series:

Translation Project Management
Callum Walker

Translation Ethics
Joseph Lambert

Translation Tools and Technologies
Andrew Rothwell, Joss Moorkens, Maria Fernández Parra, Joanna Drugan and Frank Austermuehl

Writing a Translation Commentary
Penélope Johnson

For more information on any of these and other titles, or to order, please go to https://www.routledge.com/Routledge-Introductions-to-Translation-and-Interpreting/book-series/RITI
Additional resources for Translation and Interpreting Studies are available on the Routledge Translation Studies Portal: http://routledgetranslationstudiesportal.com/

Writing a Translation Commentary

Penélope Johnson

Routledge
Taylor & Francis Group

LONDON AND NEW YORK

Designed cover image: © Getty Images

First published 2024
by Routledge
4 Park Square, Milton Park, Abingdon, Oxon OX14 4RN

and by Routledge
605 Third Avenue, New York, NY 10158

Routledge is an imprint of the Taylor & Francis Group, an informa business

British Library Cataloguing-in-Publication Data
A catalogue record for this book is available from the British Library

ISBN: 978-1-032-22704-7 (hbk)
ISBN: 978-1-032-22703-0 (pbk)
ISBN: 978-1-003-27379-0 (ebk)

DOI: 10.4324/9781003273790

Typeset in Sabon
by Deanta Global Publishing Services, Chennai, India.

Access the Support Material: www.routledgetranslationstudiesportal.com

To Betty and Tonecho

Without whom I would not be where I am today.

Contents

List of Appendices   *viii*
Series editor's foreword   *ix*
Acknowledgements   *xi*

Introduction   1

PART I
Before translating   7

1   Source text analysis   9

2   Statement of the translation strategy   33

PART II
While translating   59

3   Selecting illustrative examples   61

4   Writing your commentary   90

5   Writing your commentary in practice   113

PART III
Beyond the written word   143

6   Writing a reflective report for interpreting   145

7   Writing a reflective report for audiovisual translation,
    localisation, and transcreation   173

Afterword   *201*
Appendices   *203*
Index   *227*

Appendices

Appendix 1   Table for example selection   203
Appendix 2   Sample assessment rubric for a translation
              commentary   205
Appendix 3   Translation commentary checklist   210
Appendix 4   Sample assessment rubric for an interpreting
              reflective report (with a focus on error
              detection and analysis)   212
Appendix 5   Sample assessment rubric for an interpreting
              reflective report   214
Appendix 6   Interpreting reflective report checklist   219
Appendix 7   Sample assessment rubric for a reflective
              report for audiovisual translation,
              localisation, or transcreation   221
Appendix 8   Checklist for a reflective report for
              audiovisual translation, localisation,
              or transcreation.   225

Series editor's foreword

Translator and interpreter training programmes have become an integral feature of the present-day professional educational landscape all over the world. There are at least two good reasons for that. On the one hand, it has been realised that to work as a translator or interpreter, one needs more than to speak a couple of languages; a special training in translation and interpreting is a must. On the other hand, translator/interpreter training programmes are seen as a practical way to start a career in the language-service provision industry or to earn a degree as a Translation/Interpreting Studies scholar. These programmes may be part of the university curriculum or stand-alone courses in various formats of continuing studies or qualification upgrading.

Yet there is still a dearth of teaching materials geared at novices in translation or interpreting. In every class, students are either given sheaves of handouts which, by the end of the course, build up into a pile of paper or are referred to a small library of publications for a chapter here and a chapter there. As a result, the student struggles to imagine the subject area as a coherent whole and there is no helpful textbook for references while in the course or after.

The lack of coursebooks makes life little easier for translator/interpreter trainers. Even if they find a suitable book or monograph, a great deal of adaptation must be done. The instructor would have to adjust the book to the length of the course and individual teaching sessions, to add exercises and assignments, questions, and topics for presentations to facilitate students' engagement with the materials and to help them go beyond the 'read-only' mode of working with the recommended book(s).

The purport of the *Routledge Introductions to Translation and Interpreting* series is to put into the hands of the translator/interpreter trainee and trainer ready-made textbooks. Each textbook is written by an expert or a team of experts in the subject area under discussion; moreover, each author has vast experience of teaching the subject of their textbook. The series reflects what have already become staple courses and modules in the translator/interpreter training – but it also introduces new areas of teaching and research. The series is meant as a kind of library of textbooks – all books present various aspects of a translation and interpreting training programme viewed as a whole. They can be taken as a basis for developing new programmes and courses or reinforcing the existing ones.

The present textbook is on translation commentary. All translator/interpreter training programmes ask their students to explain and justify their translation or interpreter decisions. In the majority of programmes, producing commentaries is a part of the mandatory assignments, whether performed orally in classroom discussions or in writing in formative and summative tests and/or exams. Paradoxically, the student can find few publications that would provide guidance on what translation commentary is, what elements and components it may be comprised of, and what criteria might be applied to its assessment. Even fewer are of an accessible and systematic nature, leaving the student with some, more or less helpful, ad hoc pieces of advice offered by his or her teacher, who, in turn, may be equally perplexed by how to verbalise in an orderly manner an assortment of dos and don'ts and the rationale behind all of them.

Both students of translation and interpreting and their instructors will find in the textbook written by Dr Penélope Johnson both a comprehensive and comprehensible guide to translation commentary. Relying on her own and her colleagues' collective experience and expertise, Dr Johnson elucidates what translation commentary is, why it is needed, what forms it may take, and how to write and assess it. Moreover, she discusses not only commentary on written translation but also on interpreting and such key contemporary translational practices as audiovisual translation, localisation, and transcreation. The textbook offers a great deal of exercises and topics for discussion that make it suitable for classroom learners and autodidacts alike.

Sergey Tyulenev
June 2023

Acknowledgements

First and foremost, I would like to thank the series editor, Dr Sergey Tyulenev (Durham University) for all the guidance, help, and support he gave me during the writing of this book. I would also like to thank Jin Huang (Durham University), Noelia Cacheiro Quintas (Newcastle University), Mercedes García de Quesada (Granada University), and my PhD student, Eva Corchado, who is also a professional transcreator, for sharing their experience on audiovisual translation, interpreting, and transcreation.

I am particularly indebted to the 2020/21 cohort of the UG Spanish Translation module and the 2021/22 cohort MA in Translation Studies who, very kindly, gave permission to use their commentaries to include in this textbook. I would also like to thank all of my translation students, past and present, who allowed me to gain inspiration and try out the ideas for this book.

I would also like to thank all my friends and colleagues for their constant support and encouragement. Finally, I would like to thank my husband, John, for his patience, help, and support, and my children, Ian and Neil, who gave me constant encouragement.

Introduction

Despite the fact that most Masters of Arts in Translation, at least in the UK, include a translation project and a commentary as a way of assessment (which is also the case in many undergraduate translation modules), and although there are several books that students can resort to for guidance on how to proceed when writing a commentary (such as Routledge's *Thinking Translation* series), there are hardly any textbooks dedicated explicitly and specifically to the writing of a translation commentary.

Therefore, this textbook aims to provide guidance on how to write a translation commentary that is a coherent academic piece of writing, underpinned by theoretical concepts and illustrative examples, where students can present their rationale and justification for the translation decisions taken. Commentaries or reflective reports are not as widely used as a form of assessment in interpreting, audiovisual translation, localisation, and transcreation, as is the case with translation. Nevertheless, this textbook still provides guidance on writing them, following similar principles to the writing of a translation commentary.

This textbook can be used for self-study, or as a complementary manual to be used in practical translation courses. It can also be used as a resource that supervisors may want to refer their supervisees to for guidance on how to write a balanced, articulate, and convincing commentary or reflective report. It might also be useful for professional translators and interpreters, when explaining, for example, their translation decisions to their clients, which is often required in the case of localisation and transcreation, for instance.

This textbook is underpinned by theories on translator training, previous studies on translation commentaries, and relevant Translation Studies theories. It is also based on cognitive theories such as Bloom's taxonomy (1956) and issues of Higher Order Thinking (HOTS) and Lower Order Thinking (LOTS); social constructivism (Kilary 2000), which focuses on the learner constructing knowledge through interactions with others; theories on academic writing (Bacha 2002; Cottrell 2019; Zamel 1987); and experiential learning (Kolb 2014) with Kolb's experiential four-staged learning cycle (2014: 43–44), which is a recursive process that includes: experiencing, reflecting, thinking, and acting.

DOI: 10.4324/9781003273790-1

0.1 Rationale for using a translation commentary or a reflective report for language professionals training and assessment

Bloom's taxonomy (Bloom 1956) covers different levels of learning, going from the low to the higher level. In the lowest level, students would mainly recall or repeat information, while at the highest level they will create, construct, and develop. The six levels are organised as follows:

1. Remembering.
2. Understanding.
3. Applying.
4. Analysing.
5. Evaluating.
6. Creating.

Hence, at level 1, students remember the information, at level 2 they can explain ideas and concepts, at level 3 they can apply the information in different contexts or in new ways, at level 4 they can compare, contrast, and criticise the different parts, at level 5 they can argue, appraise, and justify their decisions, and at level 6 they can construct or create a new product or formulate a new point of view.

The three last levels are considered to be higher order thinking skills or HOTS, and the three lower levels are lower order thinking skills or LOTS. A commentary or reflective will help you move from the lowest to the highest levels of learning. Any reflective activities such as these activate higher order thinking skills, hence enhancing your educational experience. As Mazzei and Aibo (2022: 33) claim, '[t]he more obvious way to foster meta-cognitive skills in translation and interpreting students is to require them to produce journals, reflections, and self-assessment of their practice.'

When you first start writing a translation commentary or reflective report, it may seem time consuming and slow, but it is arguably the most efficient way of learning the necessary skills to be an informed translator and interpreter. The analysis, reflection, and decision-making processes will gradually become second nature. Adab (2000: 219) gives a particularly good analogy of this when we are learning how to drive and 'have to be able to undertake various independent procedures (such as changing gear, controlling speed, looking in the mirror), without losing sight of the overall purpose towards which these processes all contribute – namely, being a safe driver.' However, once you pass your test and become an experienced driver, you do all of these things without really having to think about them. In the same way, by practising writing translation commentaries and reflective reports while training, you will eventually be able to activate your critical and analytical skills and carry out these tasks almost in autopilot.

Writing a commentary or reflective report is valuable not only as a way to demonstrate that the learning outcomes of a particular module or assessment task have been satisfied, but, more importantly, as a way of acquiring the tools necessary to make informed and justified decisions when translating or interpreting. A translation commentary or reflective report is the link between translation theories and practice, which facilitate the development of confident and skilled translators and interpreters.

Learning 'requires self-reflection on learning' and is also 'lifelong and lifewide' (Washbourne 2022: 10). Writing a translation commentary or a reflective report allows you to reflect on your own learning and become a self-regulated student. The concept of self-regulated students is underpinned by socio-constructivist theories which put you, as a student, in the centre of the learning process (Postigo Pinazo 2008: 174). The learning occurs through reflective practice in combination with both peer and instructor feedback (Mazzei and Aibo 2022: 32). This self-regulation can be provided with a reflective report, which will give you the opportunity to develop lifelong learning skills and could, ideally, still be used after becoming a certified professional (Shreve 2006: 32). A combination of traditional proficiency tests with a portfolio which includes a self-assessment report makes the assessment more comprehensive and holistic (Sawyer 2004: 225).

Apart from the above, learning to translate and write commentaries teaches students many valuable transferrable skills, such as, for example, developing an eye for detail, which will enable you to produce a publishable text. Your teachers' insistence on observing all the requirements is not a whim or fault-finding but aims to prepare you for the most professional performance in today's competitive translation/interpreting industry.

0.2 How to use this book

This textbook is aimed at both undergraduate and postgraduate students as well as instructors of Translation and Interpreting, not only at universities in English speaking countries but also beyond the Anglophone world. Although many of the examples are in English, efforts have been taken for them to be applicable to any language combination.

Throughout this textbook, particularly in the first five chapters, which are dedicated to writing a translation commentary, you will be directed to the Routledge's *Thinking Translation* series, which is considered to be complementary and has a focus on actual translating. This series includes books in several language combinations. However, if your particular language combination is not covered in the series, you will still benefit greatly by reading them. In fact, even if it is covered by the series, it is still a good idea to read the rest of the books, as then you will get different perspectives about the issues at hand.

It might also be a good idea to familiarise yourself, or brush up on, text stylistics of the languages you work with so that you understand fully the terminology used in this textbook. Each chapter starts with a list of key concepts, has tasks and activities throughout, and finishes with a summary of the main points discussed. Some of these activities may have to be done before reading a particular section of the book. The reasons for this are pedagogical, as it will make you think about the issues discussed before reading about them, thus activating the higher order thinking skills mentioned above. Many of the activities are to be done in groups, but they could also be easily done individually if, for example, you are using this textbook as self-study.

0.3 Guide to chapters

This textbook is divided into three parts:

Part I – Before Translating: The big picture, focuses on the source text (ST) analysis (Chapter 1) and formulation of a translation strategy (Chapter 2). More specifically, **Chapter 1** provides a rationale as to why it is important to carry out a ST analysis; then it takes us through identifying the ST's genre, text type, skopos, intended readership, and medium of publication. **Chapter 2** provides a guide for formulating a translation strategy and setting up translation priorities by mirroring the issues looked at in Chapter 1.

Part II – While translating: The specifics, focuses on how to make a selection of illustrative examples for discussion (Chapter 3); on how to write and structure a translation commentary (Chapter 4), and on managing your time and fulfilling the assessment criteria (Chapter 5). More specifically, **Chapter 3** discusses the desirable and undesirable features of a translation commentary and guides us through how best to select illustrative examples and categorise them by loosely following some of the matrices of Routledge's *Thinking Translation* series. **Chapter 4** looks at different structures of a translation commentary and provides suggestions on how best to integrate illustrative examples and relevant translation studies theories and concepts, into a coherent narrative. **Chapter 5** provides practical advice such as managing your time, preparing for supervision sessions, and selecting a ST if required.

Part III – Beyond the written word, is dedicated to writing reflective reports for interpreting (Chapter 6) audiovisual translation, localisation, and transcreation (Chapter 7). More specifically, **Chapter 6** looks at the differences between translation and interpreting and the different skills set necessary for each discipline, then, after discussing the rationale for using a reflective report in the training and assessing of interpreting, it provides suggestions on how to write them. **Chapter 7** discusses the use of a reflective report for audiovisual translation, localisation, and transcreation training and suggests how best to go about writing it.

0.4 List of acronyms

SC	Source culture
SL	Source language
SC/L	Source culture/language
ST	Source text

TC	Target culture
TL	Target language
TC/L	Target culture/language
TT	Target text

List of references

Adab, Beverly (2000) 'Evaluating Translation Competence.' in Christina Schäffner and Beverly Adab (eds) *Developing Translation Competence*. Amsterdam and Philadelphia: John Benjamins, 215–228.

Bacha, Nahla N. (2002) 'Developing Learners' Academic Writing Skills in Higher Education: A Study for Educational Reform', *Language and Education*, 16: 161–177.

Bloom, Benjamin S. (1956) *Taxonomy of Educational Objectives: The Classification of Educational Goals. Handbook 1, Cognitive Domain*. Michigan: Association of College and University Examiners.

Cottrell, Stella (2019) *The Study Skills Handbook*, 5th ed. London: Bloomsbury Academic.

Kiraly, Donald C. (2000) *A Social Constructivist Approach to Translator Education: Empowerment from Theory to Practice*. Manchester: St. Jerome.

Kolb, David (2014) *Experiential Learning: Experience as the Source of Learning and Development*. Englewood Cliff, NJ: Prentice Hall.

Mazzei, Cristiano and Laurence Jay-Rayon Ibrahim Aibo (2022) *The Routledge Guide to Teaching Translation and Interpreting Online*. London and New York: Routledge.

Postigo Pinazo, Encarnación (2008) 'Self-Assessment in Teaching Interpreting', *TTR*, 21: 1: 173–209.

Sawyer, David B. (2004) *Fundamental Aspects of Interpreter Education*. Amsterdam and Philadelphia: John Benjamins.

Shreve, Gregory M. (2006) 'The Deliberate Practice: Translation and Expertise', *Journal of Translation Studies*, 9: 1: 27–42.

Washbourne, Kelly (2022) 'Introduction', in Cristiano Mazzei and Laurence Jay-Rayon Ibrahim Aibo (eds) *The Routledge Guide to Teaching Translation and Interpreting Online*. London and New York: Routledge, 1–13.

Zamel, Vivian (1987) 'Recent Research on Writing Pedagogy', *TESOL Quarterly*, 21: 697–712.

Part I
Before translating
The big picture

1 Source text analysis

Key concepts

- The importance of source text (ST) analysis and contextual information.
- Skopos (function or purpose).
- Genre and text type.
- Intended audience or readership.
- Medium of publication.
- Use of paratextual devices.
- Salient features of the ST.
- Tone and effect on the ST's intended readership.

Task 1.1

Think about, or discuss in small groups, the following questions:

1. In your opinion, is it important to analyse the ST before starting to translate? Why?
2. In what ways would this analysis help us with our translation?
3. What aspects should we look at in the analysis?
4. Which of the aspects you mention above do you consider more important?

1.1 Introduction

The general advice given by most of the literature (Nord 2005; Carreres et al. 2018; Andrews and Maksimova 2009: 3; Cragie et al. 2015: 185; Dickins et al. 2016: 285; Haywood et al. 2009: 265; Hervey and Higgins 2002: 260–261) is that a ST analysis will allow us to decide what features of the ST are the most salient and what relevance they have for the creation of meaning, which will help us minimise the loss that inevitably takes place in translation as well as help justify our translation decisions. Therefore, a careful reading

DOI: 10.4324/9781003273790-3

of the ST combined with this analysis will deepen our understanding of it (Carreres et al. 2018: 23–24). It will allow us to prioritise and rank certain features of the ST and sacrifice others, if we need to do so, in line with our translation strategy (discussed in Chapter 2). In other words, the ST analysis will inform our translation strategy.

Even though it might not be possible to provide a model of ST analysis that is applicable to all text types, we can still create a list of the issues that we can analyse, regardless of the ST text type, since many of these issues are likely to be relevant to varying degrees in most text types and in most cultures.

The order of the ST analysis, which is reflected in the structure of this chapter, is not intended to be linear or chronological, although it has been ordered this way for methodological reasons. The conclusions reached with the analysis will be modified according to the findings made at different stages. For example, even though in this textbook the discussion of ST genre and text type comes very early in the analysis, in *Thinking Italian Translation* (Cragie et al. 2015) it is discussed in Chapter 11, because, in their opinion, the rest of the analysis will help us decide what genre or text type the ST belongs to. The important thing to do is to analyse the different aspects of the ST regardless of the order in which this is done.

As well as your translation strategy, the ST analysis will inform the decisions you make at the lower levels. It will more than likely bring to light challenges at different levels of the text and will allow you to plan and do the necessary research. For example, you might need to research unfamiliar terminology, or find out more about certain cultural references, idiomatic expressions, etc.

The ST analysis will be the starting point of the commentary. There is one important pitfall that needs to be avoided when articulating it, so that it can be integrated into the commentary in a clear and coherent manner. We need to be absolutely clear and explicit when we are discussing the ST and when we are talking about our translation. Therefore, it is imperative to avoid just simply referring to 'the text' and to specify whether we are referring to the ST or the target text (TT). This is why many institutions prefer students to structure the commentary by putting the ST analysis first and then the translation strategy. However, as we have seen in the introductory chapter, which will also be discussed further in Chapter 4, this is not the only way to structure a translation commentary.

Another important pitfall to avoid is to not dedicate too much of the space available, in terms of word count, to the ST analysis. This is a common mistake, particularly in the case of novice translators who are perhaps more familiar with literary studies. A good rule of thumb is for the ST analysis and statement of translation strategy combined to be about a third of the whole commentary, and for this third to be roughly equally divided into ST analysis and statement of translation strategy.

A final point to keep in mind is that by 'ST analysis,' we are not just referring to textual analysis. In order to have sufficient understanding of the ST to do an informed translation, we need some contextual information about the ST, its author(s), and the source culture (SC). Then we need to carry out the analysis at the macrolevel, looking at issues that are not within the text itself (such as for example, its skopos, intended reader, use of paratextual devices, etc.). Finally, the analysis of the textual features at the microlevel will allow us to identify the salient features of the ST, which in turn will help us decide our translation priorities (discussed in Chapter 2). The structure of this chapter is as follows: first we will look at the contextual information of the ST, then the analysis at the macrolevel (looking at genre, text type, skopos, intended readership, medium of publication, use of paratextual devices) and the analysis at the microlevel (looking at the subject matter, how to identify the salient characteristics of the ST, and the tone and effect on the reader).

Task 1.2

In small groups, put the points below in order of importance when doing an ST analysis. If, in your opinion, some of them have the same importance, indicate so and provide a rationale for your hierarchy.

- Contextual information.
- Skopos.
- Genre and text type.
- Intended audience or readership.
- Medium of publication.
- Theme, structure and tone.
- Use of paratextual devices.

1.2 Background information/contextualisation/ST author and SC context

---

Task 1.3

Think about, or discuss in small groups, the following questions:

1. Is it important to include background and/or contextual information about the ST author(s), the ST, and the SC in a translation commentary? Why?
2. In what ways would this information help us with our translation?
3. Which of the aspects you have mentioned above do you consider more important?

Contextual information may help us decide what the function or purpose of the ST is (Nord 2005: 42) and will also help us interpret its meaning in an informed way. Some translation briefs include contextual information, however, often these are either non-existent or incomplete. In other words, as we will discuss in Chapter 2, not every translation commission or assignment includes a brief. Cragie and Pattison (2018: 5) recommend doing some contextual research and 'to piece together the information and reassemble it logically.' Contextual information early on in your commentary will centre the readers and allow them to have a better understanding of your whole argument and the decisions taken.

You will need to spend some time doing research on the background and contextual information on the ST, its author(s) and the sociocultural and political situation of the SC at the time of the ST's publication (see Nord 2005: 50–52 and Carreres et al. 2018: 24, for some ideas on what questions to ask and where to find the information). This might be time consuming, but it will be time well invested, which will enhance your understanding of the ST, prevent misinterpretations, and inform your translation strategy. For example, if the time when the ST was published was some time ago, you will need to check that the norms for what is politically correct or not in the target culture (TC) are not different now and whether or not you will have to be sensitive about the choices you make in your translation (Pattison and Cragie 2022).

One thing to keep in mind, however, is that only a small percentage of the data gathered will be relevant to include in your commentary. This does not mean that you must ignore the information you have. In fact, it is recommended that you put your findings in writing in a coherent manner, as it will be a resource you might be able to use to interpret the text and to make informed translation decisions, like, for example, choosing between alternative solutions that are, at first sight, equally valid.

Due to space restrictions, you will need to select from this information only what is relevant for your commentary. In fact, it is not just due to space restrictions, but also the need to present the information in a precise, concise and relevant manner, which is one of the features typically assessed in commentary writing.

Obviously, the longer the commentary, the more background and contextual information you might be able to include. However, this does not mean that for a short commentary you need to do less contextual research. In other words, the background and contextual information will be a resource to inform your translation strategy and the translation techniques used at the microlevel.

Task 1.4

Activity 1

Please read the 3 excerpts below and identify where the contextual information is given. The first two excerpts are both part of a 5000-word commentary of a 10000-word translation project. The last excerpt is part of a 1000-word commentary of a 1000-word translation assignment.

Then discuss the following:

1. What contextual information has been given?
2. In your opinion, is all the contextual information relevant? Is any information missing? What would you delete and/or add?
3. Has it been written in a sufficiently precise and concise way? If not, please rephrase it.
4. The excerpt that is part of a 1000-word commentary has the same number of words and a similar amount of contextual information as the other two. Do you think this is appropriate? Why?

Excerpt 1

Part of a 5000-word commentary for a translation from English into Chinese.

ST: Cha, Frances (2020) *If I had your face*. New York: Ballantine Books.

If I Had Your Face, written by Korean American author Frances Cha, was first published by Ballantine Books in April 2020. Frances Cha graduated from the University of Columbia with a degree in Creative Writing and worked as an editor and journalist for the Cable News Network (Park and Greene, no date). She spent time in many different countries in her formative years –including Hong Kong, the United States and Korea – in which she witnessed numerous incidents of both invisible and blatant discrimination against women because of their appearances, inspiring her to reflect deeply on the social causes of the cosmetic surgery craze. According to Cha, people often view women – especially Korean women – who have had cosmetic surgery as superficial and vain without considering the true reasons for their decisions or considering the harsh and sometimes unnatural beauty standards set for women by male-dominated society (Balanescu 2020). In light of this situation, she set out to write the novel *If I Had Your Face* in hopes of encouraging people to think about the social factors underlying cosmetic surgery obsession.

Excerpt 2

Part of a 5000-word commentary for a translation from English into Spanish.

ST: Kaur, Jasmin (2019) *When you ask me where I'm going*. New York: Harper Collins.

The source text (ST) is a poetry book by Jasmin Kaur, published in 2019 by Harper Collins Publishers. In her poems and prose, the author explores various social themes, mainly focusing on feminism, immigration, and xenophobia. Kaur was born and lives in Canada, but she also identifies herself as a Punjabi woman; her cultural identity is widely present in her writing, which provides the book with references to both lands and both languages. Even though the book is originally written in English, Punjabi words and names are present although scarcely, throughout its pages. The book can be regarded as a statement of the author's identity and her feelings towards this identity.

Excerpt 3

Part of a 1000-word commentary from Spanish into English.

ST: Grandes, Almudena (1998) 'El vocabulario de los balcones,' in Grandes, Almudena, *Modelos de mujer*. Barcelona: Tusquets: 135–160.

The source text (ST) is a short story titled *El vocabulario de los balcones*, written by the Madrid-born author Almudena Grandes. It is included in her collection, *Modelos de mujer*, a publication that compiles stories about women at different stages of their lives. The ST is a literary text and, consequently, its function is expressive (Reiss 2000: 25–26). Its level of language complexity and its subject matter indicate that its intended audience is adults, with a specific focus on women who are primarily but not exclusively middle-class. Moreover, the setting of the story relies on the reader's familiarity with several Madrid locations and therefore is also intended specifically for those who have a particular interest in the city. The complexity of the ST language and its style are consistent with the demands of the literary genre, the register is informal, and several cultural references, especially place names, are present throughout the ST.

Activity 2

Select a ST, do some research on it, and write contextual and background information about it. You can choose a ST which you have translated before or any other text you are interested in.

1.3 ST analysis at the macrolevel

To analyse the ST at the macrolevel, we need to look at the bigger picture and consider issues such as its genre and text type, its skopos (function or purpose), the intended audience or readership, the medium of publication and the use of paratextual devices. All these points are interrelated and will give us the ST's profile so that we can articulate a translation strategy based on this analysis (cf. Nord 2005: 42).

1.3.1 ST's skopos

A good starting point for the ST analysis is to identify the function, purpose, or skopos of the ST. It was mainly through the work of Nord (1997), Snell-Hornby (2006), Schäffner (2012), and Chesterman (2010) that Skopos theory was introduced to the academic community in the Anglophone world (Martín de León 2000: 201). 'Skopos' ('skopoi' in the plural) is a Greek word meaning 'aim' or 'purpose.' Reiss and Vermeer (1984/1991) often use the terms 'skopos,' 'purpose,' and 'function' as synonyms, which, some have argued, has caused 'terminological confusion' (Schäffner 2012: 120). In this textbook we will use the term 'skopos.' Hatim and Mason (1990: 138, 146) have pointed out that, although most texts are multifunctional and therefore have several skopoi, one of these functions or 'rhetorical purposes' tends to dominate at any one time.

Some institutions require that students integrate or refer explicitly to Translation Studies theories in their commentaries, and throughout this textbook we will refer to any theories that are potentially relevant in a commentary. Functional theories or skopos theories are one type of the theories that you can integrate within your commentary, both when doing the ST analysis and when articulating your translation strategy. We will discuss skopos theory further in Chapter 2, as it is more relevant to the articulation of a translation strategy.

1.3.2 ST's genre and text type

After identifying the ST's skopos, we can classify the ST with regard to genre and text type. These two terms have often been used interchangeably, and some consider that the notions overlap (Baker 2011: 123). In the glossary of some texts of the *Thinking Translation* series (Spanish, French, Arabic, Italian and English) 'genre' is defined as 'a category to which, in a given culture, a given text is seen to belong and within which it is seen to share a type of communicative purpose with other texts; that is, the text is seen to be more or less typical of the genre.'

In other words, in this definition the concept of 'genre' is considered to be culturally bound and related to the communicative purpose of any particular text. Nevertheless, although the two terms are not completely different, as they share points in common, 'genre' and 'text type' are not quite synonyms and some scholars make a distinction between them (cf. Nord 2005: 20).

As will be discussed in Chapter 2, due to the cross disciplinary nature of Translation Studies, there is both an abundance of terminology, inherited from linguistics, literary studies, sociology, etc., and a certain lack of consistency among the different theorists and scholars. In fact, there is no consistency with regard to the taxonomy used to classify genres and/or text types across the different manuals of translation that are currently in the market. This is because different manuals use different criteria for this classification, which can go from the communicative function or purpose, to the intended readership, to the medium of dissemination. This lack of consistency may also stem from the fact that the concept of genre originates in literary studies while the concept of text-type tends to be used more in linguistics.

According to Nord (2005: 20), whereas English speaking scholars tend to use the term text type for both concepts, German linguists, such as Reiss and Vermeer (1984), generally make a distinction between text type (*texttyp*) and text class (*textsorte*). Reiss (1971/2000: 23) believed that it was imperative to develop a way of classifying texts to be used by both translators and their critics, but thought that 'the classifications thus far advanced have been inadequate, primarily because they have shown no consistent principles in defining the various types of text, and the reasons given for the distinctions that are drawn (if given at all) have been variable and weak' (23).

Therefore, she used Bühler's (1965/1990: 28) three linguistic functions – informative, expressive, and appellative – to classify text types. Hence, informative texts, such as an instruction manual to use a particular type of machinery, are content-focused, expressive texts, such as a poem, are form-focused and operative or appellative texts, such an advertisement or a political pamphlet, are focused on eliciting a particular effect on the audience (Reiss 1971/2000: 26).

The problem with this classification is that it is based on the communicative function of the text in question and often a text has several functions (Carreres et al. 2018: 90; Hatim and Mason 1990; Reiss 1971/2000: 25), even though, as we discussed earlier, usually one of the functions tends to be dominant (Hatim and Mason 1990: 138, 146).

Genres, on the other hand, are classified on the basis of their function in the sociocultural context (Carreres et al. 2018: 93). That is, going back to the definition in the *Thinking Translation* series, genre is the category that a given culture gives to a text. In other words, text types are categorised according to their skopos or function and text class (*textsorte)* are texts that occur 'in standard situations (e.g. weather report, prayer, folk-ballad, operating instructions)' (Nord 2005: 20). Thus, Nord (2005) uses the term 'genre' to translate *textsorte* and so, a text can be, for example, informative (its text type according to its skopos) and belong to the genre of 'weather report.'

As Carreres et al. (2018: 94) point out, there are many classifications of textual genres and subgenres, such as a recipe, a textbook, a poem, a letter, a contract, etc. We might, therefore, want to use either the term 'text type' or 'genre' depending on the ST we are analysing and what criteria we use to classify it.

Regardless of whether we use the term 'genre' or 'text type,' the important thing to keep in mind, however, is that genres or text types usually have their own set of conventions and characteristics, which affect the readers' expectations. This set of features tends to be culturally bound and often the equivalent genre or text type in a different culture does not follow the same set of rules and characteristics, expected by the readers. This, as we will see, is also applicable to the rules of the different publication media, which are also culturally bound. What we need to remember for our analysis is that classifying the ST will help us prioritise the features that we want to preserve in our translation to articulate our translation priorities.

Apart from the above, when analysing the ST, we also need to take into account the possibility of having 'embedded texts' (cf. Nord 2005: 110–118). This will be discussed again when we look at the use of paratextual devices. An example of an embedded text could be a verbatim quotation, which may or may not belong to the same genre or text type. A more complex situation is when the embedded text belongs to a different genre or text type to the text it is embedded in, for example, an autopsy report in a crime novel. This means that we need to be aware of the conventions and characteristics of both the ST and its embedded text, so that we can check whether these are different in the TC and act accordingly.

Task 1.5

Find three different texts in one of the languages you work with that belong to three different text types as discussed above (for example, an excerpt from a novel or a poem, an instruction manual, or a tourist brochure). Then articulate a realistic skopos for each one of the texts.

1.3.3 ST's intended audience/readership

The contextual and background research that you have done about the ST, its author, and the SC will provide some of the information about the ST's intended readership, particularly at the time the ST was published. You will need to take this into account when articulating your translation strategy, as your TT will likely to be intended for contemporary readers.

The particular language variety of the ST may also indicate who the intended reader is, and again you will need to decide what to do with this (this is one of the aspects the microlevel analysis focuses on, following the matrices of the *Thinking Translation* series). The ST's intended reader may also have particular knowledge, assumptions, and expectations. Therefore, at this stage, we also need to consider the pre-knowledge of the subject matter the ST readership may have, and to what extent the readers of the ST and TT differ in this respect. Then you will have to decide how much information you will need to add or even omit in your TT. With regard to this, you might be able to integrate theories on translation and relevance (Gutt 2000; Sperber and Wilson 1986/1995 and 2004) within your commentary.

Task 1.6

In small groups brainstorm about what sort of information would be useful to have about the intended reader and think about the best way to find it.

Here are some of the issues that might be useful to know about the ST's intended reader. This list is not intended to be exhaustive.

- Age.
- Level of education.
- Social and/or geographical group.
- Occupation.
- Level of specialisation.
- Previous knowledge.

It is important to provide evidence of why you think the ST's reader is of a particular age, has a particular level of education, belongs to a specific social or geographical group, etc. This evidence could be deducted, for instance, from the linguistic profile of the text (e.g. from the use of certain grammatical and lexical structures). For instance, the use of complex grammar and a specialised vocabulary may point to an educated reader.

As we will discuss in the next chapter, the ST's and your TT's intended readers may or may not share some of the same characteristics. Therefore, it is important to know beforehand what the ST's intended reader's profile is, as it will make you aware of the changes and adaptations you may need to make for your TT's intended readership.

1.3.3.1 Age

Is the ST intended for adults or children? If it is intended for children, what is their age? Very small children, teenagers, etc.? What features of the ST indicate that this is the case?

1.3.3.2 *Occupation, level of education and of specialisation, previous knowledge*

Here we need to decide whether the ST is intended for the general reader or not. Does the intended reader have a basic level of education, or are they educated to degree level or above? Are they an expert on the subject matter? Many occupations use a particular jargon or language variety, with its own terminology, and lexical, syntactical, and stylistic choices. If this is the case, what features of the ST indicate it?

1.3.3.3 *Social and/or geographical group*

Does the intended reader belong to a particular geographical space or to a particular social group with their own dialect or language variety? What features of the ST indicate that this is the case? We need to take into account, however, as we will see in the next chapter, that the fact that a text is written in a particular language variety such as, for example, teen speech, does not necessarily mean that the intended reader belongs to that particular social group. The time and place of publication will give us clues to this.

Task 1.7

Activity 1

Look at the excerpts below and identify the aspects of the intended reader that have been described. Indicate whether there is any information missing on any of these aspects and rewrite any parts of the excerpts that might be confusing or unclear.

Excerpt 1

Part of a 5000-word commentary for a translation Spanish into English.
    ST: Sánchez-Andrade, Cristina (2022) *La nostalgia de la Mujer Anfibio*. Barcelona: Anagrama.

The source text (ST) is the historical novel *La nostalgia de la Mujer Anfibio* written by the Galician author Cristina Sánchez-Andrade and published by Anagrama in 2022. Given that the text 'expresses' as well as 'states' (Reiss 2000: 34) and prioritises form alongside content, it can be classified as a literary work and its primary function is expressive (Reiss 2000: 25–26). The mature themes of the text (coming of age, infidelity, death) as well as the complexity of the language indicate that adults are its intended audience. More specifically, the text seems to be targeted at those with a particular interest in the history of Galicia. This is evidenced by the wide variety of Galician terms and place names specific to the novel's setting that the text is rife with, unaccompanied by any form of explanation.

Excerpt 2

Part of a 5000-word commentary for a translation English into Chinese.
ST: Clements, Andrew (2002) *A Week in the Woods*. New York and London: Simon & Schuster.

The ST is a children's novel, which tells a story between a kid Mark and his teacher Mr Maxwell. Initially, the teacher judged the boy, because he thought the boy was lazy and a spoiled rich kid. After joining in the woods adventure, the teacher changed his mind, and their relation became close. The book was originally published in 2002 and its author is Andrew Clements, who is an American writer of children's literature. Over 80 of his books have been published, including a series of novels about school life. This novel is one of them and was nominated for a number of awards, including California Young Reader Medal and Golden Sower Masterlist.

...

Additionally, the book is not difficult to understand. As a children's novel, the original readers are American children, so it contains few complex sentences and words. Compared with others, although this one is relatively straightforward to translate, it still contains issues particular to translating children's literature. A translator should not only seek to translate a good ST, but also ensure the quality of the TT.

Excerpt 3

Part of a 5000-word commentary for a translation English into Chinese.
ST: Foley, Lucy (2022) *The Paris Apartment*. London: HarperCollins.

The text for translation tends to be for a literate readership without restrictions on the class, age, and gender. And this book was written for most people who can speak English and have an interest in mystery and crime stories. Based on Peter Newmark's theory of language functions (1995), the text is expressive and narrates in the forms of unplanned oral discourse and the mind of the narrator, like a special monologue. The register of the text is highly changeable as a result of the changes in narrators, situations, and occasions. And the present translation should be written in a standard language, while some stylistic freedom is allowed to a certain extent.

Activity 2

Select three texts and articulate the profile of the intended reader. Remember to provide evidence from the text features to support your conclusions and claims. You can use the same texts you used in Task 1.5.

1.3.4 ST's medium of publication

As is the case with genre, text type, and the intended readership, the ST's and TT's medium of publication might differ substantially. Therefore, we need to be aware of the ST's medium of publication in order to decide the type of changes, if any, we need to make in our translation. We also need to be careful if the media of both the TT and ST appear to be very similar or almost the same, such as, for example, a newspaper, an encyclopedia, or a website, as there might be conventions for these media in the TC which are different from those of the SC. These are issues that will be further discussed in Part III, when we will examine audiovisual translation, localisation, and transcreation.

Task 1.8

Activity 1

In small groups, brainstorm as many types of media for written communication as you can and articulate the type of reader each type would have, by referring to the different reader profiles discussed in the previous section.

Activity 2

Look at the excerpts below and identify the aspects of the ST's medium of publication that have been described. Indicate whether there is any information missing on any of these aspects and rewrite any parts of the excerpts that might be confusing or unclear.

Excerpt 1

Part of a 2500-word commentary for a 5000-word translation English into French.
   ST: *Plan Your Visit to York* | Visit York

The source text is a collection of extracts from *Only in York: Visitor guide 2020*, a tourism brochure written by 'Visit York' and self-published on the 6th of January 2020. The 'Visit York' team are part of 'Make It York,' a leisure and tourism brand which aims to present York (a cathedral city in North Yorkshire, England) as a must-see world-class destination to the leisure and business visitor' (Visit York 2022). As this is a commercial and informative tourism brochure with the aim of attracting visitors, its primary purpose is to inform as 'Visit York' wants readers to know what the area has to offer.

Excerpt 2

Part of a 5000-word commentary for a translation English into Chinese.
ST: Goldstein, Jack (2013) *1001 Amazing Jokes*. Luton: Andrews UK.

1001 Amazing Jokes is from a UK master of comedy – Jack Goldstein. The author intends to pique the readers' interest and keep their attention by collecting different kinds of hilarious jokes in the UK. This collection contains 1001 of the funniest typical British jokes and is divided into different categories, such as food jokes, animal jokes, jokes in the bar, crisscross jokes, crossing-the-road jokes, knock-knock jokes, and so on. The book not only provides information but also amusement to the intended readers.

Excerpt 3

Part of a 1000-word commentary for a translation Spanish into English.
ST: POLÍTICA CULTURAL CUBANA (gob.cu)

The ST comes from the website of Cuba's *Ministerio de Cultura*, a government agency that regulates the country's cultural policy. This site informs on the Ministry's activities and objectives, this particular extract constituting a general overview of their public policies. The information given is based on observation rather than theoretical assumptions (e.g. ST 22–27), and therefore belongs to the empirical genre. The ST aims to enlighten readers as to the current and historical cultural processes of the country, so the function is correspondingly informative.

Activity 3

Select up to three texts and discuss concisely their medium of publication, indicating how it has affected the text itself.

1.3.5 *ST's use of paratextual devices*

The term 'paratext' was first coined by Genette in 1962 (cf. Genette, 1997). Loosely based on his work, paratextual devices, in this textbook, are considered to be all of the materials that surround the text such as the cover, the title, blurbs, notes (both footnotes and endnotes), illustrations and images, introductions, appendixes, hyperlinks, copyright page, etc. Many of these devices often indicate the intended readership. For example, the use of footnotes usually points to a reader with a more than average level of education.

Nord (2005: 110–118) calls these elements 'in-texts' embedded in a unit of a higher rank or 'embedding text.' As mentioned above, we could be dealing with a ST that has other texts embedded within it, which will need to be taken into account when we are categorising the ST with regard to genre and text type.

Paratextual devices

Most assignments will not require a lengthy analysis of the use of paratextual devices in the ST, but it is important to be aware of these elements so that we can make an informed decision on how to deal with them.

Paper books in many cultures will usually have most if not all of the following parts:

- *The front matter*, comprised of all the parts that appear before the main text: half title page, frontispiece, series title page, title page, copyright page, dedication page, epigraph, table of contents, list of illustrations or tables, foreword, preface, acknowledgements, and prologue.
- *The body of the text:* epilogue, afterword, postscript, images or illustrations, tables, figures (diagrams, charts, etc.), and footnotes.
- *The back matter:* appendix or addendum, endnotes, glossary, bibliography, list of contributors, and author's bio.

If we are dealing with ebooks, we need to add hyperlinks to the above list, which would normally be used instead of footnotes or endnotes and will appear in the content page, a glossary, if there is one, etc.

Some of the issues that might emerge from the use of paratextual devices are linked to intertextuality, which is discussed later in this chapter and also, at greater length, in Chapter 3. In order to find out about the use of paratextual devices in the ST, we suggest the following questions:

- Have the paratextual elements originally been written in the source language (SL)?
- Have the paratextual elements originally been written in the target language (TL)?
- Have the paratextual elements originally been written in a language other than the SL or the TL?
- Do some of the paratextual elements (such as quotes or embedded texts, for example) belong to a text type and/or genre different to that of the ST?

Task 1.9

Chose two texts from the language you translate from and analyse the use of paratextual devices by making explicit reference to the possible intended readership.

1.3.6 Macrolevel ST analysis

There are several elements, discussed above, that are important to consider when doing a ST analysis at the macrolevel. However, depending on the ST in question and our translation strategy, some of these elements will be more relevant to our commentary, while others not so much. As we have limited space, it will be necessary to decide when to be concise and when some aspects might need further development.

According to Nord (2005: 83), sometimes we obtain information about a certain factor, such as, for example, the intended reader, by analysing other factors, such as the style or format of the ST, or the medium of publication. This is why Nord (2005) talks about 'recursiveness,' that is, an analysis that has several loops 'in which expectations are built up, confirmed, or rejected, and where knowledge is gained and extended and understanding constantly modified' (2005: 83). This recursiveness also applies to our translation strategy, since, as we will see, often some of our translation decisions will cause us to revise our strategy.

Task 1.10

Activity 1

In small groups, look at the excerpt below (part of a 5000-word commentary for a translation from English into Chinese) and identify the elements mentioned in this chapter that have been included in the ST analysis.

ST: O'Brien, Karen (2009) *Women and Enlightenment in eighteenth-century Britain*. Cambridge: Cambridge University Press.

1. Introduction of the project

An excerpt from Professor Karen O'Brien's book *Women and Enlightenment in Eighteenth-Century Britain* was chosen for translation. The book was published by Cambridge University Press in 2009 and comprises 318 pages. The source text is taken from the second chapter of the book, which discusses the history of femininity.

Three points will be covered in this section. First, an overview of the book and its author will be offered, covering the book's general content, the author's background, and the book's academic significance. Second, the examination of the source text, particularly its significant challenges in terms of text type, grammar, substance, and so on, will take precedence. Finally, the commentary's structure will be provided.

1.4 About the book and the author

Professor Karen O'Brien is the first woman to serve as Vice-Chancellor and Warden of Durham University. She specialises in the Enlightenment and eighteenth-century literature as an English literature scholar, and she has published substantially in both subjects. Her academic background in English literature and history, as well as her significant writing experience, allow her to write fluently, thoughtfully, and professionally. And her study of feminism will be considerably more intriguing and engaging since she is a distinguished woman.

The Age of Enlightenment produced numerous brilliant, progressive, and classic literary and philosophical works, as well as the start of Western feminism. Feminism, a popular subject in the world today, has garnered increasing public attention and has been intensively studied over the ages. O'Brien mixes intellectual history with literary criticism in *Women and Enlightenment in Eighteenth-Century Britain*, analysing the writings of diverse authors such as John Locke, David Hume, Montesquieu, Adam Smith, and others to examine the crucial contribution of women in the Enlightenment. The book serves as a thorough examination of the Enlightenment and feminism and is a valuable guide for readers interested in the Age of Enlightenment, eighteenth-century history, literature, philosophy, feminism, and related topics.

1.2 Analysis of the source text: key issues and difficulties

The source text is excerpted from Chapter 2 of the book, *From Savage to Scotswoman: The History of Femininity*. The whole book is divided into six chapters, each discussing the role of women in the Enlightenment from a distinct woman-related dimension, a different regional context, or a variety of scholarly perspectives. Due to word limits, only the second chapter has been chosen for translation, which is clearly structured and is based on a categorical discussion of different scholars' claims to femininity, introducing important concepts such as femininity and conjectural history, as well as writings by scholars such as Hume, Montesquieu, and Adam Smith.

The source text is an academic one, comprising multiple disciplines, and is a formal informative text abundant in academic expertise. Therefore, the primary difficulty of translation lies in the extensive extended reading required to understand the text, to properly convey the author's intention, and to effectively translate the terminology. Secondly, owing to the author's professional attainment in English literature, her writing includes numerous sophisticated and lengthy sentences, which add to the high professionalism of the text but also increase the difficulty of comprehension and translation for the translator. Finally, given that the target readers of the source text have a higher education level and are academically interested in feminism, the Enlightenment, literature, philosophy, and other related fields, the wording of the translation should be refined by all means. In general, the translation of the source text is challenging at the lexical, discourse, and syntactic levels.

Activity 2

Decide on the following, giving a rationale for your answers:

1. Are there any elements that, in your opinion, are relevant, missing from the analysis?
2. Are any elements that have been analysed not relevant?
3. Is the length of the analysis for each element appropriate or does it need to be more concise or further developed?

1.4 Microlevel analysis

As mentioned previously, the ST analysis is usually not linear but 'recursive,' as it will be done in several loops, where 'expectations are built up, confirmed, or rejected, and where knowledge is gained and extended and understanding constantly modified' (Nord 2005: 83). Therefore, as we are doing the analysis at the microlevel, we should also be refining our translation strategy and the analysis at the macrolevel. In fact, our translation strategy needs also to be revised as we translate the ST, which, in turn, will actually inform our translation. Due to this, most of the issues that need to be analysed at this level are discussed in Chapter 3. Following the nomenclature of the *Thinking Translation* series, these are cultural, formal, semantic, varietal, and intertextual issues. Apart from these, at this level of the analysis we need to identify the ST's subject matter, theme-rheme structure, tone, and effect on the reader created by the ST's salient characteristics identified in the analysis.

1.4.1 ST's subject matter and theme-rheme structure

According to Nord (2005: 93–94), it is important to identify the ST's subject matter early on in the analysis because it will help us decide whether we need to do research on issues such as terminology, referential content, etc., in advance, and may give us some information that will help with the macrolevel analysis.

We also need to be aware of whether the ST deals with more than one subject matter and, if this is the case, whether there is a dominant one and several secondary ones. Once this has been identified, we should decide whether the conventions of the TC require us to specify the subject matter in an explicit manner or not (cf. Nord 2005: 98).

The subject matter can usually be elicited from the title, from the abstract (if there is one), and/or from the 'topic sentence' of the first paragraph (cf. Nord 2005: 95–96). Other sources of information are the key words which are often included in academic texts such as articles and the blurbs that accompany books such as monographs. It might be a good idea to include a few lines about the ST's subject matter somewhere at the beginning of the commentary, perhaps where you might have provided background and contextual information.

As for the analysis of the ST's theme-rheme structure, which has an impact on textual coherence, it may be worth bearing in mind that certain languages may have different rules on how to make a text coherent and require that the information is given in a particular order. The 'theme' is usually defined as the given information and the 'rheme' as the comment or new information on the theme (Nord 2005: 117; Rogers et al. 2020: 121). The theme-rheme structure will be further discussed alongside formal issues in Chapter 3.

Please read Chapter 3 before conducting your analysis at this level.

Task 1.11

Activity 1

In small groups, look at the excerpt below (part of a 5000-word commentary for a translation from English into Chinese), and identify where the ST's subject matter is discussed. Indicate whether there is any information missing on any of these aspects and rewrite any parts of the excerpts that might be confusing or unclear.

Excerpt

ST: Walliams, David (2022) *The world's worst pets*. London: HarperCollins.

About the book

The World's Worst Pets is the newest instalment in David Walliams' *World's Worst* series. This book features ten of the weirdest pets who have habits of upsetting their owners and wreaking havoc in their lives. The hilarious stories will make readers giggle as well. To make the novel more dynamic and intriguing, as well as to keep children's attention, the author used a significant variety of onomatopoeic terms. What's more, the book is meticulously and beautifully organised, with several typefaces and graphics on each page. It's also quite aesthetically attractive, with bright drawings and glossy pages. The great majority of proper nouns and onomatopoeic words in the book employ distinctive designs to catch the reader's attention, such as bold and expanded, shifting font size, shape, colour, and so on. As a result, translating the novel's vast number of onomatopoeic terms in a way that produces the same impact as the original text is a critical concern for translators during the translation process.

Three of the ten short tales were chosen for this research. The first is about Frup, a goldfish that is always hungry and makes a loud chomping sound whenever he wants something to eat. After devouring many items, the goldfish is ultimately consumed by an octopus with an equally great hunger. The second narrative is about Monty, a pet dog that aspires to be a musician and embarks on an exciting voyage with his companion to prove that dogs can be excellent musicians. Finally, the composer who created the renowned musical *CATS* creates a musical for dogs and plays it in a theatre. The last narrative is about Zoom, an enormously old tortoise that, by coincidence, obtains the power to move quickly (zoom) and therefore leads his youthful master on a series of fascinating adventures.

Activity 2

Select two of the texts you have chosen in this chapter (for Tasks 1.4, 1.5, 1.8, or 1.9) and articulate their subject matter in a few lines.

1.4.2 *Salient characteristics of the ST*

Despite not being the only possible way to do it, using the matrices of the *Thinking Translation* series will allow our analysis to be systematic, which will help you decide which are the salient characteristics of the ST. Hence, we will use the cultural, formal, semantic, and varietal matrices. We will also look at intertextual issues and any other matters that do not really fit within any particular matrix. Please read Chapter 3 before conducting your analysis at this level.

You will also need to consider any possible deviations from the rules either grammatical, stylistic, or otherwise. For example, when the ST is written in an ungrammatical manner for a particular effect or to make a particular statement. This is linked to the concept of 'ostranenie,' which is defined by *The Oxford Dictionary of Critical Theory* as the Russian Formalists 'attempt to describe and define what constitutes *literaturnost* (literariness).' It is a literary device that writers use to make their readers see as unfamiliar or strange that which, in their culture, is familiar.

1.4.3 Tone of the text and effect on the reader

The tone of a text could be sarcastic, ironic, humorous, neutral, informal, formal, objective, subjective, vulgar, etc. We can determine what tone the ST has by looking at the features of the ST at the microlevel and the effect it has on the reader. Sometimes we could also identify the tone because it is signalled by what Nord (2005: 131–132) calls 'suprasegmental elements,' such as the use of font and punctuation (for example, use of capitalisation or exclamation marks to express anger or shock). Most importantly, the tone and/or the effect that the ST has on the reader is a product of the overall interaction of its features rather than of one particular characteristic (Nord 2005: 42).

According to Nord (2005: 143), readers 'compare the intratextual features of the text with the expectations built up externally, and the impression they get from this whether conscious, unconscious or subconscious, can be referred to as "effect".' That is, the effect of a text is created by the interplay of the subject matter with the ST textual features at the microlevel and the interaction with the reader's expectations.

When we analyse the ST, we need to select the 'effect-producing features' (Nord 2005: 148), that is, we need to select those features that work together to create a particular tone and effect, rather than providing a disconnected list of features. This will be further discussed in Chapter 3. Often, not all the features have the same effect and sometimes, some of them may elicit opposite or contradictory effects within the same text, but, according to Nord (2005: 148), there is normally a 'dominant effect intended by the sender.' What is important to remember is that we cannot or should not try to reproduce every single effect that we identify in our ST analysis (Nord 2005: 148). This is why we need to articulate a set of translation priorities.

Another thing to consider is that conventions, aesthetic norms, and certain skopos linked to a particular text type are often culturally bound and might elicit a particular effect in the SL readers. However, these features will not necessarily elicit the same effect in the TL readers (Nord 2005: 149). Therefore, we need to focus on the effect itself rather than the ST features so that we can decide how best to preserve it in our TT if that is one of our translation priorities. The preservation of the ST's tone and effect could be the main topic of a thematically-structured commentary.

1.5 Conclusion

The ST analysis will allow us to decide what the most salient features of the ST are and what relevance they have for the creation of meaning, which will help us minimise the loss that inevitably takes place in translation as well as help justify our translation decisions. It will allow us to prioritise and rank certain features of the ST and sacrifice others, if we need to do so, in line with our translation strategy. That is, it will inform our translation strategy.

The ST analysis is usually not linear but 'recursive,' which means that as we are doing the analysis at the microlevel, we should also be refining our translation strategy and the analysis at the macrolevel. In fact, when we are translating the text, we will also need to refine our translation strategy which, in turn, will affect our translation.

A good rule of thumb to avoid dedicating too much of the space in terms of word count is for the ST analysis and statement of translation strategy combined to be about a third of the whole commentary, and this third to be roughly equally divided into ST analysis and statement of translation strategy.

1.6 Summary

The focus of this chapter was on articulating a ST analysis, which will allow us to decide which are the most relevant features of the ST we need to preserve in order to follow our translation strategy and priorities. It discussed the relevance of contextual information for our understanding of the ST, as well as other issues that will need to be considered for the analysis such as: skopos, genre, text type, intended audience, medium of publication, and paratextual devices. The chapter finished with advice on how to identify the salient features of the ST, as well as the tone and effect that it might elicit on the intended reader, all of which will have a bearing on our translation strategy and translation priorities discussed in Chapter 2.

Further reading

ST analysis in general

Nord, Christiane (2005) *Text Analysis in Translation: Theory, Methodology, and Didactic Application of a Model for Translation-oriented Text Analysis*, 2nd ed. Amsterdam & New York: Rodopi.

Skopos, genre and text type

In the *Thinking Translation* skopos, genre and text type are discussed in the following publications: Andrews and Maksimova (2009, chapter 6), Cragie et al. (2015, chapter 11), Cragie and Pattison (2018: 14–15), Dickins et al. (chapter 6), Haywood et al. (2009, chapter 4), Hervey and Higgins (1992, chapter 5), Pellatt and Liu (2010, chapters 3–8) and Rogers et al. (2020, chapter 4).

Skopos more specifically

Nord, Christiane (1997) *Translating as a Purposeful Activity: Functionalist Approaches Explained*. Manchester: St. Jerome.
Schäffner, C. (2009) 'Functionalist Approaches', in Mona Baker and Gabriela Saldanha (eds) *Routledge Encyclopedia of Translation Studies*, 2nd ed. London and New York: Routledge, 115–121.

List of references

Andrews, Edna and Elena Maksimova (2009) *Russian Translation: Theory and Practice*. London and New York: Routledge.
Baker, Mona (1992/2011) *In Other Words: A Coursebook on Translation*, 2nd ed. London and New York: Routledge.
Bühler, Karl (1965/1990). *Theory of Language: The Representational Function of Language*. Philadelphia: Benjamins.
Carreres, Ángeles, María Noriega-Sánchez and Carme Calduch (2018) *Mundos en palabras: Learning Advanced Spanish Through Translation*. New York: Routledge.
Chesterman, Andrew (2010) 'Skopos Theory: A Retrospective Assessment', in Werner Kallmeyer, Ewald Reuter and Jürgen F. Schopp (eds) *Perspektiven auf Kommunikation: Festschrift für Liisa Tittula zum 60. Geburtstag*, Berlin: SAXA, 209–225.
Cragie, Stella, Ian Higgins, Sándor Hervey and Patrizia Gambarotta (2015) *Thinking Italian Translation*, 2nd ed. London and New York: Routledge.
Cragie, Stella and Pattison, Ann (2018) *Thinking English Translation. Analysing and Translating English Source Texts*. London & New York: Routledge.
Dickins, James, Sándor Hervey and Ian Higgins (2016) *Thinking Arabic Translation*, 2nd ed. London and New York: Routledge.
Genette, Gerard (1997) *Paratexts: Thresholds of Interpretation*, trans. Jane E. Lewin. Cambridge: Cambridge University Press.
Gutt, Ernst-August (2000) *Translation and Relevance: Cognition and Context*. Manchester: St. Jerome.
Hatim, Basil and Ian Mason (1990) *Discourse and the Translator*. Harlow, Essex: Longman.
Haywood, Louise M., Mike Thompson and Sándor Hervey (2009) *Thinking Spanish Translation. A Course in Translation Method: Spanish to English*. London & New York: Routledge.
Hervey, Sándor and Ian Higgins (1992) *Thinking Translation, a Course in Translation Method: French-English*. London: Routledge.
Hervey, Sándor and Ian Higgins (2002) *Thinking French Translation*, 2nd ed. Abingdon: Routledge.
Martín de León, Celia (2000) 'Functionalism', in Baker, Mona and Saldanha, Gabriela (eds) *Routledge Encyclopedia of Translation Studies*, 3rd ed. London and New York: Routledge, 199–203.
Nord, Christiane (1997) *Translating as a Purposeful Activity*. Manchester: St. Jerome.
Nord, Christiane (2005) *Text Analysis in Translation: Theory, Methodology, and Didactic Application of a Model for Translation-oriented Text Analysis*, 2nd ed. Amsterdam & New York: Rodopi.

Pattison, Ann, and Stella Cragie (2022) *Translating Change*. London and New York: Routledge.

Pellatt, Valerie and Eric Liu (2010) *Thinking Chinese Translation*. London and New York: Routledge.

Reiss, Katharina (1971/1989) 'Text Types, Translation Types and Translation Assessment', trans. Andrew Chesterman, in Andrew Chesterman (ed) (1989) *Readings in Translation Theory*. Helsinki: Finn Lectura, 105–115.

Reiss, Katharina (2000) *Translation Criticism- Potentials and Limitations: Categories and Criteria for Translation Quality Assessment*, trans. Erroll F. Rhodes. Manchester: St Jerome.

Reiss, Katharina and Hans J. Vermeer (1984) *Groundwork for a General Theory of Translation*. Niemeyer: Tubergen.

Rogers, Margaret, Michael White, Michael Loughbridge, Ian Higgins and Sándor Hervey (2020) *Thinking German Translation*, 3rd ed. London: Routledge.

Schäffner, Christina (2012) 'Functionalist Approaches', in Mona Baker and Gabriela Saldanha, (eds) *Routledge Encyclopedia of Translation Studies*, 2nd ed. London and New York: Routledge, 115–121.

Snell-Hornby, M. (2006) *The Turns of Translation Studies: New Paradigms or Shifting Viewpoints?* Amsterdam & Philadelphia: John Benjamins.

Sperber, Dan and Deirdre Wilson (1986/1995) *Relevance: Communication and Cognition*. Oxford: Blackwell.

Sperber, Dan and Deirdre Wilson (2004) 'Relevance Theory', in Laurence R. Horn and Gregory Ward (eds) *The Handbook of Pragmatics*. Oxford: Blackwell, 607–632.

2 Statement of the translation strategy

Key concepts

- The translation brief.
- What is the difference between strategy and technique?
- Genre and text type. What are the norms and conventions in the target culture (TC) of the chosen genre and text type?
- Target text's (TT's) skopos.
- TT's intended readership.
- TT's medium of publication.
- Use of paratextual devices.
- How to set out translation priorities.

2.1 The translation brief

A translation brief often accompanies a translation assignment regardless of whether the setting is professional or educational and contains the instructions to follow. The amount of detail and explicit instructions vary; therefore, we may find information on the medium of publication of the TT, such as, for example, a newspaper, a website, an encyclopaedia entry, etc. It might also include information on the TT's purpose or skopos, such as, for instance, to inform, to persuade, to promote a product, to entertain, and so on. Regardless of how detailed it is, in those cases where a translation brief accompanies an assignment, part of the assessment criteria will be to see how effectively it has been followed.

According to Nord (1997a: 60), the translation brief should contain the following information, whether implied or explicit:

- The (intended) text function(s).
- The target text addressee(s).
- The (prospective) time and place of text reception.
- The medium over which the text will be transmitted.
- The motive for the production or reception of the text.

DOI: 10.4324/9781003273790-4

This could be mapped onto the analytical framework that was used for analysing the source text (ST) in Chapter 1:

- *The (intended) text function(s)* refers to the skopos of the TT in the TC.
- *The target text addressee(s)* refers to the TT's intended audience. Here we strongly advise that, in the commentary, for the sake of clarity, the word 'target' is reserved for referring to the 'target culture' and 'target text,' and to refer to the readership we use the term 'intended,' thus preventing any ambiguity.
- *The (prospective) time and place of text reception* gives specific information about exactly where and when the translation is going to be published. This will be relevant when discussing varietal features. However, this information could be included when describing the TT's 'intended readership.'
- *The medium over which the text will be transmitted* refers to the medium of publication.
- *The motive for the production or reception of the text* could be discussed along with the skopos.

What is missing here is information about the TT's genre and text type, which, as we have seen in Chapter 1, will not necessarily be the same as those of the ST. This is, in fact, very important, because when translating we need to consider that the TC may have norms and restrictions that are specific to particular genres and text types, which are often different from those of equivalent or similar genres and text types in the SC.

Often, however, there is no translation brief to accompany the assignment, or, if there is one, it does not contain all of the above points. If this is the case, we still need to make decisions with regard to the TT's genre, text type, skopos, intended audience, and medium of publication. This is in fact the translation strategy, further discussed below, which will inform the setting out of the translation priorities. The statement of the translation strategy and the translation priorities, together with the ST analysis, will be part of the introduction to the commentary. In our experience, the more specific and precise we are in formulating a strategy, the more informed the decisions of detail will be and the easier it will be to justify them. In addition, we need to take into account that 'the translation brief does not tell the translator *how* to go about their translating job, what translation strategy to use or what translation type to choose. These decisions depend entirely on the translator's responsibility and competence' (Nord 1997a: 30). This means that our input at this stage is still crucial, regardless of how specific and directive the brief we might have been given is.

This brings us to the next section, which is one of terminology. In the quote above, the use of the word 'strategy' is rather ambiguous and even misleading. In the following section we will operationalise the concepts of 'translation strategy' and 'translation technique' by discussing their different meanings and how they are used in this textbook.

2.2 Terminology: Translation strategy and translation technique

As has often been pointed out, there is a lack of consistency in some of the terminology used in Translation Studies (Carreres et al. 2018: 12; van Doorslaer 2007: 221; Muñoz Martín 2000: 119; Bardají 2009: 161), and we also find that 'the conceptualisation and the interrelationships between concepts ... are often used ambiguously or even in an idiosyncratic way' (van Doorslaer 2007: 217) with 'unnecessary overlaps' and an 'unclear division of levels' (van Doorslaer 2007: 221). This is apparent, for instance, when the same term is used to describe different levels of analysis. Ironically, despite the lack of consistency in the use of terminology in Translation Studies, one of the assessment criteria used when marking commentaries is often, in fact, the accurate and precise use of terminology. A way to overcome this issue is to operationalise the terminology when it is first mentioned (by including what these terms mean within a particular commentary and also acknowledging the source they were selected from) and to be consistent in its use.

With regard to the words 'strategy' and 'technique,' the problem arises, much to the confusion of translation students and trainee translators, mostly because the word 'strategy' is often used both to refer to the global strategy and to the techniques used at the textual level or below. The situation is aggravated when the term 'strategy' is used together with the binary concepts, which are often called methods or strategies, and which usually refer to the decision to have a TT that is more source language (SL) oriented or more target language (TL) oriented. Thus, for example, we may find binary terminology that goes from the more traditional 'faithful' or 'literal' vs 'free,' through Nida's (1964) 'formal equivalence' vs 'dynamic equivalence,' and Newmark's (1988) 'semantic' vs 'communicative,' all the way to Venuti's (1995) 'foreignising' vs 'domesticating.'

Looking at these terms more closely, as pointed out by Hurtado Albir (2001: 121), a 'literal' translation tends to be seen as 'faithful,' and this way of thinking is misleading and even wrong. Similarly, the concepts of 'foreignising' and 'domesticating' have been criticised for not having been 'carefully define[d]' (Tymoczko 2000: 34). In fact, according to Tymoczko (1999), certain aspects of a text might be foreignised (source culture/language [SC/L] oriented), while other aspects might be domesticated (target culture/language [TC/L] oriented), which means that the TT is oriented simultaneously towards both cultures. This opinion is shared by Lane-Mercier (1997: 56), who believes that both strategies can come into play 'for different reasons, at different textual sites, with varying effects, in the course of the translation process' (1997: 55–56), which is the opinion supported in this textbook.

The imprecise use of the word 'strategy' in combination with the rest of the terms discussed above, may cause the wrong assumption that if the translator were to decide to use a domesticating strategy (i.e. TL oriented), they would have to follow this method throughout the whole of their translation, which, as mentioned above, is not necessarily the case. However, if, for instance, we think of the terms 'foreignising' and 'domesticating' as translation techniques applicable to the textual level and below, like, for example the use of a foreignising technique to translate a certain set of cultural specific items (Franco Aixelá 1996), then the discussion is much more clear and precise.

Similar to Carreres et. al. (2018: 12), in this textbook the term 'strategy' is used in a superordinate way to refer to the global, overall strategy taken by the translator. In fact, this particular use coincides with the definition of the word 'strategy' in the *Oxford English Dictionary* as a 'plan of action designed to achieve a long-term or overall aim.' Therefore, to a certain extent, it could be considered to be a synonym of the translation brief and, therefore, it needs to include decisions about the following aspects, which mirror the framework use in Chapter 1 for ST analysis and will be discussed at greater length later in the chapter:

- The TT's genre and text type.
- ↦The TT's skopos/purpose/ function in the TC.
- The TT's Intended audience/readership.
- The TT's medium of publication.
- The TT's use of paratextual devices.
- The ST's salient characteristics which are important to preserve in the TT and will inform the setting out of the translation priorities.

We need to remember that if a particular assignment includes a translation brief, some or all of these decisions may have already been made. However, it is advisable to make sure that the decisions regarding all of the above points have been made before proceeding with the translation. This will prevent an excessive focus on the so-called decisions of detail (Haywood et al. 2009: 9) and will give the commentary a more coherent and convincing structure (rather than a list of unconnected points), as well as a firm basis to justify the decisions taken at the textual level.

However, as is the case with the translation brief, the translation strategy does not specify *how* to do the translation (Nord 1997a: 30). This means that translators 'sometimes find during translating that problems of detail arise that lead them to refine the original strategy, the refined strategy in turn entailing changes to some of the decisions of detail already taken' (Haywood et al. 2009: 9). In other words, as Haywood et al. (2009: 10) point out, understanding the ST and formulating a TT occur simultaneously and translators often come to a better understanding of the ST once they start translating.

Therefore, in this book, the term 'translation techniques' is used to refer to the procedures used at the textual level and below, which will clearly be informed by the overall translation strategy (cf. Carreres et al. 2018: 12–13).

Task 2.1

Activity 1

Please read the excerpts below where the terms 'strategy' and 'technique' have not been used consistently. Taking into account what has been said in this section about terminology, discuss in groups your opinion about these excerpts and make any amendments that you deem necessary.

Excerpt 1

Part of a 5000-word commentary for a translation from English into Chinese.

ST: Foley, Lucy (2022) *The Paris Apartment*. London: HarperCollins.

When a sociolect unit carries less important cognitive information or has an explicit inner form, the translator can boldly choose to translate it into a less standard language, resorting to a wide range of translation techniques, including loan translation, term coining and borrowing. ... Therefore, in the TT, the translation techniques of explanatory translation and amplification are restrainedly employed to make them understandable and not ruin the sociolect nature of the text.

The phrases 'butter up,' 'crash on someone's sofa,' are highly intelligible and have very important cognitive information, which means employing a foreignisation strategy is very likely to create cultural bumps and great difficulties to impede understanding. ... On the one hand, a strategy of standardisation of the discourse, on the other hand, a strategy of preservation of the social difference between the speakers by the use of non-standard features.

Excerpt 2

Part of a 5000-word commentary for a translation from English into Chinese.

ST: Watson, Casey (2022) *I Just Want to be Loved*. London: HarperCollins.

Under the guidance of relevance theory and domestication and foreignisation strategies, the following specific translation techniques are typically used in translation. ... Finally, the most important and common ones: addition and omission. These two translation techniques can be simply understood as adding or deleting words in order to ensure a rational sentence structure and to make the translation fluent and natural.

Activity 2

Look at the excerpts below and decide whether they are discussing the translation strategy or the translation techniques, as understood in this textbook. Provide a rationale for your opinion.

Excerpt 1

Part of a 5000-word commentary for a translation from English into Chinese.

   ST: Cha, Frances (2020) *If I Had Your Face*. New York: Ballantine Books

1.2 Statement of Translation Priority and Strategy

Since the author intends to present the Korean cosmetic surgery industry and the oppressions Korean women face in family and society, the ST inevitably involves terms that are deeply rooted in Korean culture and demonstrate distinct customs, materials, and lifestyles of Korea. These terms not only reflect the deep historical accumulation of a nation, but sometimes the cultural connotations behind them can also serve to foreshadow the plot. If they are not correctly understood, the TT will be challenging for intended readers to access, and at the same time the author's intention will be missed. Therefore, the author's intention will be missed. My top priority is to improve readability as much as possible without compromising the functional equivalence of the TT. To achieve this goal, I have applied domestication to rhetorical expressions and terms that have Chinese equivalents, including 'room salon,' 'Bruce,' 'Nonhyeon,' 'cloudy white,' and 'gape like fish.' However, for terms without Chinese equivalents, including 'iljin,' 'Ajax,' and 'officetel,' foreignisation was adopted to maintain the text's foreignness. Furthermore, when translating religious terms, a different strategy was used: for the term 'God,' although it exists in the target society, domestication was used to make the TT more accessible to readers, while for 'the Virgin Mary,' a term with a foreshadowing function in the text, foreignisation with annotation was employed to ensure that the target readers understand the author's intention.

Excerpt 2

Part of a 2500-word commentary for a translation from English into French.

   ST: *Plan Your Visit to York* | Visit York

   When considering Vermeer's (1978) skopos theory, the purpose of this target text is to deliver a French translation of this tourism brochure for 'Visit York' so that they can appeal to French speakers who do not understand English and gain more tourism from French-speaking countries. Overall, the target text's translation strategy is to maintain an equivalent French-speaking target audience through keeping the informal and unspecialised register and vocabulary of the source text. Venuti's (1995) notion of foreignisation and domestication are used in varying levels throughout the target text in order to keep French idiomaticity on the one hand, but also to flaunt British exoticism to a French-speaking reader on the other hand, to conform to a tourism brochure's ultimate goal of encouraging a visit. Throughout this translation, it was imperative to remain faithful (see Nord 2005) to the translation of places and names. Fidelity in this sense meaning not taking liberties such as coining translations for places and names in England which do not exist in their own right in French. Otherwise, a visiting tourist would be unable to locate the places they would be reading about.

2.3 Skopos, text type, and genre

As discussed in Chapter 1 on ST analysis, a text type is linked to its skopos, that is, its function or purpose in a particular culture. Each text type is comprised of several genres which are usually associated with them, and many texts are hybrid (Reiss 1971/1989). These concepts are important because, depending on the skopos and text type of both the ST and the TT (regardless of whether they are the same or not), certain aspects of the ST will need to be prioritised when translating. For example, if the ST is informative, such as an instruction manual to set up a domestic appliance or a patient information leaflet, the focus is usually on the content and on writing as clearly and as unambiguously as possible; in the case of an expressive text, such as a poem or the lyrics of a song, the focus will be on the form; and in the case of an operative text, such as advertisement or a text from a promotional campaign against drug taking, the focus will be on the desired effect on the reader (Reiss 1971/2000: 108–109). If the ST is a hybrid text, then we will need to decide which skopos should be prioritised in the TT.

Most of the time, the ST and TT will be very similar in this regard, but there will be cases where their skopos and, hence, their text type will be different (Munday 2016: 309). This is because 'the situation in which the source text fulfils its functions is, by definition, different from that of the target text' (Nord 1997: 59). Thus, for example, a political manifesto in the US, with a clear operative skopos of convincing the ST's intended readership, might have a more informative skopos in the TC, as, for instance, in the case of the translation of political speeches to be included in an encyclopaedia, or to be used 'to inform foreign policy analysts' (Haywood et al. 2009: 48).

Before starting to translate, it is important to decide the TT's skopos, text type, and genre, so that the restrictions and conventions in the TC that certain text types and genres may have can be taken into account. For instance, the use of footnotes might not be appropriate in journalistic texts, whereas they might be expected in an academic article. Nord (1997b: 53) recommends the use of parallel texts, that is, texts belonging to the same text type or genre in the TC, which can then be used as textual models or as a source of information and even vocabulary and terminology. They can also be used to help justify certain, perhaps controversial, decisions at the textual level.

Task 2.2

Activity 1

Select up to three texts among the STs analysed in Chapter 1 and articulate at least three different skopoi for a possible translation of each one of them, including information on the text type and genre.

Activity 2

Look at one translation that you have previously done and articulate its skopos. Then think of a different possible skopos and explain how the translation would be different.

Activity 3

Think of a particular genre or text type in the languages you work with, research the differences in norms and conventions between them, and discuss it in small groups in class.

2.4 Intended audience/readership

Unless it is specified in the translation brief, it is necessary to create a profile of the TT's intended readership. As mentioned above, we strongly advise using the word 'intended' when referring to the TT's readership and to avoid using the word 'target' in this context, to prevent the type of confusion discussed at the beginning of this chapter.

The more specific the description of the TT's intended readership is, and the greater amount of detail it has, the easier it will be to justify the decisions of detail. Therefore, even in those cases where the TT's intended readership has been specified, it might be necessary to add further information for our own purposes. It is crucial to avoid generalisations and vague statements such as 'the intended readership of my TT is the same (or similar, or equivalent) as that of the ST.' Statements such as this are often misleading and, in fact, inaccurate. Even if the ST is fairly recent, the TT's intended readership cannot be the same as that of the ST, not even similar or equivalent. The TL speakers belong to a totally different sociocultural and political context, with different shared knowledge, assumptions, and expectations. This is even more so, when the ST was created years, or even centuries ago. Furthermore, when the TL is a language that is spoken in several parts of the world, like, for example, Spanish, the situation becomes rather complex because of the different sociocultural and political contexts of the countries where Spanish is spoken. In such cases it is particularly important to decide which language variety of the TL is going to be chosen and link it to the intended reader. This will affect the decisions of detail, not only with regard to varietal features, but also regarding formal features (such as grammatical choices), semantic features, and cultural features. This is due to the fact that a particular language variety will use different vocabulary and idiomatic expressions (further discussed in Chapter 3).

As was the case in the ST analysis, among the variables that are useful to look at when creating the profile of the TT's intended reader are the following:

- Age.
- Level of education.
- Social and/or geographical group.
- Occupation.
- Level of specialisation.
- Previous knowledge.

If the translation assignment includes a translation brief, some information on the intended reader might have already been provided. However, this does not prevent us from adding further detail to make the translation decisions more informed. Most of these aspects are interlinked and they are not discrete categories, as they frequently overlap each other. Furthermore, not all of the aspects will be relevant in all of the cases. An important thing to keep in mind is that this part of the commentary should be articulated in a coherent narrative rather than an unconnected list of different points.

2.4.1 Age

This is particularly relevant in the case of children, especially in those cases when the ST was written for an adult readership but needs to be adapted for a younger audience. Furthermore, a 3-year-old has very different needs than a 15-year-old or even than a 7-year-old. We also need to take into account that small children, before becoming confident readers, have the books read to them. Therefore, in such cases, the intended reader will actually be adults. In the case of teenagers, they often have their own sociolect, which tends to date fairly quickly. It may also be hard to motivate them to read the text and to hold their attention, probably much more than with any other reader. If the TT's intended readers are children, it might be useful to read theories on the translation of children's literature (a list of which is recommended at the end of this chapter). At the other end of the spectrum, older readers might also have different expectations. The most important thing here is to be as specific as possible. Once the age of the intended reader has been decided it is advisable to consult parallel texts in the TC that have been written for an audience of the same age range. This will provide resources for consultation to make informed decisions and choose between two or more possible alternatives, for example.

2.4.2 Level of education

To a certain extent this is also linked to the reader's level of specialisation, discussed below. If the intended readership is the general reader, we need to think about what we actually mean by this. Once again, it is advisable to be as specific as possible and decide, for example, whether this reader would have basic secondary education (which, for example, would be equivalent to being educated until the age of 16 in the UK) and what this would entail for the TT. On the other hand, the intended readership might be educated, which may indicate having a university degree or above. Thinking about the level of education is important, as it will inform the choice of vocabulary and grammatical structures. It will also influence the decision to use, or not, certain paratextual devices such as footnotes or endnotes, since they may not be appropriate for all readers. For example, footnotes or endnotes usually appear on texts aimed at the educated, or specialised readers.

2.4.3 Social and/or geographical group

This relates to the social and/or geographical background of the TT's intended readership and will inform the decisions taken at the varietal level. The TT's intended reader might belong to a particular social group with its own sociolect or to a particular geographical space with their own dialect or language variety. For example, different decisions may be made with regard to varietal features such as choices of certain vocabulary, syntactical structures, register, and so on, depending on whether the intended readership is, for instance, Canadian or European French; or whether the audience is teenagers, young adults, etc.

Here, it is important to differentiate between features related to the intended readership that are linked to the varietal filter, and varietal issues that are a feature of the ST. In other words, as pointed out in Chapter 1, the fact that a text or part of a text is written in a particular sociolect such as, for example, teen speech, does not necessarily mean that the intended reader belongs to that particular social group (i.e. a teenager in the above case). That is, even though the social and/or geographical background of the intended reader is not totally unrelated from the varietal characteristics of the ST, it is better to keep it separate at this stage of the analysis and when articulating the translation strategy.

Apart from the above, this part of the commentary can also include the time and place of publication, as suggested by Nord (1997a: 60). That is, we need to decide where in the world the TT is going to be published. It might be in two different places at once, such as, for example, London and New York and, hence, we would need to consider how it is going to affect our decisions when translating varietal features. As for the time of publication, if, at the time, certain global sensitive issues are at the forefront of the minds of the intended readers, this might also affect our lexical choices, tone, and so on. Varietal issues are discussed in greater depth in Chapter 3.

2.4.4 Occupation and degree of specialisation

These two categories are interlinked. Certain occupations use a particular jargon, which will involve lexical, syntactical, and stylistic choices, and within each occupation there might be different levels of specialisation. When we look at these two factors, it is easier to understand the way the TT's intended readership may be very different to that of the ST. For instance, a text could have been written in the SC for medical researchers, but the TT could be intended for medical practitioners (which, not being a homogeneous group, have different degrees of specialisation; for example, a brain surgeon as opposed to a care nurse), or for patients. The TT's intended reader might even have a totally different occupation to that of the ST, such as, in the example above, a patient as opposed to a medical practitioner. Another example could be the translation of a political speech addressed in the SC to the general public, but translated, for instance, for linguists, historians or political experts. The important thing here is that once we have decided the profile of the TT's intended readership with regard to their level of specialisation, we will need to abide to their expectations.

2.4.5 Previous knowledge

This is also linked to the level of specialisation; that is, how much previous knowledge of the subject matter the intended reader may already have. However, it also refers to their previous knowledge of the source culture. This will inform our use of translation techniques such as explicitation and omission, as well as the use of certain paratextual devices such as glosses (intratextual glosses and extratextual glosses), as well as explanatory or introductory prefaces, glossaries, and so on.

Theoretical approaches particularly useful here are relevance theory (Gutt 2000; Sperber and Wilson 1986/1995, 2004) and pragmatics and translation (Baker 1992/2011), particularly regarding issues to do with presupposition and implicature. Grice (1975) proposed four maxims for effective communication based on the cooperative principle: the maxim of quantity, the maxim of quality, the maxim of relation, and the maxim of manner. The maxim of relation or relevance means that we need to decide whether to omit information that the intended reader might already know or to add more information so that the intended reader can fully understand the text. For example, if you were to translate a sentence such as, 'Number 10 has decided to start vaccinating under 18s,' unless the intended reader knows what 'Number 10' refers to, we will need to add more information, such as 'the UK government' or, 'the UK Prime Minister,' in the TT.

If the chosen structure of the commentary is thematic, issues to do with the TT's intended readership and how its profile has informed the decisions of detail could be the main line of argument, which will need to be underpinned by the theories mentioned above. In any case and regardless of the structure of the commentary, it is still necessary to do a ST analysis and articulate the translation strategy.

Task 2.3

Activity 1

Look at the excerpts from sample commentaries and translation briefs below and decide what aspects of the intended reader have been described. If there is any information missing on any of the aspects, add your own detail and write down how this would affect your translation.

Excerpt 1

Part of a 5000-word commentary for a translation from English into Spanish.

ST: Kaur, Jasmin (2019) *When You Ask Me Where I'm Going*. New York: Harper Collins.

Nevertheless, before discussing the problems posed by the ST, as well as the strategies adopted for the TT, it is necessary to define who the audience of the latter would be, which raises its own issues. Since the selected target readers were Spanish speakers from the American continent, I attempted to align with a standard American Spanish, although in order to obtain a creative tone, it took some distance, in occasions, from the 'neutral' variety, so that words or expressions that would give a more lyrical content to the poems could be selected.

Excerpt 2

Part of a 5000-word commentary for a translation from English into Chinese.

ST: Clements, Andrew (2002) *A Week in the Woods*. New York and London: Simon & Schuster.

Every translation is a text produced with a target purpose for the target audience in target contexts (Colina 2015: 44). Especially in children's literature, children at different ages have different linguistic abilities that are linked to their different stages of language acquisition. Thus, the target readers (TRs) must be identified. Searched on Amazon, the reading ages of the ST are 9 to 13, and the TRs are Chinese students in the same age group.

Activity 2

Select up to two texts among the STs analysed in Chapter 1 and formulate at least two different intended readership profiles for a possible translation of each one of them, including information on how this would affect your translation priorities.

Activity 3

Look at one or two translations that you have previously done and formulate the profile of their intended reader. Think of a possible different intended reader for each one of your chosen TTs and explain how the translation would be different.

2.5 Medium of publication

The medium of publication of a text is linked to its skopos, genre, and text type, as well as to its intended readership. Usually, as in the case of the genre and text type, there are conventions, norms, and restrictions linked to the medium of publication, some of which might be shared between different cultures, but others might be more culturally specific. In addition to this, we also need to remember that the TT's medium of publication may not necessarily be the same as that of the ST. For example, we can translate a text that was published as a newspaper article in the SC into a text which will form part of a website. Moreover, your TT might have other elements which are either non-verbal (images) or outside the text itself (theatre directions). This is discussed in the next section, on the use of paratextual devices. Part III is dedicated to audiovisual translation, localisation, and transcreation, which are, to some extent, related to the medium of publication.

Task 2.4

Activity 1

Select up to two texts among the STs analysed in Chapter 1 and formulate at least two different media of publication for a possible translation of each one of them, including information on how this would affect your translation priorities.

Activity 2

Look at one or two translations that you have previously done and formulate the medium of publication for each one of them. Think of a different possible medium of publication for each one of your chosen TTs and explain how this would affect the translation.

2.6 Paratextual devices

As mentioned in Chapter 1, in this textbook, we consider to be paratextual devices all of the materials that surround the text, such as the cover, the title, blurbs, notes (both footnotes and endnotes), illustrations and images, introductions, appendixes, hyperlinks, copyright page, etc. Many of these devices are often linked to the intended readership.

Here we need to make a distinction between the paratextual devices used in the ST, which would have formed part of the ST analysis discussion, and the extra paratextual devices that might be used in the TT and are not in the ST, such as translator's notes (either footnotes or endnotes), a preface or introduction providing contextual information and/or a justification or explanation for certain translation decisions, glossaries, and so on. These are discussed separately in what follows.

2.6.1 *Paratextual devices in the ST*

As mentioned before, most assignments will not require an explanation into the use of the paratextual devices in great depth, but it might be necessary to make important decisions with regard to some of these features. Paper books usually have most, if not all, of the following parts (for a more detailed description of each part, go to Chapter 1):

- *The front matter.*
- *The body of the text.*
- *The back matter.*

As for ebooks, they usually have hyperlinks.

As is the case with the medium of publication, different cultures have different norms about the use of paratextual devices. For example, the contents page might be part of the back matter rather than the front matter. Therefore, it is important to become familiar with these norms before articulating the translation strategy. Also, in some universities, the use of hyperlinks might not be allowed, so it is advisable to check first what is, or is not, possible to use in a particular assignment.

The parts of a text from the above list that will be relevant for formulating the translation strategy are the epigraph, tables, figures, footnotes, endnotes, bibliography, and the glossary. Some of these elements may contain or consist of a quotation, a phrase, or references to sources that may not have necessarily been written originally in the SL. Furthermore, some of the issues that might emerge from the use of paratextual devices are linked to intertextuality, which is discussed at greater length in Chapter 3. Thus, we suggest the following:

- *If these paratextual elements have originally been written in the SL*, we need to find out whether there is already a published translation of these elements in the TC and decide whether we want to use this rather than our own translation. If we decide the former and there are several different translations, we need to discuss the criteria used to choose between the available alternatives.
- *If these paratextual elements have been translated into the SL from a text originally written in the TL*, it is advisable to go back to the TL original source and discuss this fact in the commentary.
- *If these paratextual elements have been translated into the SL from a text originally written in a language other than the SL or the TL*, in a similar way to the case above, we need to find out whether there is already a published translation of these elements in the TC and decide whether we want to use this rather than our own translation. If we decide the former and there are several different translations, we need to discuss the criteria used to choose between the available alternatives.
- *If these paratextual elements are written in the TL*, we need to decide whether to indicate this fact to the reader or not, or whether to use a particular translation technique to deal with them. If we choose the latter, we recommend reading theoretical issues relating to the translation of multilingual texts (a list of which is recommended at the end of this chapter).
- *If these paratextual elements are written in a language other than the SL or the TL*, we need to decide whether to leave it in that language or, as was the case above, whether to use a particular translation technique to deal with them. If we choose the latter, we also recommend reading theoretical issues related to the translation of multilingual texts.

2.6.2 Paratextual devices in the TT

If the decision has been made to use any extra paratextual devices that are not present in the ST, it is necessary to specify it in the commentary as part of the translation strategy. All of these extra devices are linked to the TT's intended readership, particularly to their previous knowledge and degree of specialisation. If the reader needs added information, contextual and/or explanatory, it is necessary to decide whether this information will be given as an intratextual gloss (within the text), in which case it would not be considered a paratextual device, or whether it would be given as an extratextual gloss, in the form of a footnote and/or endnote. If this is the case, it is important to differentiate these from the notes already present in the ST, by using acronyms or phrases such as 'TN,' 'Translator's note,' or something similar in the relevant language. Instead of extratextual glosses or even in addition to them, it might be possible to use a preface or introduction where some contextual information is provided in order to justify translation choices. Another possible paratextual device is a glossary at the end of the TT. Both the preface and the glossary have the advantage of not stopping the flow of the narrative. It is important to also remember that, as mentioned above, the use of footnotes usually indicates an educated reader, so the use of paratextual devices needs to be consistent with the TT's intended reader. As was the case with the use of hyperlinks, we will also need to check first what is, or is not, possible to use in a particular assignment.

Task 2.5

Activity 1

Look at the two STs that you selected for Task 9 in Chapter 1, which you have analysed for their use of paratextual devices. Explain how you are going to deal with these devices in your TT.

Activity 2

Using the same STs as in the previous activity, think of what extra paratextual devices you could use in your TT, explaining how they are linked to your TT's intended readership and adding any other aspect of your translation strategy that you might consider relevant.

2.7 Salient characteristics of the ST important to preserve. Setting out translation priorities

It is important to explicitly formulate the translation priorities, which will inform the decisions at the textual level and provide a coherent justification for them. Haywood et al. (2009: 25) suggest that, if we consider that translation loss is inevitable, the challenge then is 'not to eliminate it completely but to reduce it by deciding which of the relevant features in the ST are most important to respect, and which can most legitimately be sacrificed in doing so.' In other words, we need to set out our translation priorities by selecting those aspects of the ST that we want to preserve in the TT. This process needs to be informed by our strategy, that is, by the TT's genre, text type, skopos, intended reader, and medium of publication, keeping in mind that these are not necessarily the same as those of the ST. For example, we might be translating a political speech, with a persuasive skopos in the SC, but the TT's skopos is informative. In this particular case, one of the translation priorities will be to use a clear language and to avoid ambiguity, and the focus will be on the content rather than on the form or on the effect on the reader. Similarly, we may be translating a medical ST originally intended for experts, but we have been instructed to adapt it to a patient's information sheet. In this case, the main priority would be to determinologise and provide an explanation for the technical vocabulary, as well as to simplify the syntactical structures when needed.

Another reason why it is important to set out our translation priorities is because, as we mentioned in Chapter 1, we cannot or should not try to reproduce every single effect that we encounter in the ST (Nord 2005: 148). Hence, some of the features will be top priority, whilst others will be middle range or even marginal priorities (Zabalbeascoa 2005: 201–202).

Task 2.6

Activity 1

Look at the two excerpts below. They are both part of a 1000-word commentary for a translation of the same ST from Cuba's *Ministerio de Cultura* website POLÍTICA CULTURAL CUBANA (gob.cu). Decide what the translation priorities are, explaining to what extent these relate to the rest of the formulated translation strategy.

Excerpt 1

The source text comes from the website of Cuba's *Ministerio de Cultura*, a government agency that regulates the country's cultural policy. The site informs on the Ministry's activities and objectives, this particular extract constituting a general overview of their public policies. The information given is based on observation rather than theoretical assumptions (e.g. ST 22–27), and therefore belongs to the empirical genre. The ST aims to enlighten readers as to the current and historical cultural processes of the country, so the function is correspondingly informative.

The target text would be part of a UK textbook on the Cuban Revolution for undergraduate students of Hispanic Studies, appearing in a section about lasting cultural impact. The aim is to reproduce the informative function of the ST in a manner accessible to young adults with an interest but only a basic knowledge in these cultural issues.

With Cuban culture at the core of the ST, the implications could not be retained if transplanted to an alternative setting. The translation priority is therefore to avoid compromising either the information given or the significant cultural element. Whilst target language readers will not be as familiar with certain cultural components as the likely overwhelmingly Cuban readership of the ST, any degree of cultural transplantation is inappropriate because figures and events such as José Martí, Fidel Castro (ST 20–21, 64, 74), and *Playa Girón* (ST 70) are indispensable to the ST's message regarding Cuban culture and freedom. To counteract any potential confusion for the TL reader and uphold the informative function, TT 73–4 elaborates on the events of *Playa Girón*, and the prior information in TT 20–21 that the following are key revolutionary ideologies should account for anyone unfamiliar with Martí or Castro. The information must be presented accurately and without any alteration to cultural referents, further evident with regard to lexical items such as 'municipio' (ST 52), translated literally in TT 55. Although this is not a classification that the TL culture would readily use, the TT references Cuba and must therefore respect the geographical organisation of that culture.

Excerpt 2

The source text is taken from the official website of the Cuban ministry of culture, and whilst the identity of the author is unknown, its structure and style are typical of an official government website: formal, with regular paragraphs and long lists of commitments. Its genre is non-fictional and explanatory; however, its function is a little less clearly defined. The passage is predominantly informative but the tone used contains a nationalistic celebration of the Cuban Revolution as well as a persuasion of the reader as to the importance of culture in maintaining the freedom it won. In this sense the text transcends the barriers of different text types proposed by Reiss: it is at once informative and operative (2000).

The target text is intended for publication on the same website, and given the same official place of publication, it aims to be as faithful to the ST as possible, whilst sounding natural in the target language. Another aim of the TT is to reproduce both functions (informative/operative) of the ST: systematically listing the information provided, whilst capturing the text's political aspect and patriotic tone. The target reader is any non-Spanish speaker worldwide, but due to various reasons the TT has adopted US English spelling (TT 5, 43, 50). These reasons include Cuba's geographic location 100 miles off the coast of Florida, and the considerably more widespread use of US English spelling across the globe (Scragg 1974). The target reader has actively decided to click on this page's link, so it is safe to assume a sufficient interest in Cuba to want to read about its cultural policies, and also an understanding that it is a communist country, but beyond that no advanced knowledge of current government policies nor of the Cuban Revolution. Given the importance of this specific revolution, it should under no circumstances be culturally transplanted into the TL, and the TT has also added the word 'Cuban' to 'Revolución' (TT 26, 35, 59, 67) to remove any ambiguity.

Activity 2

Select those excerpts used in the previous activity where the translation priorities were not satisfactorily articulated or were not linked effectively to the rest of the translation strategy and reformulate them so that they are.

2.8 Conclusion

As mentioned in Chapter 1, something particularly important to consider, which will provide coherence and clarity to the commentary, is to make it absolutely clear when we are discussing the ST and when the TT. Therefore, it is imperative to avoid simply referring to 'the text' and to always specify whether we are referring to the ST or the TT. It is not necessary to separate the ST analysis from the statement of the translation strategy as long as this is kept in mind. For example, we might want to discuss the genre, skopos, and medium of publication of both the ST and TT within the same paragraph and leave the rest of the information for the following paragraph. However, some institutions prefer for the students to put the ST analysis in a separate section from the statement of translation strategy.

Moreover, we need to consider that all of the aspects discussed so far work together to form our translation strategy, which, in turn, will inform our decisions of detail. The more specific we are when formulating our translation strategy, the easier it will be to make decisions and justify them. This formulation needs to be explicit, and therefore it is necessary to avoid leaving some of the strategy as implicit, expecting the reader to understand what we mean. Thus, we need to avoid statements such as 'the TT's intended reader has the same level of education as that of the ST' or something to that effect, without explicitly specifying whether they have any previous knowledge of the SC or of the subject matter, or whether they would need certain explanations at particular points in the TT or not.

It is also important to remember the recursive nature of a translation commentary. That is, sometimes, once we have started translating, a problem at the textual level may arise which will make it necessary for us to refine our strategy, and in turn, we may have to revise other translation decisions already taken (Haywood et al. 2009: 9). In other words, our translation strategy will inform the decisions we take at the textual level, but, at the same time, translation challenges at the textual level may force us to refine the strategy. Nothing will be totally fixed until it has been completed.

Task 2.7

Look at the two excerpts below and decide where the ST and TT are discussed. Point out where this is unclear and reformulate those passages to make them clearer and more coherent.

Excerpt 1

Part of a 1000-word commentary for a translation from Russian into English.

ST: Erlan, Karin (2020) *Операция «Жусан»*

The text is an extract from the 2020 book *Операция «Жусан»* by Erlan Karin. As specified in the translation brief, the genre of the work is investigative journalism, directed towards an educated but wide readership with an interest in the subject matter, in particular the history of modern Kazakhstan and terrorism. As the ST was intended for a Russian-speaking audience in Kazakhstan, significant changes were necessary to meet the genre expectations of the TC.

At a macro-textual level, skopos theory was used to guide the necessary adaptations. The skopos, or aim, of the ST is to provide information on a historical event while conveying the author's own assessment. The ST can therefore be categorised as an 'informative' text with a secondary 'operative' function, according to the text types laid out by Reiss and Vermeer (2014: 182). Consequently, Reiß's (translated and adapted in Munday 2012: 112) suggested translation method of 'plain prose' with 'explication as required' for informative texts was the dominant translation strategy used. As per Vermeer (2000: 222), the commission, in this case the translation brief, guided the definition of the TT's skopos, in particular the importance of accuracy in relation to stylistics and content. The function of the TT as a standalone text guided further changes at the micro-textual level to provide a more coherent reading experience and aid the TT reader's further research.

Excerpt 2

Part of a 5000-word commentary for a translation from English to Chinese.

ST: Watson, Casey (2022) *I Just Want to be Loved*. London: HarperCollins.

In this autobiographical writing, the author uses a first-person perspective to create an intimate and natural expression, giving readers a sense of authenticity and vividness. Because of the specificity of the biographical genre, the author did not use overly florid rhetoric and cumbersome descriptions in the book. However, vivid language, apt wording, fluent sentences, and a clear structure are necessary. The characterisation is done from the point of view of the person's speech, actions, and appearance. There are direct descriptions, portraying the person's speech, actions, and psychology. In addition to this, there are also side descriptions, which draw on the setting and the comments of others to show the person's character. The author's storyline is set up in a way that lays the groundwork for readers at the beginning of the story and gradually reveals the truth to stimulate the reader's interest in reading.

The large number of colloquial expressions in the work contains a number of colloquialisms, catchphrases, and meaningless inflections. These English colloquialisms and sayings are very different from the Chinese, and they can also reflect different cultural backgrounds and historical trajectories of language development. When translating these words and phrases, the choice of translation strategy is particularly important, and the use of additions, subtractions, or the reorganisation of sentence structure is one of the difficulties that translators have to overcome. The target audience for this translation are general Chinese readers, so fluency and accessibility of the language is the primary goal when translating. Therefore, the translator mostly used the method of domestication to ensure the readability of the text for Chinese readers, so that they are likely empathising with the author.

2.9 Summary

This chapter focused on the writing of a translation strategy and on the setting out of translation priorities. It discussed the elements that need to be present in a translation brief such as genre, text type, skopos, intended readership, and medium of publication. It also emphasised how, in those cases where a translation brief is not provided, or the instructions in all of the aspects are not given, it is advisable to formulate a translation strategy which includes the decisions made with regard to those elements. Then, after operationalising the concepts of translation strategy and technique within this textbook, the reader was given guidance on the issues needed to be taken into account to make strategic decisions with regard to the elements above, as well as to the issues on the use of paratextual devices. All of this will help establish the translation priorities as well as inform the translation decisions taken at the textual level, which will be discussed in Chapter 3.

Further reading

Genre, text type, and skopos

Nord, Christiane (1997a) *Translating as a Purposeful Activity*. Manchester: St Jerome.

Nord, Christiane (1997b) 'Defining Translation Functions: The Translation Brief as a Guideline for the Trainee Translation', *Ilha do Desterro*, 3: 39–54.

Nord, Christiane (2005) *Text Analysis in Translation: Theory, Methodology, and Didactic Application of a Model for Translation-oriented Text Analysis*, 2nd ed. Amsterdam & New York: Rodopi.

Reiss, Katharina (1971/1989) 'Text Types, Translation Types and Translation Assessment', trans. Andrew Chesterman, in Andrew Chesterman (ed) (1989) *Readings in Translation Theory*. Helsinki: Finn Lectura.

Translation of children's literature

van Collie, Jan (2006) *Children's Literature in Translation: Challenges and Strategies*. Manchester: St. Jerome.

Lathey, Gillian (2006) *The Translation of Children's Literature: A Reader*. Clevedon: Multilingual Matters.

Lathey, Gillian (2016) *Translating Children's Literature*. London and New York: Routledge.

Shavit, Zohar (1981) 'Translation of Children's Literature as a Function of Its Position in the Literary Polysystem', *Poetics Today*, 2: 4: 171–179.

Shavit, Zohar (2009) *Poetics of Children's Literature*. Athens, Georgia: University of Georgia Press.

Relevance theory

Gutt, Ernst-August (2000) *Translation and Relevance: Cognition and Context*. Manchester: St. Jerome.

Margala, Miriam (2009) 'Grice in Translation: The Case of Hrabal', *Journal of Language & Translation*, 10: 2: 87–128.

Sperber, Dan and Deirdre Wilson (1986/1995) *Relevance: Communication and Cognition*. Oxford: Blackwell.

Sperber, Dan and Deirdre Wilson (2004) 'Relevance Theory', in Laurence R. Horn and Gregory Ward (eds) *The Handbook of Pragmatics*. Blackwell: Oxford, 607–632.

Pragmatics in translation

Baker, Mona (1992/2011) *In Other Words: A Coursebook on Translation*, 2nd ed. London and New York: Routledge.

Use of paratextual devices

Genette, Gerard (1997) *Paratexts: Thresholds of Interpretation*, trans. Jane E. Lewin. Cambridge: Cambridge University Press.
Kovala, Urpo (1996) 'Translations, Paratextual Mediation and Ideological Closure', *Target*, 8: 1: 119–147.

Translation of multilingual texts

Grutman, Rainier (2006) 'Refraction and Recognition. Literary Multilingualism in Translation', *Target*, 18: 1: 17–47.
Meylaerts, Reine (ed) (2006) *Literary Heteroglossia in/and Translation*, special issue of *Target*, 18: 1.

List of references

Baker, Mona (1992/2011) *In Other Words: A Coursebook on Translation*, 2nd ed. London and New York: Routledge.
Bardaji, Anna Gil (2009) 'Procedures Techniques Strategies Translation Process Operators', *Perspectives: Studies in Translatology*, 17: 3: 161–173.
Carreres, Ángeles, María Noriega-Sánchez and Carmen Calduch (2018) *Mundos en Palabras: Learning Advanced Spanish Through Translation*. New York: Routledge.
Colina, Sonia (2015) *Fundamentals of Translation*. Cambridge: CUP.
van Collie, Jan (2006) *Children's Literature in Translation: Challenges and Strategies*. Manchester: St. Jerome.
van Doorslaer, Luc (2007) 'Risking Conceptual Maps', in Yves Gambier and Luc van Doorslaer (eds) *The Metalanguage of Tanslation*, special issue of *Target*, 19: 2: 217–233.
Franco Aixelá, Javier (1996) 'Culture Specific Items in Translation', in Román Álvarez and María Carmen-África Vidal (eds) *Translation, Power, Subversion*. Clevedon: Multilingual Matters, 52–78.
Genette, Gerard (1997) *Paratexts: Thresholds of Interpretation*, trans. Jane E. Lewin. Cambridge: Cambridge University Press.
Grice, Paul (1975) 'Logic and Conversation', in Peter Cole and Jerry J. Morgan (eds) *Syntax and Semantics 3: Speech Acts*. New York: Academic Press, 41-58.
Grutman, Rainier (2006) 'Refraction and Recognition. Literary Multilingualism in Translation', *Target*, 18: 1: 17–47.

Gutt, Ernst-August (2000) *Translation and Relevance: Cognition and Context.* Manchester: St. Jerome.

Haywood, Louise M., Mike Thompson and Sándor Hervey (2009) *Thinking Spanish Translation. A Course in Translation Method: Spanish to English.* London & New York: Routledge.

Hurtado Albir, A. (2001) *Traducción y Traductología.* Madrid: Cátedra.

Kovala, Urpo (1996) 'Translations, Paratextual Mediation and Ideological Closure', *Target,* 8: 1: 119–147.

Lane-Mercier, Gillian (1997) 'Translating the Untranslatable: The Translator's Aesthetic, Ideological and Political Responsibility', *Target,* 9: 1: 43–68.

Lathey, Gillian (2006) *The Translation of Children's Literature: A Reader.* Clevedon: Multilingual Matters.

Lathey, Gillian (2016) *Translating Children's Literature.* London and New York: Routledge.

Margala, Miriam (2009) 'Grice in Translation: The Case of Hrabal', *Journal of Language & Translation,* 10: 2: 87–128.

Meylaerts, Reine (ed) (2006) *Literary Heteroglossia in/and Translation,* special issue of *Target,* 18: 1.

Munday, Jeremy (2016) *Introducing Translation Studies. Theories and Applications.* 4th ed. London and New York: Routledge.

Muñoz Martín, R. (2000) 'Translation Strategies: Somewhere over the Rainbow', in Allison Beeby, Doris Ensinger and Marisa Presas (eds) *Investigating Translation.* Amsterdam: John Benjamins, 129–138.

Newmark, Peter (1988) *A Textbook of Translation.* Hemel Hempstead: Prentice Hall.

Nida, Eugene A. (1964) *Toward a Science of Translating.* Leiden: E. J. Brill.

Nord, Christiane (1997a) *Translating as a Purposeful Activity.* Manchester: St Jerome.

Nord, Christiane (1997b) 'Defining Translation Functions: The Translation Brief as a Guideline for the Trainee Translation', *Ilha do Desterro,* 3: 39–54.

Nord, Christiane (2005) *Text Analysis in Translation: Theory, Methodology, and Didactic Application of a Model for Translation-oriented Text Analysis,* 2nd ed. Amsterdam & New York: Rodopi.

Reiss, Katharina (1971/1989) 'Text Types, Translation Types and Translation Assessment', trans. Andrew Chesterman, in Andrew Chesterman (ed) *Readings in Translation Theory.* Helsinki: Finn Lectura, 105–115.

Reiss, Katharina and Hans J. Vermeer (2014) *Towards a General Theory of Translational Action. Skopos Theory Explained.* London and New York: Routledge.

Scragg, Donald (1974) *A History of English Spelling.* Manchester: Manchester University Press.

Shavit, Zohar (1981) 'Translation of Children's Literature as a Function of Its Position in the Literary Polysystem', *Poetics Today,* 2: 4: 171–179.

Shavit, Zohar (2009) *Poetics of Children's Literature.* Athens, Georgia: University of Georgia Press.

Sperber, Dan and Deirdre Wilson (1986/1995) *Relevance: Communication and Cognition.* Oxford: Blackwell.

Sperber, Dan and Deirdre Wilson (2004) 'Relevance Theory', in Laurence R. Horn and Gregory Ward (eds) *The Handbook of Pragmatics.* Blackwell: Oxford, 607–632.

Tymoczko, Maria (1999) *Translation in a Postcolonial Context*. Manchester: St. Jerome.

Tymoczko, Maria (2000) 'Translation and Political Engagement. Activism, Social Change and the Role of Translation in Geopolitical Shifts', *The Translator*, 6: 1: 23–47.

Venuti, Lawrence (1995) *The Translator's Invisibility: A History of Translation*. London and New York: Routledge.

Vermeer, H. J. (1978). Ein Rahmen für eine allgemeine Translationstheorie. *Lebende Sprachen*, 23(3): 99–102.

Zabalbeascoa, Patrick (2005) Humor and Translation - an interdiscipline. *Humor*, 18(2): 185-207.

Part II
While translating
The specifics

3 Selecting illustrative examples

Key concepts

- Translation commentary vs translator's footnotes.
- Reflective discussion.
- Characteristics of academic writing.
- Obligatory vs optional translation choices.
- Translation techniques – taxonomy.

3.1 Introduction

Since the focus of this chapter is on selecting examples for your commentary, it does not discuss the possible techniques available for the translator at the microlevel. The assumption is that you are familiar with the techniques discussed in the *Thinking Translation* series, or other translation manuals and general texts (e.g. Baker 1992/2011; Díaz Cintas and Remael 2007; Franco Aixelá 1996; Newmark 1988; Vinay and Darbelnet 1958/1995), and have made an informed choice based on your source text (ST) analysis and translation strategy. If this is not the case, please read the relevant sections of these manuals.

Due to the recursive nature of the commentary, many of the issues discussed in this chapter will be useful when doing the ST analysis at the microlevel (see Chapter 1). However, as we will see in Chapter 4, and for the sake of coherence, it is better to discuss them after we have articulated our statement of translation strategy. Nevertheless, if when analysing the ST at the microlevel we discover certain features that create a particular tone or effect on the reader, it might be worth briefly mentioning this when we discuss the ST analysis at the beginning of our commentary, indicating that it will be further developed at a later stage in the analysis.

As we will see in the next section, one of the undesirable features of weaker translation commentaries is discussing decisions that are obligatory to a particular language combination. If you are writing the commentary to justify your translation decisions, it is important that you discuss those cases where you had several, equally valid, alternatives, and to show that your ST analysis and your translation strategy have informed the choices made. However,

DOI: 10.4324/9781003273790-6

since it is inadvisable, if not impossible, to discuss every single translation decision, we need to select illustrative examples to justify the decisions taken. In fact, in many institutions one of the criteria used to assess translation commentaries is the selection of these examples, mainly in terms of their relevance to the issue discussed.

However, also consider that some institutions may want you to discuss your decisions in a linear (i.e. decision by decision from beginning to end) and comprehensive way, which is sometimes called 'annotated text for translation' or 'translation annotation' (cf. Shih 2018: 298). This type of assignment would tend to have the format of a segment of the translation decision followed by a couple of lines. If you are required to discuss all the decisions taken, rather than the 'controversial' ones, this might take as much space as the translation itself. Please check with your institution what is required in your assignments. In any case, even though in this textbook we focus on writing a reflective academic narrative, rather than a linear and unidirectional justification of the translation decisions taken, many of the principles discussed will be relevant in both cases.

Task 3.1

Discuss in small groups, the following questions:

1. What are the characteristics of academic writing?
2. What do you understand by the word 'reflective'?
3. Taking into account what has been said so far in this textbook, what do you think you are asked to reflect on in a translation commentary?
4. What is the difference between a translation commentary and translator's footnotes?

3.2 Desirable features of a translation commentary

3.2.1 Difference between a translation commentary and translator's footnotes

The types of translation commentaries mentioned above, that are done in a unidirectional way and are usually referred to as 'annotated text for translation' or 'translation annotation' (cf. Shih 2018: 298) look more like what we would consider to be translator's footnotes. Translator's footnotes (which appear at the bottom of the page) or endnotes (which appear at the end of a document, chapter, or whole document), are paratextual devices used by translators to help their readers understand the text (by providing, for example, contextual information, lexical connotations, cultural background, etc.).

Each footnote is usually independent of the others and together they form an unconnected list of several explanations.

However, the type of translation commentary that we are considering here is usually 'perceived to be a hybrid of both an academic essay and reflective narrative' (Shih 2018: 291). This means that it has characteristics of both kinds of writing. Academic writing is analytical and organised, uses a formal register, and is evidenced with examples and theoretical sources. The use of language is concise as well as precise. In reflective writing, although it is not necessary to avoid using the first person, overusing it will give your commentary an anecdotal tone, which would not be appropriate for an academic assignment. In fact, '[i]n reflective writing, you aim to achieve a balance between your personal perspective, experience and ideas and the requirements of good academic practice and rigorous thinking' (Williams et al. 2020: 95).

3.2.2 *Undesirable features of a translation commentary*

Among the undesirable features of a translation commentary found by Shih (2018: 302–303) in her research are:

- Theories that are not linked to translation examples;
- Attempting to discuss too many issues or problems without clear categorisation of the problems and an in-depth analysis on translation examples;
- Inaccurate application of theoretical concepts;
- Developing an argument based on a mistaken translation or miscomprehension in translation;
- Only discussing one issue or one type of translation problem.

To these we could add discussing generic problems of translating in a particular language combination, as well as discussing the issues in a unidirectional order as they appear in the text or without any logical order at all.

3.2.3 *Desirable features of a translation commentary*

Based on the premise that a translation commentary is a hybrid of a reflective narrative and an academic essay, it should ideally:

- Have a coherent and clear structure;
- Include a selection of examples that are representative enough to illustrate the challenging translation issues selected to be discussed rather than including a long list of unconnected examples. In fact, it is advisable to use line numbers both in the ST and the target text (TT) so that you can use them to refer to the examples, in order to be found easily by the reader;
- Discuss optional features; that is, those features where there is a choice between several alternatives where the losses and gains are weighed up,

rather than discussing obligatory changes generic to a particular language pair (for example translating a grammatically non-gendered English word into a grammatically gendered word in a target language [TL], where the gender is a given);

• Cite academic references to support or substantiate your arguments (for advice on referencing, see 4.3).

Some institutions vary on the last point. That is, some will require you to cite academic references, while others will not. You will need to check what your institution requires. Also, if you think you need help with academic writing, please ask in your institution, as this is usually a service provided to students in most educational establishments.

3.3 Selecting illustrative examples

As mentioned above, many institutions use the selection of illustrative examples as one the criteria to assess translation commentaries. It is more a matter of choosing examples that 'are representative enough to illustrate core challenges and problems that are specific to the text being translated' (Shih 2018: 303), rather than providing a long list of unconnected examples.

Although not the only way possible, the matrices in the *Thinking Translation* series will allow you to categorise your examples, as it

provides a checklist of tests that can be carried out on any text to be translated, which can be visualised as a series of filters collecting and sorting relevant textual properties so that their importance for the translation process can be gauged.

(Haywood et al. 2009: 5)

The most effective way to select illustrative examples is to do it while translating. As you come across challenging segments or places where you had to choose between several alternatives, indicate these somehow to yourself and categorise them according to the *Thinking Translation* matrices and issues discussed below. You can do this by using a note, by colour coding the segments, or by any other way that works for you. Once this is done, you will have a databank full of examples from which you can select the most illustrative ones that support and/or justify your decisions. Some of the examples that could be chosen are those features that work together to create a particular tone and effect (discussed in 1.3.3).

We will now go through the *Thinking Translation* series matrices and also other issues as follows: cultural matrix (3.3.1), formal matrix (3.3.2), semantic matrix (3.3.3), and varietal matrix (3.3.4). We will also have a section for intertextual issues (3.3.5) and other challenges (3.3.6).

At the start of each section, we include where these issues are discussed in each of the books in the series. It is advisable for you to read the relevant book for your language combination while you are preparing to write your commentary. You might also benefit from reading the relevant sections of the rest of the books in the series, as they might provide you with some useful information.

3.3.1 Cultural matrix

This section focuses on the cultural features within, rather than outside the text. That is, we will not be discussing extratextual issues (for instance, the cultural context of the ST), which have been dealt with in Chapter 1. In the *Thinking Translation* series, cultural features are discussed in the following publications: Andrews and Maksimova (2009), Chapter 4; Cragie and Pattison (2018: 35–39, 40, 57–63); Cragie et al. (2015), Chapter 5; Dickins et al. (2016), Chapter 4; Haywood et al. (2009), Chapter 5; Hervey and Higgins (1992), Chapter 3; Pellatt and Liu (2010), throughout the book; Rogers et al. (2020), Chapter 5.

3.3.1.1 Culture-specific terminology

Culture has been defined as 'the "shared values" of a group' and 'whatever is distinctive about the way of life of a people, community, nation or social group' (Hall 1997: 2), but the term 'culture' does not necessarily have the same meaning as 'nation state,' which is defined in the *Oxford English Dictionary* as

> An independent political state formed from a people who share a common national identity (historically, culturally, or ethnically); (more generally) any independent political state.

What is relevant for translation are those 'shared values' or experiences, and in addition to values shared internally within a particular culture, in today's world, there are also internationally/interculturally shared values. For example, an institution such as the UN is international, and, although it could be considered to be a cultural reference, it is not bound to any particular nation state. However, it is likely to have a different name depending on the language (for example in Spanish it is ONU, *Organización de las Naciones Unidas*, and in Ukrainian it is *Організація Об'єднаних Націй*). In addition, although some concepts may be universal, 'the same cannot be said of cultural phenomena, where source and target cultures may not share knowledge or experience of the phenomenon or phenomena referred to.' (Cragie and Pattison 2019: 44) This is what has been described as a 'lexical gap,' which will be further discussed in section 3.3.3, when we talk about semantic issues. We also need to take into account cultural references that belong to the target culture (TC) or to a third culture, that is, a culture other than the source culture (SC) or the TC, which Cragie and Pattison (2018: 62) call 'multicultural references.'

Franco Aixelá (1996: 58) uses the phrase 'culture specific items' to refer to these elements, which he defines as:

> Those textually actualized items whose function and connotations in a source text involve a translation problem in their transference to a target text, whenever this problem is a product of the non-existence of the referred item or of its different intertextual status in the cultural system of the readers of the target texts.

Others refer to them as 'cultural references,' which is the term we will use in this book. In some of the *Thinking Translation* series texts they list examples of these items (Haywood et al. 2009: 69–70, Cragie et al. 2015: 26). Within the culture-specific terminology we can include names of institutions, services, habits, customs, objects (food and drink, units of measure, currency, clothes), public notices, proverbs, idioms, conversational clichés. As pointed out by Rogers et al. (2020: 64),

> Cultural issues in translation then can be everything from dealing with translating terms with literary and cultural resonance in a narrow sense, to institutional terms, to problems that are harder to identify, such as industry regulations, modes of address, or genre norms.

In addition to this, we also need to keep up to date with the changes in attitudes about culture-specific terminology, which may take place in the SC and/or the TC (Pattison and Cragie 2022: 13), so that we deal with it accordingly in our translation.

Another relevant thing about cultural references that we need to take into account when translating and also when articulating the translation strategy is the TT reader's pre-knowledge and level of expertise. This will inform our decision on how much extra help and information this reader will need in our TT. That is, analysing the ST with regard the cultural references within it informs our translation strategy by identifying those instances that might create a comprehension problem in the TT reader (cf. Haywood et al. 2009: 69).

The translation of culture-specific terminology could be the main topic of a thematically structured commentary (Chapter 4). It might also be relevant in the case of localisation and transcreation (see Chapter 7).

3.3.1.2 *Proper nouns*

According to Cragie and Pattison (2018: 37), proper nouns tend to be the 'most common cultural items found in STs.' Among proper nouns we find 'ordinary' names, names of famous people (such as kings and queens, writers, artists, etc), forms of address, toponyms or names of places (countries, cities, towns, streets, buildings, etc.), and titles of literary works, to cite some examples.

The typical translation issues that are encountered when translating proper names mainly have to do with pre-existing translations, some of which might already be established in the target culture. An example of this are the names of the cities and countries that appear on maps and atlases; sometimes they are domesticated and others foreignised. Another example is the Spanish translation of William Shakespeare, which is usually foreignised whereas, for instance, King Charles III is domesticated as *El Rey Carlos III*.

An added translation issue that we encounter when translating proper nouns is when they are semantically loaded. In 'The dead' in James Joyce's collection of short stories, *Dubliners*, published in 1914, there is a character called 'Lily.' As the name refers to the flower, which is generally used at funerals in the UK, it is safe to assume that the name is semantically loaded and linked to the title of the story. This might be one of the cases where we have to accept a loss in translation, as the equivalent flower might not be used in funerals or it might not be a girl's name at all.

Other instances where the proper names are semantically loaded are when the 'proper names that were created by the author in a clear intention to evoke laughter' (Podleśny 2021: 97) and they actually are 'an inseparable part of the storyline' (Podleśny 2021: 206). There are many examples of this in the literature, as in Podleśny's (2021) discussion of the translation into Polish of the proper names in Terry Pratchett's juvenile stories; or the case study in Munday (2016: 192–193), where he analyses the translations of the proper nouns in *Harry Potter and the Philosopher's Stone* by J.K. Rowling. A final example is the praised English translations by Anthea Bell OBE of the Franco-Belgian *Asterix* series by René Goscinny and Albert Uderzo, which started to be published in the late 1950s. Most of the characters names include a pun: the dog, Idéfix, the druid, Panoramix, and the oldest man in the Gaul village, Âgecanonix, have been translated as Dogmatix, Getafix, and Geriatrix, thus keeping the humour and even, sometimes, adding more humorous associations.

The translation of proper nouns could be the main topic of a thematically structured commentary, discussed in Chapter 4, either as a self-standing topic or linked to the translation of humour. It might also be relevant in the case of transcreation (see Chapter 7).

3.3.1.3 *Taxonomy of techniques for translating culture-specific items*

By 'taxonomy' we mean a list of categories. As mentioned earlier, there are translation studies texts and manuals (e.g. Baker 1992/2011; Díaz Cintas and Remael 2007; Franco Aixelá 1996; Newmark 1988; Vinay and Darbelnet 1958/1995) that include a list of different translation techniques, to be used mainly with cultural references. There are also some techniques listed in some of the *Thinking Translation* series when they discuss the cultural matrix (Haywood et al. 2009: 7–8; Hervey and Higgins 1992: 5; Cragie et al. 2015: 3–4; Dickins et al. 2016: xviii), which are loosely based on Vinay and Darbelnet (1958/1995). In addition, Cragie and Pattison (2018: 67–70), although they do not include a table of matrices in their book, discuss in detail a taxonomy of techniques, which they refer to as 'micro strategies.' In your translation commentary, you can use any taxonomy or a combination of them, but you need to be clear, precise, and consistent in your use of terminology.

When we talked about the example of the translation of King Charles III into Spanish we mentioned a foreignising or a domesticating technique. In the glossary of Haywood et al. (2009: 270), a foreignising or exoticising translation is defined as a '[source language- (SL-)] biased translation strategy aiming to retain features of the ST and the SL culture in the TT,' and it is contrasted with a domesticating or naturalising translation, which is defined as 'a TL-biased translation strategy aiming to make the TT seem as accessible and familiar as possible to TL readers, especially on the cultural level' (2009: 270). Those of you familiar with translation theory will recognise Venuti's (1995/2017) concepts, which are based on an earlier work by Schleiermacher (1813/2012). Here you can see how the term 'strategy' has been used with a slight lack of precision, as it is not totally clear whether the definition for foreignisation and domestication applies to the overall translation strategy, or the translation techniques used at the microlevel.

Regardless of the lack of terminological precision found in some texts, it is important to bear in mind the difference between the concepts of strategy and technique, as we discussed in Chapter 2. It is also important not to make statements that are too vague such as, 'my strategy is to translate the text communicatively,' when you actually mean something like 'the translation strategy is TL-biased and most of the cultural references will be translated using a domesticating or communicative technique.'

Another issue to bear in mind is that the concepts of 'foreignising' and 'domesticating' are not necessarily an either/or situation. Tymoczko (1999) claims that certain aspects of a text might be foreignised, while others might be domesticated, which means that the target text is oriented simultaneously towards both cultures. This opinion is shared by Lane-Mercier (1997: 56), who believes that both strategies can come into play 'for different reasons, at different textual sites, with varying effects, in the course of the translation process' (1997: 55–56). Nevertheless, it is advisable to be consistent with sets of cultural references, for example you can decide to domesticate currency but foreignise measurements and forms of address, etc.

Venuti's (1995/2017) concepts of foreignisation and domestication, discussed above, could be some of the theoretical concepts that could be integrated within your commentary, particularly when dealing with cultural references. The use of these techniques could also be the main topic of a thematically structured commentary.

Task 3.2

Activity 1

Read the excerpt below, which discusses how the cultural references were dealt with in the translation. Identify the terminology that refers to the translation techniques used. Discuss in groups the precision and accuracy of the terms used and suggest any amendments that you deem necessary.

Excerpt

Part of a 2500-word commentary for a translation from English into French.

ST: *Plan Your Visit to York* | Visit York

On a cultural level, British cultural and historical references that do not coexist in French are largely unchanged in that they are rendered in the same way but may include a short gloss so that the reference is not entirely misunderstood. For example, 'the Domesday Book' (ST 234) is rendered as 'le livre de 1086 Domesday Book' (TT 248), just as 'King Charles I's gentleman of the bedchamber' (ST 251) is rendered as 'le "Gentleman of the Bedchamber" du roi Charles Ier, le courtisan …' (TT 266-7). This is to purposefully highlight British culture by employing Venuti's (1995) concept of foreignization, which may appeal to French tourists wanting to visit York for its history. Alternative translations could have seen the transliteration of these cultural references, though this could have led to terms being coined such as 'le Livre du judgement dernier' and 'monsieur de la chambre' respectively, which would not provide any clarification of these terms to a native French speaker.

While the addition of glosses proved useful for certain cultural items, it was also necessary in parts to omit short sections of text where glosses would add little to no value to understanding and would instead have a negative effect on cohesion. This was mostly an issue for references to the Yorkshire dialect. For example, the sentence relating to impressing the locals and calling a street 'Bishy Road' (ST 421-2) was omitted entirely as it would require a certain level of linguistic competency in English that one can assume many speakers of other languages may lack; those who otherwise have this level of linguistic competency may opt to read the tourism brochure in the original English source text.

Activity 2

Look at one translation that you have previously done and articulate how you dealt with the cultural references, taking special care to use the terminology in a precise manner.

3.3.2 Formal matrix

In the *Thinking Translation* series formal features are discussed in the following publications: Andrews and Maksimova (2009), Chapters 2, 3, 7, and 9; Cragie and Pattison (2018), Chapter 2; Cragie et al. (2015), Chapters 5, 6, and 7; Dickins et al. (2016), Chapters 9, 10, 12, and 13; Haywood et al. (2009), Chapter 6 and 7; Hervey and Higgins (1992), Chapters 6, 7, and 8; Pellatt and Liu (2010), Chapters 1, 2, 3, and 4; Rogers et al. (2020), Chapters 8, 9, 10, and 11.

The *Thinking Translation* series books propose several levels of analysis in the formal matrix. However, as there are some differences in the categories between the books, in this textbook, we will use the ones proposed in Dickins et al. 2016: xviii), as they appear to be the most applicable to most language combinations:

Phonic/graphic level.
Prosodic level.
Grammatical level: Lexis, morphology, and syntax.
Sentential level.
Discourse level.

Some books in the series (Dickins et al. 2016: xviii; Hervey and Higgins 1992: 5; Cragie et al. 2015: 4) introduce intertextual issues in the formal matrix. However, since we consider these issues to be of particular relevance to a translation commentary, they will be discussed in section 3.3.5.

3.3.2.1 Phonic/graphic level

Some of the issues to do with the phonic and graphic level will be more relevant when the language combination in question includes languages with different script; if the ST includes poems or lyrics from songs; or if it is a persuasive text, such as an advertisement or a political campaign, which use phrases or slogans that contain sound effects, such as alliteration, onomatopoeia, etc. These issues are also relevant in transcreation discussed in Chapter 7.

In some cases, we might also need to look at the use of punctuation and typography such as italics, capitals, and bold typeface, to express a certain nuance (Nord 2005: 137) such as emphasis, anger, intonation, stress, etc., but we need to keep in mind that not all languages use this typography. For example, as pointed out by Dickins et al. (2016: 163), capitals do not exist in Arabic and translators need to resort to adding an explicit comment such as 'he shouted.'

We need to bear in mind, however, that if we decide to select some examples from the phonic or graphic level, we will need to point out explicitly which of these features are relevant in the ST for the construction of meaning.

We must also remember that the equivalent features in the TL might not have the same effect.

The translation of phonic and/or graphic features could be the main topic of a thematically structured commentary. It might also be relevant in the case of localisation and transcreation (See chapter 7).

3.3.2.2 *Prosodic level*

This level has to do with 'vocal pitch' and 'rhythm,' metric, tempo, as well as syllable and/or stress patterns. As in the section above, the discussion of these features will be most relevant when dealing with poetry translation, although there are other genres and text types that might use these stylistic devices, such as, for example, advertising slogans. Again, we will only need to point this out when the features are important for meaning construction.

3.3.2.3 *Grammatical level: Lexis, morphology, and syntax*

Rogers et al. (2020: 130) refers to 'grammatical changes' as 'those changes that necessarily occur in translation at the level of the word and phrase because the available structural patterns and habits of expression in the two languages are different.' As we have been pointing out so far, due to the fact that the commentary is an opportunity to justify our translation decisions, we would need to focus on translation decisions that are not obligatory but optional. It is at the grammatical level that we need to be more vigilant not to do so. Comparative Linguistics theories will be useful here.

A point to consider here is where the formal matrix overlaps with the semantic matrix. This may happen in cases where individual morphemes carry lexical as well as grammatical information (Haywood et al. 2009: 90) and, therefore, are important for the construction of meaning. Another example could be in the use of mode or verb tenses. For instance, in Spanish the use of the subjunctive indicates uncertainty on the part of the speaker or author. It could also cast doubt on whether something is a fact. This can be illustrated by an opinion column written by Alex Grijelmo, published in *El País* (4 April 2015), entitled 'Los errores que se reconocen en subjuntivo' (literally 'the errors that are acknowledged in the subjunctive'), where the author is ironically referring to the use of the subjunctive by Spanish politicians to admit (or not admit) their mistakes. In other words, different languages use grammar differently to construct meaning.

Another issue to be borne in mind here, and a pitfall to avoid is, how idiomatic a particular grammatical structure is in the SL. An example of this is the preference in the English language to use phrasal verbs rather than cognates of Latin origins, or the extensive use of gerunds. A novice translator might tend to translate the ST by following too closely the SL structures, thus making their TT less idiomatic, awkward, and, in some cases, grammatically incorrect. However, there are some cases where the ST author deviates from the grammatical rules to create an effect; for example,

Hemingway used far fewer adjectives and adverbs in his prose than other writers. If in your ST the author deviates from the grammatical rules of the SL, you will need to decide how to deal with this and how best to reflect it in your TT. Whatever your decision is, this would be something worth discussing in your commentary.

3.3.2.4 *Sentential level*

Hervey and Higgins (1992: 105–106) give the following definition of a sentence:

> A sentence is defined as a complete, self-contained and ready-made vehicle for communication: nothing needs to be added before it can be uttered and understood in concrete situations … Note that, in this definition, a sentence does not necessarily contain a verb.

This means that a sentence could consist of just one word and, therefore, several of the points discussed in the previous subsections are also applicable here, such as syntax and punctuation for example (cf. Haywood et al. 2009: 90–91). Nevertheless, the focus at the sentential level is mainly on the order the information is given, which is particularly relevant in certain languages (such Arabic for example) and affects the overall coherence of the text, discussed in the next subsection.

Thus, in some cases the order in which the information is presented may be used to create meaning, by 'foregrounding' or 'backgrounding' part of the content (Dickins et al. 2016: 160). This is also related to the theme-rheme structure discussed in 1.3.1. The use of 'foregrounding' and 'backgrounding' techniques could also be the main topic of a thematically structured commentary.

3.3.2.5 *Discourse level*

According to Haywood et al. (2009: 91):

> In its basic linguistic sense, a discourse is a collection of sentences or utterances forming a complete text: a conversation, a speech, a letter, an instruction leaflet, an advertisement, a poem, a novel.

One of the issues to look at here is cogency, both in terms of cohesion and coherence. These three concepts are interrelated and are defined in the glossary of Haywood et al. (2009: 269) as follows: cogency is 'a "thread" of intellectual interrelatedness of ideas running through a text'; coherence is 'a tacit, yet intellectually discernible, thematic development that characterises a cogent text, as distinct from a random sequence of unrelated sentences'; cohesion is 'the explicit and transparent linking of sentences and larger sections of text by the use of overt linguistic devices that act as "signposts" for the cogency of the text.'

Cohesion can be achieved by use of discourse connectors (for example, however, nevertheless, furthermore, etc.); by using 'grammatical anaphora' (Hervey and Higgins 1992: 115), that is, expressions that refer back to something that has already been mentioned, such as 'he,' 'them,' 'the latter' (Haywood et al. 2009: 91); by repeating the same word, phrase or clause at certain points in the text or very close to each other, which is referred to as 'rhetorical anaphora' (Hervey and Higgins 1992: 117–18) and is used in 'political speeches, advertising, journalism and literary texts'; or by using a particular semantic field throughout the text, like, for instance, using a semantic field of illnesses and viruses in a text against tourism.

Coherence is the 'tacit thematic and intentional development running through the text' (Haywood et al. 2009: 92). In other words, it is the way the ideas have been ordered, such as, for example, from the general to the specific or vice versa, chronologically, in a circular manner, etc.

We must, however, keep in mind that the cohesion and the coherence of a text are not always constructed in the same way in different languages (cf. Rogers et al. 2020: 121). Even the use of punctuation (Dickins et al. 2016: 183) or the paragraphing (Dickins et al. 2016: 183) as cohesive devices might be different depending on the language. Nevertheless, as pointed out by Pellatt and Liu (2010), some of these differences may be due to an individual writer or a particular genre. This type of markedness or idiosyncrasy is linked to the concept of ostranenie, mentioned above, which would explain potential deviations from the SL rules.

Therefore, in this part of the analysis, it might be a good idea to focus both on deviations from the SL rules and markedness. That is, the author of the ST may have used these techniques to create a certain meaning and/or to produce a particular effect on the reader, as has been discussed in section 1.3.3. In addition, we might also need to identify some of the formulae used in the ST, which may traditionally be used in a particular genre or text type (such as, for instance, 'Once upon a time' at the start of a fairy tale) to be able to decide the level of adaptation we need to make to cater for the differences in the TC, of equivalent formulaic texts.

Task 3.3

Activity 1

Read the excerpt below and identify the ST's formal issues that are discussed. In groups, give your opinion of the effectiveness of this discussion in terms of the coherence of the excerpt and the representativeness of the examples chosen. Also suggest any amendments that you deem necessary.

Excerpt

Part of a 2500-word commentary for a translation from English into French.

ST: *Plan Your Visit to York* | Visit York

On a formal level, cohesion became a challenge in translation, as the English source text in places has longer sentences that were not easily translated into French. On the whole, longer sentences were separated into two or more shorter sentences in order to aid cohesion in French (see TT 27 ff.). While foreignisation was mostly restricted to the names of places and events, domestication was employed on this more sentential level in order to read naturally and give less of an impression of being a literal translation from the source language. This conforms with the translation strategy in that cohesive sentences keep French idiomaticity and sentences which are easy to understand can play a part in encouraging a visit.

Moreover, on the cohesive level, due to word order changes in French when translating from English, omission was used in cases where word repetition occurred in close proximity. For example, 'in the city … in York city centre 8' (ST 76–77) is rendered as 'du centre-ville de York [in the centre of the town of York]' (TT 77–88) in the first instance of 'city' and omitted in the second. Similarly, see also omission of 'of the Moors' (ST 381–382) wherein necessary glossing of the full name would have led to repetition of the sentence prior.

Continuing on the formal level, a difficult translation decision had to be made for a section title due to reasons of prosody. 'It's time to unwind and expand your mind' (ST 346) proved difficult to translate into French in wanting to keep the meaning of the phrase but equally retain the rhyme to conform to the text's secondary purpose of entertaining the reader. Ultimately, I decided to favour the retention of the phrase meaning to indicate the following section's content to a reader, rather than keeping the rhyme but losing any underlying meaning: 'Il est temps d'élargir l'esprit et de se détendre [It's time to broaden your mind and relax oneself]' (TT 372). As this section's purpose is to promote the relaxing and calm aspects of York, priority emphasis is to be given to the meaning of the words themselves as opposed to sticking to a rhyming scheme.

On a grammatical level, an important decision for the target text is one of the levels of pronominal formality used in sections of direct address to the reader. As this text has a primary and secondary purpose of informing and entertaining the reader, it employs direct address often. The strategy for this target text is to produce an equivalent tourism brochure for 'Visit York,' so I decided to use more direct address in the form of the second-person plural pronoun, as opposed to the second-person singular or third-person singular pronoun, with the aim of using said direct address as a means of reinforcing the brochure's ultimate goal, which is to encourage readers to visit York by actively calling upon them as a form of marketing. The plural pronoun was chosen over the singular pronoun as it is addressing multiple people and equally does not want to create too informal a rapport with a given reader. This approach is also in line with approaches taken in other tourism brochures in France with French as the source language (see Office de Tourisme de Dijon Métropole 2022).

Moreover, on the grammatical level, some words or phrases proved difficult in translation when attempting to match the source word class in the target text, so word class shifting was used in these cases. For example, 'a must do' (ST 1845) does not translate well, and so I decided to convert the word class from noun to the French verb 'devoir,' thus creating a final rendering of 'quelque chose que tout le monde doit faire [something everyone should do]' (TT 197).

Activity 2

Look at one translation that you have previously done and articulate how you have dealt with the formal features by taking special care to select representative examples of optional, rather than obligatory decisions.

3.3.3 *Semantic matrix*

In the *Thinking Translation* series, semantic features are discussed in the following publications: Andrews and Maksimova (2009), Chapters 5, 8, 10, 11, 12, 13, 14, 15; Cragie and Pattison (2018), Chapter 1: 21, 31–33, and Chapter 2: 55–56; Cragie et al. (2015), Chapters 8, 9, 12, and 13; Dickins et al. (2016), Chapters 8, 9, 12, and 13; Haywood et al. (2009), Chapters 8, 9, 12, and 13; Hervey and Higgins (1992), Chapters 9 and 10; Pellatt and Liu (2010), Chapters 3, 4, 5, 7, and 9; Rogers et al. (2020), Chapters 7, 12.2, 14, and 15. Within this matrix we can discuss the following issues: connotative and denotative meaning; ambiguities, collocations, and neologisms; technical terminology; and the translation of metaphors.

Due to the word count restrictions of your particular assignment, you might only be able to discuss one or two of the points below. What we provide here is another checklist that will allow you to subcategorise any semantic issues you may encounter while translating. You would then have to decide which examples would be more illustrative to select for inclusion in your commentary.

3.3.3.1 *Denotative and connotative meaning*

The *Thinking Translation* series differentiates between literal (or denotative) and connotative (or figurative) meaning. As mentioned in the glossary of the series, '[t]he overall meaning of an expression in context is compounded of the literal meaning of the expression plus its contextually relevant connotative overtones.' Often, these connotative overtones or associate meanings, which are usually culturally bound, accompany the referential content of a particular expression (Rogers et al. 2020: 95). To get a full understanding of the ST when we are carrying out the analysis, we need to be aware of the possible connotations the words, expressions, and phrases used might have. This will allow us to decide what to do with them in our translation, as, on the one hand, we might not be able to preserve all of the connotations of certain words or phrases and, on the other, we might not want our TT to have connotations that were not present in the ST as they may often be inappropriate. Among these connotations we can find the following:

3.3.3.2 Ambiguities

Ambiguities are any expressions that can have more than one possible meaning. Regardless of whether they are intentional or unintentional (Cragie and Pattison 2018: 55–56), we need to be aware of them in the ST as they will potentially have an effect on the tone of the text and on the readership, as was discussed in 1.3.3. In addition, we need to be careful not to create an unintentional ambiguity in the TT.

3.3.3.3 Collocations

Collocations are defined by Cragie and Pattison (2019: 28) as 'sets of words used in combination, such as nouns and verbs, nouns and adjectives or verbs and adverbs' in a particular language. For example, in English the collocation is 'to commit a crime' and 'to make a mistake' in Spanish the word for 'commit' is used both with 'crime' and with 'mistake,' as in 'cometer un crimen' and 'cometer un error,' rather than 'hacer un error.' Something to bear in mind is the author's intentional use of unusual collocations to create an effect.

3.3.3.4 Neologisms

Neologisms are newly coined words or expressions. Even though they usually appear in technical texts, they are also abundant after certain events, such as the movement 'Black Lives Matter,' the global Covid pandemic, etc. Certain genres (such as, for example, science-fiction, fantasy, and children's literature) are also full of neologisms (Cragie and Pattison 2019: 45).

3.3.3.5 Synonyms

Some languages (for example, Spanish and French) have a stylistic preference to use synonyms in certain genres. However, we need to be careful, because in certain texts, for instance legal or technical texts, the use of synonyms could be considered to be a lack of consistency and could cause confusion.

3.3.3.6 *Technical terminology*

In those cases where the ST is a technical text, you will need to make sure you understand the terminology accurately as 'most technical texts are relatively inaccessible to the non-specialist reader' due to both lexical and conceptual reasons (Hervey and Higgins 1992: 172). It might also be a good idea to create a glossary, particularly for the sake of consistency.

The texts that are likely to be categorised as technical are those that belong to specialised fields from both the sciences and the humanities (medicine, law, psychology, archaeology, engineering, etc.). These texts are characterised by the use of technical terminology which has a specific meaning within its particular field as well as 'its own technical register, its own jargon, its own genre-marking characteristics' (Haywood et al. 2009: 211).

When analysing a technical ST, it might be useful to bear in mind the difference between language for specific purposes, whose lexical items are called 'terms,' and language for general purposes, whose lexical items are called 'words'. As pointed out by Bowker (2023: 62), terms are used to refer to 'concepts in a specialised field of knowledge,' which could be linked not only to a profession, but also to other activities or hobbies. Sometimes the difference between these two concepts is fuzzy. Often, these terms or words will not have an equivalent in the TC due to a 'lexical gap.' That is, as we mentioned previously, when a concept does not exist in the TC, it is referred to as a 'lexical gap' (discussed in 3.3.1.1).

3.3.3.7 *Metaphors*

Schäffner (2004: 1253) defines a 'metaphor' as 'a figure of speech, as a linguistic expression which is substituted for another expression (with a literal meaning), and whose main function is the stylistic embellishment of the text.'

Identifying metaphors is relevant when we analyse the ST, because the meaning created by metaphors is often culturally bound and dependent on the SL linguistic structures. This means that often it is not possible to preserve the same image and its associations in translation (Schäffner 2004: 1256). This will alert you to possible procedures and techniques you can use to deal with them in your translation, which will inform your translation strategy.

The translation of semantic issues such as, for example, the translation of metaphors is also an issue which could be the main topic of a thematically structured commentary, which will be further discussed in Chapter 4.

Task 3.4

Activity 1

Read the excerpt below and identify the ST's semantic issues that are discussed. In groups, give your opinion of the effectiveness of this discussion in terms of the coherence of the excerpt and the representativeness of the examples chosen. Also suggest any amendments that you deem necessary.

Excerpt

Part of a 2500-word commentary for a translation from English into French.

ST: *Plan Your Visit to York* | Visit York

On a semantic level, some English words and expressions in the source text are difficult to translate as they do not have French equivalents. For this, I focused less on translating word-for-word but rather sense-for-sense (see Nida 2000) in order to provide an idiomatic rendering. For example, the phrase '[A new decade] is upon us' (ST 7) proved difficult to translate as semantically close as possible. I decided to translate this as '[Une nouvelle décennie] est à nos portes' (TT 5), as the original meaning of '[a time] has arrived' is retained, yet this more idiomatic expression in French humanises the notion of the new decade, which in turn adds to the text's entertaining marketing language. I believe this is a better translation than a simple sentence such as 'C'est une nouvelle décennie' which does not include any of the aforementioned imagery or create an inviting tone for touristic purposes.

Owing to the number of proper nouns and anglicisms retained in the target text as a means of foreignising language as a marketing tool, additional glossing was used to explain certain names should they not be immediately clear for non-anglophones. For example, the 'York & Beyond Explorer Pass' (ST 30) was rendered as 'carte touristique York & Beyond Explorer Pass' (TT 31). This was done so that French speakers could understand the meaning of the English, and equally understand why the name of the tourist pass was retained in the English (so they knew what they would be asking for if they were to buy it in person). Had this gloss not been added, many readers would not have been able to deduce the English name from the surrounding context. Similarly, had this name been translated word-for-word into French, the reader would fully understand what it was, but would not know what to look out for in the English should they want to buy it (assuming they have no prior knowledge of English).

In some instances, semantic addition was used to further clarify cases where English-French translation is possible, but there are subtle and nuanced differences in their meanings. For example, 'a steel walkway' (ST 115) was rendered as 'une petite passerelle' (TT 121–122), with the addition of 'petite' in the target text. This addition is subtle but helps the reader to create an image of what to expect, as the alternative translation without addition 'une passrelle' may lead one to believe this is a lot larger than a walkway.

On the other hand, some expressions with double meanings were not possible in translation, and so I decided to retain the primary purpose of the original expression itself and lose the secondary sense in order to keep text cohesion. For example, 'Have a butchers at' (ST 232) proved very difficult to translate, as it is calling the reader to look at something, while equally hinting at the content to which it is referring. As the primary purpose of this expression is to call the reader to look at something in particular, I rendered this as, 'Jetez un coup d'œil' (TT 246) by applying Minimax theory (Levý 2000), as it makes idiomatic sense and is not a considerable loss of meaning when later in the sentence the butcher's is directly described.

Activity 2

Look at one translation that you have previously done and articulate how you dealt with the semantic issues by taking special care to select representative examples of optional, rather than obligatory decisions.

3.3.4 Varietal matrix

In the *Thinking Translation* series, varietal features are discussed in the following publications: Cragie and Pattison (2018), Chapters 1 and 2; Cragie et al. (2015), Chapter 10; Dickins et al. (2016), Chapter 10; Haywood et al. (2009), Chapters 10 and 11; Hervey and Higgins (1992), Chapter 11; Pellatt and Liu (2010), Chapter 3; the rest of the books in the series do not deal explicitly with these issues. Among them we find the tenor of a text (i.e. the writer-reader relationship), as well as the different language varieties as categorised in the *Thinking Translation* series, and the concepts of multilingualism and code switching.

Within this matrix you will look at issues to do with SL language varieties and/or other languages that might be present in the ST to decide how to deal with this in your TT. You will need to understand the differences between the categories of language varieties which are described in most of the *Thinking Translation* series. In addition, please bear in mind that, often, the lexis and grammatical structures of a text and/or its cultural references may be an indication of its language variety or varieties. This just goes to show that the categorisation into matrices is simply for methodological purposes, as, often, the categories overlap.

Also, remember that, as we mentioned in section 1.2.3.3, the fact that a text is written in a particular language variety does not necessarily mean that the intended reader will use that particular language variety.

As was the case with semantic issues, what follows is a checklist that will allow you to subcategorise any varietal issues you may encounter while translating. You will then have to judge which examples would be more illustrative to select for inclusion in your commentary.

3.3.4.1 *Tenor (writer-reader relationship)*

The tenor of a text indicates the relationship between the writer and the reader, that is, its level of 'formality, politeness, impersonality and accessibility' (Cragie and Pattison 2018: 20). The tenor is usually linked to the concept of register, a term usually applied to 'a variety of language used for a particular purpose or used in a specific social setting' (Cragie and Pattison 2018: 20). In turn, the register of a text may indicate its genre or text type, its skopos, and its intended reader. For example, an academic journal written for experts or for the educated reader with an informative skopos will invariably be written in a high register. This example also illustrates the concept of accessibility mentioned in 1.2.3. The higher or more formal the register, the less accessible it would be. Some texts, however, such as opinion articles, for example, have hybrid registers where the author uses both formal and informal language to cause a particular effect on the reader (for example, to shock, to add credibility, to create a link with the reader, etc.).

Bear in mind, however, that the level of formality of the ST need not necessarily be preserved in the TT. Politeness theory is relevant at this stage of the commentary. In fact, the SC and the TC may have different expectations regarding the appropriate tonal register(s) for a given situation' Dickins et al. (2016: 212–213). The translation of register, as well as the translation of politeness, could also be the main topic to be discussed in a thematically structured commentary.

3.3.4.2 *Language variety*

Hervey and Higgins (1992: 161) define the concept of 'language variety' as 'the way the message is formulated that reveal information about the speaker or writer,' such as, for instance, social and regional information. This is usually relevant in literary or expressive texts. However, you may also find a particular language variety used in journalistic texts when there are direct quotations from people from different social and/or geographical backgrounds. What we need to identify are the markers or features that represent the characteristics of a particular group, as then, we will be able to decide how best to translate it (Haywood et al. 2009: 197).

One thing we need to consider is any possible stigma attached to a particular language variety. This will be crucial, both for replicating an equivalent stigma in the TL and to avoid any possible unintentional stigma that might be attached to the TL language variety chosen.

The *Thinking Translation* series gives the following taxonomy of language varieties: social register, sociolect, dialect, temporal dialect, diglossia, and idiolect.

3.3.4.2.1 SOCIAL REGISTER

The social register indicates the 'social stereotype the speaker belongs to' (Hervey and Higgins 1992: 162), which may be related to their occupation, level of education, etc. It is also linked to the linguistic register discussed above. As Haywood et al. (2009: 189–190) point out, 'social register is to a large extent a conscious performance,' and it is perceived as the appropriate language variety to be used by a particular type of person in a particular situation (Dickins et al. 2016: 213), complying with the readers' or the listeners' expectations. Sometimes it is difficult to differentiate between social and tonal register, so, if this were the case, it would be acceptable to use the term 'register' for both (Dickins et al. 2016: 214).

3.3.4.2.2 SOCIOLECT

A sociolect is defined 'in terms of sociological notions of class … [it] is a language variety typical of one of the broad groupings that together constitute the "class structure" of a society' (Cragie et al. 2015: 92–93). It is an 'established habit' rather than an 'adaptation for particular communicative purposes,' as in the case of social register (Haywood et al. 2009: 185). The problem here is that cultures structure their class system differently from each other, so we first need to decide which classes are represented in the sociolects used in the ST to then ascertain what to do with them in our TT.

3.3.4.2.3 DIALECT

A dialect is defined by Hervey and Higgins (1992: 166) as 'a language variety with features of accent, lexis, syntax and sentence-formation characteristic of a given region.' Unlike social registers that provide us with information about social groupings, dialect indicates regional affiliations (Haywood et al. 2009: 189–190). In the Arab world, most dialects have a sociolectal aspect (Dickins et al. 2016: 215) and, in other parts of the world, dialects may contain sociolects. However, often, sociolects exist independently of regional affiliations (Haywood et al. 2009: 202).

With regard to the word 'dialect' itself, we need to be careful and sensitive with the terminology we use because, in some cases, due to political reasons, we have what has been called the dialectalisation of minority languages, like, for example, in Spain, during Franco's regime. This tends to happen in a situation of diglossia, when, within the same nation state, there are multiple official languages which have an asymmetrical power relationship between them. During Franco's regime in Spain (1939-1975), the central government propaganda disseminated the erroneous idea that all the other languages that co-existed in Spain were dialects of Spanish.

3.3.4.2.4 TEMPORAL DIALECT

According to Dickins et al. (2016), temporal dialect, which is also referred to by Cragie and Pattison (2019: 48) as 'period language,' reflects the fact that 'the pronunciation, spelling, lexis, morphology, syntax and semantics, etc. of any language change over time' (Dickins et al. 2016: 216). Whether the ST has been written in an old language variety because of being published in the past or because the text is set in the past, it will be important to point out in your commentary which features indicate the periodicity of the language variety. It is equally important to identify a very modern or up to date language variety at the time the ST is being translated. In fact, this is particularly relevant in interpreting, audiovisual translation, localisation, and transcreation (issues which will be dealt with in Part III of this book). In these cases, the interpreter or translator has to keep up with new emerging lexical and grammatical structures as well as lexical trends and obsolete language (cf. Pattison and Cragie 2022: 1).

3.3.4.2.5 DIGLOSSIA

Diglossia has been defined as 'a situation where two very different varieties of a language co-occur throughout a community of speakers, each having a distinct range of social functions' (Dickins et al. 2016: 218). Usually, one of the coexisting varieties has greater prestige than the others. In turn, the varieties with less prestige might have some kind of stigma attached to them (see dialectalisation above). Each of these varieties might be used in some contexts of that particular culture and not others, which makes it particularly difficult for the translator.

3.3.4.2.6 IDIOLECT

An idiolect refers to an idiosyncratic language variety used by a particular author, or a particular character.

To sum up, according to Dickins et al. (2016: 211), tonal and social registers can be categorised as registers, but sociolect, dialect, and temporal variety or period language are sublanguages. You need to bear in mind that the categories of language varieties above may not be clear cut and might often overlap or coexist with each other. Once again, being culturally bound, this overlap is likely to not be shared between different cultures. The crucial thing to do in your analysis is to identify the function a particular language variety has in the ST (Cragie et al. 2015: 91–92) and decide how important it is for the overall effect of the ST (Hervey and Higgins 1992: 166), as well as its meaning and skopos. For example, one of the functions of using a particular language variety could be to create a contrast between different social classes, different geographical origins, or to portray certain characteristics of the SC (Newmark 1988: 195), all of which will be essential for the creation of the ST's meaning.

3.3.4.3 Multilingualism and code switching

There may be times where the ST includes expressions from a language or languages other than the SL. Sometimes this language might even be the TL. In such cases, identifying this multilingualism in your ST analysis will allow you to decide how to deal with it in your translation.

Multilingualism may often appear in the form of code switching, defined by Hervey and Higgins (1992: 168) as 'switching between language varieties, or even between languages.' Code switching could take place not only from one sentence to another, but also within the same sentence. The issue that we need to consider is that it might be almost impossible to reproduce in the target language the relationship between the two languages or language varieties involved. For example, if we are translating a text into French, which has been written in English, but has code switching between English and Spanish, the relationship between Spanish and French will not be the same as the relationship between Spanish and English, both in terms of the social context and the prestige and/or stigma attached to each language. This applies also to code switching between language varieties. This may even be more complex if the TL is part of the code switching, which will be discussed further in Chapter 4.

An important thing to ask ourselves, while doing the ST analysis, is the significance and function of any code switching that we may observe in the ST and how it relates to its skopos. This will help us decide how to deal with it when articulating the translation strategy (Hervey and Higgins 1992: 165). The translation of language variety, or multilingualism and code switching, could be a topic for the thematically structured commentary.

Task 3.5

Activity 1

Read the excerpt below and identify the ST's varietal issues that are discussed. In groups, give your opinion of the effectiveness of this discussion in terms of the coherence of the excerpt and the representativeness of the examples chosen. Also suggest any amendments that you deem necessary.

Excerpt

Part of a 2500-word commentary for a translation from English into French.

ST: *Plan Your Visit to York* | Visit York

Finally, on a varietal level, I decided to employ a relatively informal register, especially on the level of vocabulary. The aim of this was to use approaches of foreignization and exoticism to conform to this text's secondary purpose of entertaining the reader and marketing the city of York in a desirable way. An example of this comes from the rendering of 'street food' (ST 25, 77, 238, 469, 495, 518, 520, 521) in the same way in French (TT 25, 78, 252–253, 509, 537, 561, 563, 565) as the alternative more literal translation of 'nourriture vendue dans la rue' is much less succinct and would not give as exotic an image to a reader. The term 'look' (ST 73) is a similar example of using an anglicism and calque to embrace this strategy of foreignization (TT 74).

Furthermore, this informal register can be seen in cases where polite calls to action were used in the source text. 'Please share [your experiences]' (ST 32) is rendered as a polite imperative 'Partagez la joie' (TT 33) in order to retain the call to action from the source text and equally be of an informal register to show the light-heartedness of the text. An alternative rendering of 'merci de partager' was not chosen in this case as the level of formality would be too high and less likely to create a friendly rapport with the reader.

Moreover, the target text employs idioms as a way of conforming to this informal register, especially in areas of the source text where speech is transcribed, giving the reader an illusion of talking directly to someone from York. For example, '[the locals are a chatty bunch that] will do anything to help you' (ST 159–160) is rendered as '[les gens du coin sont bavards qui] se mettraient en quatre pour vous' (TT 170–171). This idiom was well suited here as it conforms to the source's more colloquial style of speech and also retains the meaning of the source expression. In addition, this idiom helps to balance out any omission in speech where dialect-specific references to English would have been lost in translation for French speakers and were therefore omitted.

Activity 2

Look at one translation that you have previously done and articulate how you have dealt with the varietal issues by taking special care to select representative examples of optional, rather than obligatory decisions.

3.3.5 Intertextual issues

In the *Thinking Translation* series, intertextual issues are included either in the 'formal matrix' (Hervey and Higgins 1992; Cragie et al. 2015; Dickins et al. 2016) or the 'cultural matrix' (Haywood et al. 2009). This is because they share features that could be placed in either matrix, which is why in this textbook it has its own subsection. In the *Thinking Translation* series, intertextuality issues are discussed in the following publications: Andrews and Maksimova (2009), Chapter 9; Cragie et al. (2015), Chapter 7; Dickins et al. (2016), Chapter 13; Cragie et al. (2015), Chapter 5; Haywood et al. (2009), Chapter 5; Hervey and Higgins (1992), Chapter 8.

According to Andrews and Maksimova (2009: 97):

> The term 'intertextuality' is used when a set of texts are perceived to share important characteristics to other texts within the same language or culture. This *sharing of characteristics* may occur at any level of the text, including exact quotes (with or without quotation marks), thematic content or structural principles of the text (including genre and register).

That is, the term is used to refer to the relationship a particular text has to other texts within a culture or cultures (Hervey and Higgins 1992: 124). Intertextuality can take the form of a quotation, an allusion, a parody of a text, or even a parody of a whole genre. We have already discussed quotations when we talked about paratexts and embedded texts (1.2.5).

Sometimes a particular SC genre is being parodied in the ST, like, for example, *Bored of the Rings* by Henry Beard and Douglas Kenney published in 1969, which is a parody of J.R.R. Tolkien's *The Lord of the Rings*. This might happen not only in literary texts, but also in advertising and journalism (Hervey and Higgins 1992: 125). What might be problematic is when the genre parodied does not exist in the TC.

As for allusions or quotations, if they are too culturally bound to be understood by the TT intended reader, but you consider them to be important for preserving the ST's meaning, you might decide to make exegetic additions, by including extra information either within the text, in a footnote or endnote.

3.3.6 Other challenges

There might be other issues that you want to discuss in your ST analysis which do not fit easily within any of the matrices above. Among these issues we can find the following (please take note that this list is not meant to be exhaustive):

- Translating sensitive texts, such as for example those texts dealing with or having aspects related to gender, race, political correctness, decolonialism, inclusivity, etc.
- Translating humour.
- Translating politeness.
- Translating expletives, obscenities, profanity, and taboo words.

All of these issues will be discussed in Chapter 4, when we look at themed structured commentaries.

Task 3.6

1. Think of two or three translations you have done in your practical translation classes or in your working experience and recall which aspects discussed above you have come across: cultural, formal, semantic, varietal, intertextual, or other challenges, such as the translation of sensitive texts, humour, politeness, profanity, etc. You can find a table for example selection in Appendix 1, which you can use to make a list of these aspects.
2. Discuss these aspects in small groups.

3.4 Conclusion

In Chapter 1, we said that a good rule of thumb in structuring our commentary was to use the first third of the whole commentary in discussing the ST analysis and our statement of translation strategy (divided roughly equally between them). This means that two-thirds of the commentary will be dedicated to discussing and justifying your translation decisions at the microlevel, called in the *Thinking Translation* series 'decisions of detail' (Haywood et al. 2009; Hervey and Higgins 1992). Since the translation commentary is a hybrid between an academic essay and a reflective report, it needs to be coherent. This means that you have to select your examples with care, and an effective way of doing this is by using the matrices as a framework or checklist. Finally, as we have been saying throughout this text, it is important to select examples that illustrate translation decisions that were not obligatory in your language combination.

3.5 Summary

In this chapter, we looked at the desirable and undesirable features of a translation commentary, which needs to be coherent and include examples and secondary sources to justify your translation decisions. The focus of the chapter was the matrices of the *Thinking Translation* series and other issues and their use as a set of criteria or check list to select examples. In Chapter 4, we will look at the possible structures that a translation commentary can have and how best to integrate illustrative examples and relevant theories into a coherent narrative.

Further reading

Academic writing

Gillett, Andy, Angela Hammond and Mary Martala-Lockett (2009) *Successful Academic Writing*. Harlow: Pearson.

Strongman, Luke (2013) *Academic Writing*. Newcastle upon Tyne: Cambridge Scholars Publishing.

Reflective writing

Williams, Kate, Mary Woolliams and Jane Spiro (2020) *Reflective Writing*, 2nd ed. New York: Palgrave Macmillan.

Translation techniques taxonomy

Baker, Mona (1992/2011) *In Other Words: A Coursebook on Translation*, 2nd ed. London and New York: Routledge.

Díaz Cintas, Jorge and Aline Remael (2007) *Audiovisual Translation: Subtitling*. Manchester: St. Jerome.

Franco Aixelá, Javier (1996) 'Culture Specific Items in Translation', in Román Álvarez and M. Carmen-África Vidal (eds) *Translation, Power, Subversion*. Clevedon: Multilingual Matters, 52–78.

Newmark, Peter (1988) *A Textbook of Translation*. Hemel Hempstead: Prentice Hall.

Vinay, Jean-Paul and Jean Darbelnet (1958/1995) *Comparative Stylistics of French and English: A Methodology for Translation*, translated and edited by Juan Sager and Marie-Jo Hamel. Amsterdam and Philadelphia: John Benjamins.

List of references

Andrews, Edna and Elena Maksimova (2009) *Russian Translation: Theory and Practice*. London and New York: Routledge.

Baker, Mona (1992/2011) *In Other Words: A Coursebook on Translation*, 2nd ed. London and New York: Routledge.

Bowker, Lynne (2023) *De-mystifying Translation. Introducing Translation to Non-translators*. London and New York: Routledge.

Catford, John C. (1965) *A Linguistic Theory of Translation*. Oxford: Oxford University Press.

Cragie, Stella, Ian Higgins, Sándor Hervey and Patrizia Gambarotta (2015) *Thinking Italian Translation*, 2nd ed. London and New York: Routledge.

Cragie, Stella and Ann Pattison (2018) *Thinking English Translation: Analysing and Translating English Source Texts*. London and New York: Routledge.

Cragie, Stella and Ann Pattison (2019) *Translation: A Guide to the Practice of Crafting Target Texts*. London and New York: Routledge.

Díaz Cintas, Jorge and Aline Remael (2007) *Audiovisual Translation: Subtitling*. Manchester: St. Jerome.

Dickins, James, Sándor Hervey and Ian Higgins (2016) *Thinking Arabic Translation*, 2nd ed. London and New York: Routledge.

Franco Aixelá, Javier (1996) 'Culture Specific Items in Translation', in Román Álvarez and M. Carmen-África Vidal (eds) *Translation, Power, Subversion*, Clevedon: Multilingual Matters, 52–78.

Gillett, Andy, Angela Hammond and Mary Martala-Lockett (2009) *Successful Academic Writing*. Harlow: Pearson.

Hall, Stuart (1997) *Representation: Cultural Representations and Signifying Practices*. London Thousand Oaks, CA: Sage in association with the Open University.

Haywood, Louise M., Mike Thompson and Sándor Hervey (2009) *Thinking Spanish Translation. A Course in Translation Method: Spanish to English*. London and New York: Routledge.

Hervey, Sándor and Ian Higgins (1992) *Thinking Translation, a Course in Translation Method: French-English*. London: Routledge.

Lane-Mercier, Gillian (1997) 'Translating the Untranslatable: The Translator's Aesthetic, Ideological and Political Responsibility', *Target*, 9: 1: 43–68.

Levý, Jiří (2000) Translation as a decision process, in Lawrence Venuti (ed.) *The Translation Studies Reader*. London and New York: Routledge, 148–159.

Munday, Jeremy (2016) *Introducing Translation Studies: Theories and Applications*, 4th ed. London and New York: Routledge.

Newmark, Peter (1988) *A Textbook of Translation*. Hemel Hempstead: Prentice Hall.

Nida, Eugene (2000). Principles of Correspondence, in Lawrence Venuti (ed.) *The Translation Studies Reader*. London and New York: Routledge, 126–140.

Nord, Christiane (2005) *Text Analysis in Translation: Theory, Methodology, and Didactic Application of a Model for Translation-oriented Text Analysis*, 2nd ed. Amsterdam and New York: Rodopi.

Office de Tourisme de Dijon Métropole (2022) *Expériences & Escapades*. (Retrieved from Office de Tourisme de Dijon Métropole on 29 May 2022): https://www.destinationdijon.com/brochure/experiences-et-escapades/

Pattison, Ann and Stella Cragie (2022) *Translating Change*. London and New York: Routledge.

Pellatt, Valerie and Eric Liu (2010) *Thinking Chinese Translation*. London and New York: Taylor & Francis.

Podleśny, Damian (2021) 'Of Dragons, Wizards, and Distant … Rugs: Proper Names in Terry Pratchett's Juvenile Stories in Polish Translation', in Joanna Dybiec-Gajer and Agnieszka Gicala (eds) *Mediating Practices in Translating Children's Literature: Tackling Controversial Topics*. Berlin: Peter Lang, 96–108.

Rogers, Margaret, Michael White, Michael Loughbridge, Ian Higgins and Sándor Hervey (2020) *Thinking German Translation*, 3rd ed. London: Routledge.

Schleiermacher, Friedrich (1813/2012) 'On the Different Methods of Translating', translated by Susan Bernofsky, in Lawrence Venuti (ed) *The Translation Studies Reader*, 3rd ed. London and New York: Routledge, 43–63.

Schäffner, Christina (2004) Metaphor and translation: some implications of a cognitive approach. *Journal of Pragmatics*, 36: 1253–1269.

Shih, Claire Yi-yi (2018) 'Translation Commentary Re-examined in the Eyes of Translator Educators at British Universities', *The Journal of Specialised Translation*, 30: 291–311.

Strongman, Luke (2013) *Academic Writing*. Newcastle upon Tyne: Cambridge Scholars Publishing.

Tymoczko, Maria (1999) *Translation in a Postcolonial Context*. Manchester: St. Jerome.

Vinay, Jean-Paul and Jean Darbelnet (1958/1995) *Comparative Stylistics of French and English: A Methodology for Translation*, translated and edited by Juan Sager and Marie-Jo Hamel. Amsterdam and Philadelphia: John Benjamins.

Venuti, Lawrence (1995/2017) *The Translator's Invisibility: A History of Translation*. London and New York: Routledge.

Williams, Kate, Mary Woolliams and Jane Spiro (2020) *Reflective Writing*, 2nd ed. New York: Palgrave Macmillan.

4 Writing your commentary

Key concepts

- Types of commentary structure.
- Translation topics for a thematically structured commentary.
- The role of Translation Studies theories.
- Obligatory vs optional translation choices.

4.1 Introduction

As long as your commentary is coherent, clear in formulating ideas, concise, and relevant enough to justify your translation decisions, you can structure it in several different ways. However, you need to have a plan, select your ideas, and organise them logically.

Among the marking criteria used by institutions to assess a translation commentary, we find the following:

- Structure.
- Source text (ST) analysis.
- Formulation of translation strategy.
- Selection of illustrative examples.
- Use of appropriate terminology and presentation (e.g. referencing).

The list above, which has not been ordered in level of importance, shows the need for having a checklist or something similar, so that we can plan and select the issues to be discussed in a comprehensive and systematic manner (Haywood et al. 2009: 5). It might be the case that you spend quite a few hours analysing your ST, writing up your strategy, selecting examples, and gathering information, to find that only a small part of this material will be used in your commentary due to restrictions of word count. This should not bother or demotivate you. As mentioned in the introduction to this textbook, the rationale for writing a translation commentary is to make informed decisions when you translate. You need to learn to single out the most strategically important points. This is similar to how a translation project manager formulates a strategy for translating a text.

DOI: 10.4324/9781003273790-7

The more you translate, the better translator you become, but at the same time, the more versed you become in analysing STs and formulating a translation strategy, as well as selecting those examples that justify your decisions, the more informed and confident a translator you will become. In fact, this will be good practice for when you need to write a translation report for your publishers or clients, or to justify your decisions to the project manager, etc. In fact, in many professional translation contexts, such as, for example, in the case of transcreation, translators are required to send a report to their clients.

The important thing is to do the ST analysis both at the macro- and micro-level, formulate a translation strategy, set up the translation priorities, and then decide, in light of our strategy and our translation priorities, how to deal with challenging issues, or those issues where we have more than one equally valid solution. As mentioned above, each time one of these issues emerges, we should categorise them (by using the matrices, for example). In fact, you can even write up a draft of your discussion of several translation decisions without taking into account word count or space restrictions. This could perhaps take the form of a journal. Then, you will have sufficient material and data to select from to include in the actual commentary. This will need to be structured, organised, and should include a particular content, depending on the specific instructions of the assignment in question.

In the rest of the chapter, we will look at how you can structure your commentary and integrate relevant theoretical concepts and illustrative examples into the narrative.

4.2 Structuring your commentary

Following on from the previous section, once we have some notes or drafts to select from, we can decide what to include in the commentary and how to organise it.

Even though there are several possible ways to structure your commentary (please check whether your institution has any particular requirements on this and read the instructions of your assignments carefully), as mentioned above we are going to focus on structuring the commentary in two ways: one using the *Thinking Translation* matrices and the other using a thematic structure.

Regardless of which structure you decide to use, you will always need to analyse the ST at the macrolevel (ideally finding out information in terms of background and contextual information, genre and text type, skopos, intended readership, and medium of publication). You will also need to analyse the ST at the microlevel (in terms of cultural, semantic, formal, varietal and intertextual issues), identify the ST's salient features, formulate a translation strategy, and set out your translation priorities. All of these would then need to be included at the start of the commentary, which is why a thematic structure is not advisable for a short commentary (of 1000 words or less), as there would not be enough space to discuss the theories in depth and still provide a sophisticated and critical reflection on the translation decisions taken.

A possible organisation of the space could be as follows:

- Up to one-third of the commentary could be dedicated to the ST analysis and the statement of a translation strategy (including your translation priorities).
- Slightly less than two-thirds of the commentary could be dedicated to discussing and justifying your translation decisions and the techniques used (if you are using the matrices) or to discussing a particular topic (if you are writing a thematically structured commentary).
- A few lines at the end to make conclusive remarks on how your translation strategy has influenced your decision-making, thus producing your final target text (TT).

This organisation is applicable to both types of structure which will now be discussed in the following sections.

4.2.1 *Using the* Thinking Translation *matrices*

After writing your ST analysis and the statement of translation strategy you are ready to select which issues to discuss in the rest of the commentary.

For a short commentary of 1000 words or less you would only have around 600 words to discuss your decisions of detail. Therefore, since you will not be able to discuss issues that belong to all of the matrices, and you will have to decide which aspects are more relevant to justify your decisions, possibly limiting yourself to two of the matrices would be a good idea.

Task 4.1

Select three different text types (e.g. a medical text, a tourist brochure, the lyrics of a song) and decide which two matrices would be more relevant in selecting illustrative examples to discuss potential translation decisions for each of the texts.

As the task above has shown, some text types and genres have certain features and issues that are more relevant for discussion than others. For instance, the cultural matrix will be very relevant in a tourist brochure, the semantic matrix when translating a technical text (such as medical or legal), the formal matrix in the translation of lyrics, and the varietal register will be important for literary texts and plays that have characters from different social or regional backgrounds. However, you need to be careful, because, as mentioned in Chapter 1, most texts are hybrid and therefore we cannot predict what matrices will be more relevant until we do the ST analysis.

In longer commentaries you might be able to include more issues if you wish, or if you consider it important to justify some of the decisions you have made. You may still want to select issues from only two or three matrices. This would just mean that you can go deeper into the discussion.

In commentaries of 5000 words or more you will have enough space to discuss more issues, which you might want to discuss by going systematically through all of the matrices. However, in commentaries of this length, you might want to consider writing a thematically structured commentary as you will be able to explore your topic in depth. Nevertheless, regardless of what you decide, remember to always justify your decisions by referring back to your strategy and translation priorities.

4.2.2 Having a themed structure

The other structure that we are going to look at is thematic, which entails focusing on a particular topic throughout your commentary. Remember that you still need to start with the ST analysis, your statement of translation strategy, and your translation priorities. In fact, it is by doing the ST analysis that you will be able to identify a topic that is particularly relevant to your translation. For example, by analysing the meaning constructing or the effect creating features of the ST, you will be able to identify its overall tone and/ or effect. For instance, one of the effects might be humour. Another point that might emerge as particularly relevant is the translation of cultural references, for example in a tourist brochure, a website of an institution, etc. Here, Venuti's (1995) concepts of foreignising and domesticating will be useful. We can even be more specific within the cultural references and focus the commentary on the translation of proper nouns. Another issue could be the translation of politeness, which relates to both the varietal filter and pragmatics. Other relevant topics might be the translation of metaphors, and the translation language variety, code switching and multilingualism, as well as the translation of sensitive texts and the translation of profanity. If you decide to discuss any of these issues it is recommended that you consult the suggested further reading at the end of the chapter. The list of topics listed below is not intended to be exhaustive as it is merely an illustrative selection. Some of the topics listed overlap with others, so you might want to discuss a combination of two or three topics rather than a single one.

Task 4.2

In groups, brainstorm other possible topics to use in a thematically structured commentary that have not been included in the sections below.

4.2.2.1 Preserving the tone and effect of the ST

As mentioned in Chapter 1, the tone and/or effect that any text has on its reader is created by the overall interaction between its features (Nord 2005: 42) and their interplay with the reader's expectations (Nord 2005: 143). Often, however, certain features of the ST might elicit a particular effect on the source language (SL) readers, but the preservation of similar features in our TT might not necessarily elicit the same effect in the target language (TL) readers because of being culturally bound. This is why it is important to focus on the actual tone and effect of the ST rather than on the features themselves.

Nida's *dynamic equivalence*, defined as 'the relationship between receptor and message should be substantially the same as that which existed between the original receptors and the message' (1964: 159), might be a theoretical concept relevant here. In other words, in order to have dynamic equivalence the effect of the TT on its intended readers should be as close as possible to the effect the ST had on its intended readers.

Haywood et al. (2009: 22) believe this approach to be 'unhelpful and misleading' because, according to them, '[b]efore one could objectively assess textual effects, one would need to have recourse to a fairly detailed and exact theory of psychological effect, a theory capable, among other things, of giving an account of the aesthetic sensations that are often paramount in response to texts' (2009: 22). However, they do believe that as long as we do not consider 'equivalence' as an absolutist concept and the focus is on 'minimising relevant dissimilarities' rather than 'maximising sameness' (2009: 23), we could aim at preserving an equivalent effect in the TT understood as 'not dissimilar in certain relevant respects' (2009: 23).

As mentioned in Chapter 1, the tone or effect of a text could be sarcastic, ironic, humorous, neutral, informal, formal, objective, subjective, vulgar, etc. The ST's features that interact to create this tone or effect could be categorised as belonging to different matrices, which is why it is useful to do the analysis at the microlevel and create a bank of examples of the translation techniques used, so that you can select those examples to include in your thematically structured commentary. This recommendation is also applicable to the translation of humour, politeness, sensitive texts and profanity, which are discussed below. In brief, once you identify the tone and/or effect of the reader in the ST, you can discuss the translation techniques you have used to preserve them. You can then structure this discussion by using some matrices, as you will still need to select illustrative examples.

4.2.2.2 Translating humour

As Vandaele (2002a: 267) points out, 'humour is a matter of interpretation ... not of text-immanent features alone.' This is also applicable to the discussion about tone and effect above. That is, it is we as translators and readers who will interpret the text and identify its effect. However, we need to bear in mind that only if we know the object of the joke, will we be able to identify the humour (Bendi 2019: 87). This is important in the case of translation, as often the object of humour is obvious for SL readers, but not necessarily for TL readers. Hence, much has been said about the untranslatability of humour due to the fact that it is particularly culturally bound, and it depends on 'local beliefs, symbolic items and societal behaviours that belong to a network of meaningful relations in the source culture' (Bendi 2019: 89). Sometimes the humorous effect is elicited from puns or wordplay, which are also culturally bound (Delabastita 1996). Often these puns and wordplays make up the proper names of the characters in a text (Podleśny 2021: 102), which will be discussed further below. Similarly, the humour might be created by the use of taboo language and profanity, also discussed below. A technique that can be used to translate humour is the use of annotations to explain puns and jokes. However, as Nord (2003: 195) points out, this technique tends to 'kill' the joke and make it not funny.

What needs to be done when translating humour is 'to weigh the relative importance of humour, along with the importance of a given type of humour, when deciding how to deal with it' (Zabalbeascoa 2005: 187), but without sacrificing other textual features that might be more important for the creation of the ST's meaning (2005: 189). Herein lies the importance of setting up our translation priorities when we formulate our translation strategy. Translating humour is one of the issues that will give you more than one alternative translation solution, which is why it is a particularly interesting topic to discuss in a commentary. The translation of humour is also relevant for interpreting, audiovisual translation, and transcreation, discussed in Chapters 6 and 7.

4.2.2.3 Use of foreignisation or domestication to translate the ST cultural references

The concepts of foreignisation and domestication have been discussed in Chapter 3. To recap, according to Venuti (1995), domestication is a strategy which produces a fluent and readable translation by minimising the foreign elements and, thus, creating the 'illusion of transparency.' A foreignising strategy, on the other hand, emphasises the foreign provenance of a text. However, this does not necessarily mean literalism or a preservation of source language grammatical structures and/or lexis.

Venuti has been criticised by several scholars (e.g. Tymoczko 1999, 2000; Lane-Mercier 1997; Robinson 1997; Palaposki and Oittinen 1998; Pym 1996). One of these criticisms is that Venuti does not 'carefully define' the terms he has developed (Tymoczko 2000: 34). In fact, the vague use of the term 'strategy' above highlights one of the problems with the definition of these terms, as they have been applied to the process of text selection as well as to the translation techniques at the microlevel.

Both these terms are useful if we think of them as translation techniques to be used with culture-specific items. Thus, as we mention in Chapter 3, a foreignising technique will be SL-oriented and a domesticating technique would be TL-oriented. Using as an example the translation of 'King Charles III' into Spanish, as we did in Chapter 3, a foreignising technique would be 'El Rey Charles III' and a domesticating one 'El Rey Carlos III.'

When choosing the techniques you are going to use to translate culture-specific items, remember that we do not need to use either a foreignising or a domesticating technique with all of the cultural references, but we can use one or the other for different sets of cultural references (Tymoczko 1999; Lane-Mercier 1997: 55–56). If this is the topic of your thematically structured commentary, you could, for example, provide a rationale for using a foreignising or domesticating technique throughout, if this is what you have done, or why you have used one technique in certain cases and not in others.

4.2.2.4 *Translating proper nouns*

As mentioned in Chapter 3, proper nouns tend to be the 'most common cultural items found in STs' (Cragie and Pattison 2018: 37). In the case of famous people's names, their translation might be problematic because of pre-existing or established translations, as well as changing norms (preferring at some points a domesticating translation and at others a foreignising translation), such as for example in the case of names of places in maps and atlases.

The other problematic issue is when the proper noun is semantically loaded and when they are actually formed by a wordplay or pun, which would be culturally bound and also linked to the translation of humour mentioned above. In your commentary you can then discuss, for example, why you went against the norms of the TL or the readers' expectations and translated the name of a famous person following a domestication technique when a foreignising technique might have been expected. Or you might want to justify certain sacrifices you might have to make to preserve a humorous pun in a name, etc., always remembering to refer to your translation strategy and priorities.

4.2.2.5 *Translating metaphors*

According to Newmark (1988: 104), a metaphor has two purposes: one referential and cognitive; the other pragmatic and aesthetic. '[I]ts referential purpose is to describe a mental process or state, a concept, a person, an object, a quality or an action more comprehensively and concisely than is possible in literal or physical language.' Its pragmatic purpose 'is to appeal to the senses, to interest, to clarify "graphically," to please, to delight, to surprise' (1988: 104). He also gives definitions for the terminology used to talk about metaphors such as '*Image*: the picture conjured up by the metaphor'; '*Object*: what is described or qualified by the metaphor'; and '*Sense*: the literal meaning of the metaphor; the resemblance or the semantic area overlapping object and image' (1988: 104). When translating metaphors, we have the option of prioritising either the sense or the image (1988: 113). However, as mentioned in Chapter 3, often it is not possible to preserve the same image and associations in our TT (Schäffner 2004: 1256), as most of the time these are culturally bound.

If this is the topic you decided on to discuss, you can talk about whether to prioritise the sense of the image and why; or whether sometimes you might have been able to preserve the image or metaphor but not others, but you might have used some sort of compensation (Newmark 1988: 90). You might also discuss how you weighed out the importance in the creation of meaning of some of the metaphors present in the ST and decided not to preserve them.

4.2.2.6 *Translating language varieties and/or multilingualism*

If you have chosen the translation of language varieties or multilingualism as the main topic of your commentary, you will need to first identify what type of language varieties are present in the ST (social register, sociolect, dialect, temporal dialect, diglossia, and idiolect, already discussed in Chapter 3) and then you can discuss how you dealt with them in your TT, basing your decisions on your translation strategy and translation priorities as well as theoretical sources. As for the translation of social register, since it is a language variety that is used in a particular situation or context, it is sometimes linked to expressing politeness (discussed below).

Regarding multilingualism and code switching, further to what was discussed in Chapter 3, the situation becomes more complex when one of the languages that coexist in the ST is the TL. If this were the case, you would need to decide how to reflect the interplay between both languages and avoid doing a monolingual translation, which would thus efface the multilingualism present in the ST.

4.2.2.7 *Translating politeness*

The translation of politeness or impoliteness (Mapson 2019) is an aspect of pragmatics, and it is also relevant for interpreting. The translation of impoliteness has also been discussed by Hatim and Mason (1997/2000) in the context of audiovisual translation. Therefore, we will discuss it further in Chapter 7. Haywood et al. (2009: 273) define pragmatics as

> the study of language as used for particular purposes in particular situations, focusing on communicative acts rather than grammatical structures (what users are doing or intending to achieve by expressing themselves in particular ways).

The degree of politeness necessary in any interaction is determined by the power relationship between the parties involved (whether asymmetrical or not); the social distance; and the expectations imposed on them (Mapson 2019: 29). It is culturally bound and, therefore, the strategies used to express politeness or impoliteness will be different in different cultures (cf. Kecskes 2015), even though, as criticised by Eelen (2001), early politeness theories claimed that politeness was universal.

There are several issues that could be analysed in the translation of politeness:

- Politeness markers such as 'please' and 'thank you' in English, which may not exist in other languages, may be used differently, or there are totally different markers in the TL.
- The T-V distinction, in languages that use different pronouns (such as the French *tu* and *vous* or the Spanish *tú* and *usted*). These are related to social distance and the asymmetrical power relationship between the parties involved in the interaction.
- The use of polite icebreakers such as, for example, the use of small talk in English (Mapson 2019: 33).
- The degree of directness or indirectness as a way of expressing politeness.
- Solidarity politeness common in non-Western cultures (Mapson 2019: 33).
- Apologising.
- Giving advice or suggestions.
- Forms of address depending on age, gender, and status (Kasper 1990).

As with the topics above, you will first need to identify the issues to do with politeness that you would like to discuss and then justify the choice of translation techniques used to preserve the particular polite or impolite tone of the ST. Issues of politeness are also relevant in the case of interpreting and audiovisual translation. Therefore, we will discuss this further in Chapters 6 and 7.

4.2.2.8 *Translating sensitive texts*

Sensitive texts might deal with or have expressions related to gender, race, political correctness, inclusivity, etc. They may also contain aspects of profanity and taboo or sex-related topics, which are discussed in the next section. According to Lung (2003: 255), cultural specificity is 'one of the major determinants for making a text sensitive.' Therefore, a translation of a text might be considered sensitive in the target culture (TC), regardless of whether it was considered sensitive in the source culture (SC) or not. For instance, Western societies might be more open to express explicitly issues to do with 'love, emotion, fear, sex and intimacy' (Lung 2003: 257) than other cultures. Conversely, in some cultures, it might be more appropriate to translate a euphemistic expression in the ST more explicitly, to comply with the readers' expectations.

Those texts which are considered sacred and are among 'the most trans-lated texts across the largest number of languages' (Israel 2020: 505) are also sensitive texts. A text is classed as sacred 'when faith communities ascribe sacred value to it by inferring specific meanings from it or by using it for ritual purposes. By implication, sacred texts may also lose their sacrality for the same reasons' (Israel 2020: 506).

This takes us to the fact that sociocultural change, either in the SC or the TC, will mean that a text that was not considered sensitive in the past might be considered sensitive now, and vice versa. For example, '[s]ensitivity to matters of race and history has been on the increase for many years, albeit gradually to start with' (Pattison and Cragie 2022: 14). Hence, we often see in the media news about re-editions or revisions of works that when they first appeared were not seen as problematic; for example, films such as *Gone with the Wind* (1939) or books by Roald Dahl, Agatha Christie, and Enid Blyton, to cite just a few examples in the Anglophone world. The problem for the translator is to find a solution 'between conveying the tone of the source text and striking a balance of present-day correctness as the attitudes of yes-teryear' (Pattison and Cragie 2022: 16). Furthermore, and to complicate the situation with regard to translation, social change takes place at different rates in different societies (Pattison and Gragie 2022: 14). This means that translators need to keep themselves up to date with what is acceptable or appropriate in the TC.

If this is the topic you have chosen to discuss in your commentary, you need to first identify whether the ST is considered to be a sensitive text in the SC, or, if this is not the case, whether the style and/or content of the ST are considered sensitive issues in the TC. Then you will need to discuss how you dealt with it and made any adjustments necessary. This is something that is also relevant to interpreting, audiovisual translation, localisation, and tran-screation, and will be discussed in Chapters 6, 7 and 8.

4.2.2.9 *Translating expletives, obscenities, profanity, and taboo words*

According to Allan and Burridge (2006: 1) taboos include:

- Bodies and their effluvia (sweat, snot, faeces, menstrual fluid, etc.).
- The organs and acts of sex, micturition, and defecation.
- Diseases, death, and killing (including hunting and fishing).
- Naming, addressing, touching, and viewing persons and sacred beings, objects, and places.
- Food gathering, preparation, and consumption.

'We learn about taboos through the socialization of speech practices, which creates an oral or folk knowledge of swearing etiquette' (Jay 2009: 154). That is, we learn in what context the use of taboo words is acceptable or appropriate. Hence, it is culturally bound.

Sometimes humour is based on the usage of profanity and taboo (Zabalbeascoa 2005: 194) and taboo language is also linked to sensitive texts and impolite language. In fact, Culpeper (2019: 29) considers taboo language to be 'a subgroup within impoliteness,' as both depend on their conflict with people's expectations in a particular context (Culpeper 2019: 29). For instance, you would not expect swear words on the minutes of a meeting or an academic essay (unless it was about profanity). In addition, as mentioned above, the perception of a text or expression as sensitive, impolite, or taboo might change according to sociocultural changes (Pattison and Cragie 2022: 14–16; Valdeón 2015: 367). That is, issues that were considered taboo two decades ago might not necessarily be considered taboo now.

Profanity and taboo might be part of the characterisation of the narrator or one of the speakers in your ST. If this is the case, you will need to decide how to deal with it. According to Nida (2000: 139), in these cases 'each character must be permitted to have the same kind of individuality and personality as the author himself gave them in the original message.' This might prove particularly difficult to do, especially when translating profanity into a culture that is less receptive to it than the SC. The most common translation techniques used in this situation are 'omission' or 'softening.' In other words, translators may delete the profanity completely or 'maintain the expressive quality but not the profanity itself' (Azura et al. 2019: 45). The risk of using softening or omission, however, is actually creating a totally different character from that of the ST (Azura et al. 2019: 52).

If you have selected the translation of profanity as the main topic of your commentary, you will need to justify your decisions by weighing up the gains and losses that result from the use of particular translation techniques, linking them to your translation strategy. For example, you might disagree with the use of omission or softening and might have found a way to preserve the expressive quality of the ST while still using a style or expressions that are acceptable in the TC.

Much research has been done on the translation of profanity in interpreting and in subtitling, which will be discussed in Chapters 6 and 7.

4.3 Integrating Translation Studies (and other relevant) theories into your discussion

It might be easier to integrate concepts and theories in a thematically structured commentary.

However, you can also integrate them if you structure your commentary by using the *Thinking Translation* series matrices. One pitfall you need to avoid is to make sure that your commentary does not become a pseudo translation theory essay which is written in a very superficial manner because of not having enough word count to explore the issues discussed in depth. This is why a thematic structure is not recommended for commentaries of less than 5000 words, as you will still need to analyse the ST, formulate your translation strategy and translation priorities, and justify your translations decisions in a sophisticated and critical manner.

As mentioned in Chapter 3, many institutions require students to cite secondary sources in their commentaries. We have also pointed out some of the undesirable features found in commentaries when theoretical concepts were applied inaccurately and when theories were not linked to translation examples (Shih 2018: 302–303). Therefore, and related to the latter point, you need to be careful to not simply mention a claim, thought, or principle of a particular scholar, for the sake of including secondary references, and then not refer to them at all for the rest of the commentary. That is, you need to make sure that the theoretical sources are relevant and an essential part of your discussion. In this section we will look at how to integrate concepts and theories from Translation Studies and other relevant disciplines within your discussion.

Task 4.3

Before you read the following pages, brainstorm in small groups which theories and concepts you could integrate into the ST analysis, the statement of your translation strategy, the setting up of your priorities, and the discussion of the translation decisions taken at the microlevel.

One of the ways of integrating Translation Studies concepts and theories is by the use of appropriate terminology. This is usually one of the criteria used to assess translation commentaries. You can use Translation Studies terminology to discuss your translation techniques at the microlevel, but you might also use it in your ST analysis and statement of translation strategy (see Chapters 1–3). The important thing to remember is to use the terminology you have chosen consistently, accurately, and precisely, and also to acknowledge the sources used when required.

Newmark (1988), Nida (1964), Venuti (1995), and Vinay and Darbelnet (1958/1995) might be useful when discussing the translation techniques used at the microlevel. Functional theories, such as skopos theory (Nord 1997 and Schäffner 2012), will be relevant both in the ST analysis and the statement of translation strategy. There are also theoretical sources that might be useful when talking about formal issues at the discourse level, such as, for example, coherence (Baker 1992/2011; Hatim and Mason 1990; etc.). Other theories that can be used have to do with the genre or text type of the ST; for example, children's literature, technical texts (legal, medical, scientific, etc.), theatre, etc. Apart from these, there are also the theories that relate to the topics mentioned above, such as the translation of humour, of profanity, etc.

There are also theories and approaches that might be more useful for a dissertation than for a translation commentary, such as, for example, those theories that relate to the so-called turns in Translation Studies: cultural, ideological, sociological, power turns. However, some of these theories could be used to justify the selection of a particular text and/or the general approach or strategy taken in the translation. You might also be able to integrate some of these theories into your commentary if the ST's content or style has elements that deal with the issues discussed by them (for example, a ST that contains racist or politically incorrect language). You can then discuss how these theories have informed your translation decisions.

A final, but very important, point with regard to theoretical sources is that you always need to acknowledge the sources of your information and reference them both within the text and in a list of references. When sources are not acknowledged, this is considered to be plagiarism.

There are many ways of referencing, and you need to familiarise yourself with your institution's preferred way of referencing. Most institutions offer sessions in academic writing which include referencing and plagiarism. You could also ask your teacher if you have any questions about it (also, see further reading at the end of this chapter). The most important thing is consistency. For example, some forms of reference put the date in brackets and a full stop afterwards; others put the date at the end of the reference. Others write the surname in full and then just the initials of the given name, rather than the full name, etc.

As mentioned in the introduction, as a future translator and text creator you need to develop an eye for detail to be able to produce publishable texts. In fact, as a professional translator all of the elements of your texts, from content and grammar to formatting, should be of the highest possible quality; otherwise you will risk losing a client.

Task 4.4

In groups, read the excerpts below and identify the theories that have been integrated into the discussion. Decide whether the theories have been integrated in a coherent manner and suggest any improvements you might think necessary. Finally, suggest any other theories that might also be relevant to include in these excerpts.

Excerpt 1

Part of a 2500-word commentary for a translation from English into French.

ST: Sánchez-Andrade, Cristina (2022) *La nostalgia de la Mujer Anfibio*. Barcelona: Anagrama.

On a cultural level, my goal was to immerse TT readers in the novel's setting and preserve the cultural context of the ST as well as avoid what Fawcett refer to as 'information overload' (Fawcett 1997: 46) by foregoing extratextual glosses, restricting intratextual explicitation and including the latter only where necessary for the sake of TT readers' comprehension. Although Catford defines translation as 'the replacement of textual material in one language (SL) by equivalent textual material in another language (TL)' (Catford 1965: 20), to attempt to find terms equivalent to the Galicia-specific vocabulary included in the ST would only arguably be an endeavour doomed to failure, given that most of those terms simply do not have an equivalent in the TL, but would also run the risk of contributing to producing, in Venuti's words, an 'aggressively monolingual, unreceptive to the foreign' culture and presenting the target readership 'with the narcissistic experience of recognising their own culture in a cultural other' (Venuti 1995: 15). Considering the importance that the setting of the novel has for the narrative and the author's deliberate choice to include Galician terms, which appear in italics in the ST and are not guaranteed to be any more familiar to ST readers than they are to TT readers, I have chosen not to translate those terms and employed the technique of borrowing (Fawcett 1997: 34), restricting myself to minimal glosses in order to 'carry forward on an irresistible stream of narrative' (Cohen 1962: 33). This approach has the disadvantage of potentially alienating the reader; however, I judged that the target audience will likely be able to easily infer the meaning of most of the Galician terms based on their location in the text. It is clear from the context that *faiado* (ST 13) must be a room, *avoa* (ST 50) is a form of address, *lura* (ST 98) is a type of food, whereas a *xesta* (ST 199) must be a plant species. The less transparent term *marusía* (ST 131), which refers to a low-tide smell, has been preserved in the TT to emphasise the lyrical effect of the line 'the merciless air of the marusía,' but the epithet 'low-tide' has been added to help the readers better envision the scene and help them identify the smell described in the text (TT 130–131). Similarly, terms such as *o Cachán* and *o Maligno* (ST 222) have not been translated but, to make their meaning more explicit, the term 'the Devil' (TT 222) has been used as the subject of the following sentence.

Excerpt 2

Part of a 5000-word commentary for a translation from Russian into English.
 ST: Dyachenko, Marina and Sergey Dyachenko (2000) *Volch'ia syt'*. http://www.rusf.ru/marser/books/text/volk_01.htm

5.2 Dialogue

The dialogue of the characters differs on the level of social register, reflecting their backgrounds and relationships. As Nord (2014: 99) explains, dialogue is a crucial component of literary translation, since 'characters are implicitly described by the way they talk or address each other,' which 'may be one of the functions of the literary text.' Therefore, the creation of an equivalent effect in the TT, as suggested by Reiß (translated and adapted in Munday 2012: 112), was important to fulfilling the TT's skopoi. The story's setting grants the dialogue the further function of implicitly developing the society for the reader, as, in the context of an imagined world 'the smallest utterance can contribute to the world and can be analysed for its contribution' (Ekman and Taylor 2016: 14).

While important context about the text world, such as class hierarchies within the protagonists' society, are not explicitly described, they can be inferred from the different social registers that the characters use. In particular 'the headman' uses more colloquial language than many other characters. The section of part two in which Smoke visits the headman's village illustrates Ekman and Taylor's (2016: 13) conceptualisation of imagined worlds as 'places designed with a certain *form* to fulfil a certain *function* and express a certain *meaning*,' as the village functions as a foil to Smoke's way of life, allowing further thematic exploration of the compromise between freedom and security. During this part of the story, Smoke shows a great concern for the state of education within the village, which he sees as important to the survival of civilisation (ST 271). Furthermore, the headman and Cary-Woods both express a disdain for the centre, with the headman disdainfully stating that 'Я и в столице всего раз был' (ST 280-281). In this way, the presentation of dialogue in the ST also reflects contemporary regional and social divisions within Russia. Consequently, the headman's social register can be interpreted through ST analysis as corresponding to a stereotypical idea of someone who is 'uneducated,' which manifests in the increased frequency of slang and colloquialisms in his dialogue.

In order to fulfil these functions in the TT, equivalent slang and colloquial forms were used to recreate a casual tone:

ST Line 280: -Сроду я не был в Высоком доме, - с неприязнью сказал
 староста.
TT Line 306: 'I've sure never been to the High House,' the headman
 said hostilely.

To replicate the emphatic effect of the colloquial adverb 'сроду,' the word order was changed to convey the speaker's contempt for the High House, as well as his social register, as the grammar is marked rather than conventional.

In addition to grammatical changes, compensation was used to convey the overall tone of the headman's dialogue:

ST Line 292: - Въедливый ты, - сказал староста. - Чувствуется, что чиновник.
TT Line 321: 'Damn you're thorough,' said the headman. 'Sound like a civil servant well enough.'

Swearwords are stereotypically associated with less educated speech, fulfilling the function of the headman's dialogue on a broader level, while, at a semantic level, the use of swearwords can 'increase the emotional intensity of certain passages,' including to 'emphasize a particular identity' (Bosseaux 2018: 133). The addition of 'damn' in this case emphasises the attitude of the headman towards both the centre and Smoke, as it is followed by an expression of distaste for government officials, who the headman implicitly positions in contrast to his own marginal position. In this way, the addition of slang and swearwords facilitates the ST authors' intent of exploring different social groups' reactions to the moral dilemmas presented in the story. In this way, the translation strategies applied to dialogue in the TT reflect the Dyachenkos' tendency to 'set up complex social experiments and watch the outcome together with their readers' (Mironciuc 2013: 37).

4.4 Integrating the examples into the narrative of your commentary

As mentioned above, one of the criteria used to assess commentaries is how relevant and illustrative the examples selected are. In Chapter 3, using the *Thinking translation* series matrices as a guide, we discussed the issues you can look at to create a databank from where you can select your examples to illustrate the justification of the decisions taken at the microlevel.

By analysing the ST, you will be able to identify its salient features, that is, those meaning creation features that you deem essential to preserve in your target text (the tone, humour, imagery, etc.). In addition, and as we suggested previously, while you are translating, you can take note of the challenging issues you encounter. The important thing to do after this is to categorise them, by creating a list of issues and following the matrices, by colour coding them, by creating a database, or by any other method that works for you.

You can then select those examples that better illustrate the reasons for the translation decisions taken at the microlevel to integrate within your commentary. As mentioned previously, it is better to discuss fewer examples at length than to present a long, unconnected and incoherent list of examples. This will give you enough space to justify your decisions in a sophisticated and critical way, always relating back to your strategy and how it has informed your actions. Hence, you could select those examples that are more relevant for your discussion. For instance, one of the examples you can choose is using a general and accessible vocabulary and avoiding complex grammar because the TT's intended readership is the general reader.

Something worth selecting are those examples where your decisions are slightly controversial or where they go against the expectations of the TC readers, such as using an exoticising or foreignising technique when what was expected was domestication. For example, translating the name of pilgrimage route '*El Camino Inglés a Santiago de Compostela*' from Spanish into English as 'The Camino Inglés to Santiago de Compostela' to preserve its Spanish identity, rather than 'The English Way to Santiago de Compostela' (which is the preferred translation of the Spanish authorities and tourist board). You can also include in your narrative alternative translation solutions that, at first sight, appeared to be equally valid and discuss why they were rejected.

Other examples you can select are those where the techniques used either contradict your strategy or are not consistent with other techniques used in the same text. For instance, imagine you are translating a tourist brochure about a particular town. You might have decided to domesticate measurements such as, for example, miles into kilometres, but you foreignised the names of the streets, as these would be the names that the prospective tourists would have seen in the maps and street signs.

Task 4.5

Read the excerpts that were used for Task 4.4 and discuss whether the selection of illustrative examples is relevant for the issues discussed and whether they have been integrated into the narrative in a coherent manner. Finally, suggest any improvements you think necessary.

4.5 Conclusion

Something to bear in mind is that the two different types of commentary we have seen in this chapter are not an either/or situation. That is, they should be seen more like two extremes in a cline. In other words, a translation commentary that has been structured based on the *Thinking translation* series matrices could have a particular topic running through it, for example, discussing the translation of humour by going through the matrices.

Remember that a thematically structured commentary is not recommended for short assignments of 1000 words or less. If you decide to discuss one of the topics listed in this chapter, you will find, in the relevant further reading section below, some useful sources. Regardless of the structure you decide to use, you will still need to integrate the theoretical sources and illustrative examples you have selected in an effective and coherent manner.

4.6 Summary

In this chapter we looked at two different ways of structuring a translation commentary, by using the *Thinking Translation* series matrices as a guide or by having a thematic structure. We also discussed how best to integrate relevant theories and concepts as well as your selection or illustrative examples into your translation commentary. Chapter 5 will help you to put into practice what you have learnt so far in the first four chapters. It first looks at different types of translation commentary assignments and provides you with advice on how to manage your time and prepare for supervision sessions.

Further reading

Referencing and plagiarism

Williams, Kate and Jude Carroll (2009) *Referencing and Understanding Plagiarism*. London: Palgrave.

Preserving the tone and effect of the ST

Haywood, Louise M., Mike Thompson and Sándor Hervey (2009) *Thinking Spanish Translation: A Course in Translation Method: Spanish to English*. London and New York: Routledge, 22–25.

Nord, Christiane (1997) *Translating as a Purposeful Activity*. Manchester: St Jerome (Chapter 3).

Translating humour

Attardo, Salvatore (2002) 'Translation and Humour', *The Translator*, 8: 2: 173–194.

Vandaele, Jeroen (2002a) '"Funny Fictions": Francoist Translation Censorship of Two Billy Wilder Films', *The Translator*, 8: 2: 267–302.

Vandaele, Jeroen (2002b) (ed) *Translating Humour*, Special Issue, *The Translator*, 8: 2.

Zabalbeascoa, Patrick (2005) 'Humor and Translation - An Interdiscipline', *Humor*, 18: 2: 185–207.

Use of foreignisation and domestication to translate ST cultural references

Lane-Mercier, Gillian (1997) 'Translating the Untranslatable: The Translator's Aesthetic, Ideological and Political Responsibility', *Target* 9: 1: 43–68.

Palaposki, Outi and Oittinen, Riita (1998) 'The Domesticated Foreign', in Andrew Chesterman et al. (eds) *Translation in Context*. Amsterdam and Philadelphia: Benjamins, 373–390.

Venuti, Lawrence (1995/2017) *The Translator's Invisibility: A History of Translation.* London and New York: Routledge.

Translating proper nouns

Nord, Christiane (2003) 'Proper Names in Translations for Children: Alice in Wonderland as a Case in Point', *Meta* 48: 1–2: 182–196.
Podleśny, Damian (2021) 'Of Dragons, Wizards, and Distant … Rugs: Proper Names in Terry Pratchett's Juvenile Stories in Polish Translation', in Joanna Dybiec-Gajer and Agnieszka Gicala (eds) *Mediating Practices in Translating Children's Literature. Tackling Controversial Topics.* Berlin: Peter Lang, 96–108.

Translating metaphors

Guldin, Rainer (2016) *Translation as Metaphor.* London and New York: Routledge.
Newmark, Peter (1988) *A Textbook of Translation.* Hemel Hempstead: Prentice Hall. Chapter 10, 104–113.
Schäffner, Christina (2004) 'Metaphor and Translation: Some Implications of a Cognitive Approach', *Journal of Pragmatics*, 36: 1253–1269.
St. André, James (ed) (2010) *Thinking Through Translation with Metaphors.* Manchester: St. Jerome Publishing.

Translating language varieties and/or multilingualism

Armstrong, Nigel (2004) 'Voicing "The Simpsons" from English into French: A Story of Variable Success', *The Journal of Specialised Translation*, 2: 97–109.
Grutman, Rainier (2006) 'Refraction and Recognition. Literary Multilingualism in Translation', *Target* 18: 1: 17–47.
Johnson, Penelope (2018) 'Border Writing in Translation: The Spanish Translations of Woman Hollering Creek by the Chicana Writer Sandra Cisneros', in Jean Boase-Beier, Lina Fisher and Hiroko Furukawa (eds) *Palgrave Handbook of Literary Translation.* London: Palgrave, 427–442.
Lane-Mercier, Gillian (1997) 'Translating the Untranslatable: The Translator's Aesthetic, Ideological and Political Responsibility', *Target* 9: 1: 43–68.
Meylaerts, Reine (ed) (2006) *Literary Heteroglossia in/and Translation*, special issue of *Target* 18: 1.

Translating politeness and impoliteness

Culpeper, Jonathan (2011) *Impoliteness: Using Language to Cause Offence.* Cambridge: Cambridge University Press.
Hatim, Basil and Ian Mason (1997/2000) 'Politeness in Screen Translating', in Lawrence Venuti (ed) *The Translation Studies Reader*, London and New York: Routledge, 430–445.
Kecskes, Istvan (2015) 'Intercultural Impoliteness', *Journal of Pragmatics*, 86: 43–47.
Mapson, Rachel (2019) 'Im/politeness and Interpreting', in Rebecca Tipton and Louisa Desilla (eds) *The Routledge Handbook of Translation and Pragmatics.* London and New York: Routledge, 27–50.

Sidiropoulou, Maria (2021) *Understanding Im/politeness Through Translation. The English-Greek Paradigm*. Edinburgh: Springer.
Translating sensitive texts
Lung, Rachel (2003) 'Translating Sensitive Texts', *Perspectives: Studies in Translatology*, 11: 4: 255–268.
Pattison, Ann and Stella Cragie (2022) *Translating Change*. London and New York: Routledge.
Simms, Karl (1997) (ed) *Translating Sensitive Texts*. Amsterdam: Rodopi.

Translating profanity

Allan, Keith and Kate Burridge (2006) *Forbidden Words*. Cambridge: Cambridge UP.
Azura, Fachrina, Haru Deliana Dewi and Rahayu Surtiati Hidayat (2019) 'Profanity and Characterization: A Study of Translation. Strategies and Their Effects on *The Catcher in the Rye*', *Journal of Language and Literature*, 19: 2: 43–54.
Culpeper, Jonathan (2019) 'Taboo Language and Impoliteness', in Keith Allan (ed) *Oxford Handbook of Taboo Words and Language*. New York: Oxford University Press, 28–40.
Hale, Sandra, Natalie Martschuck, Jane Goodman-Delahunty, Mustapha Taibi and Han Xu (2020) 'Interpreting Profanity in Police Interviews', *Multilingua* 39: 4: 369–393.

List of references

Allan, Keith and Kate Burridge (2006) *Forbidden Words*. Cambridge: Cambridge University Press.
Armstrong, Nigel (2004) 'Voicing "The Simpsons" from English into French: A Story of Variable Success', *The Journal of Specialised Translation*, 2: 97–109.
Attardo, Salvatore (2002) 'Translation and Humour', *The Translator*, 8: 2: 173–194.
Azura, Fachrina, Haru Deliana Dewi and Rahayu Surtiati Hidayat (2019) 'Profanity and Characterization: A Study of Translation. Strategies and Their Effects on *The Catcher in the Rye*', *Journal of Language and Literature*, 19: 2: 43–54.
Baker, Mona (1992/2011) *In Other Words: A Coursebook on Translation*, 2nd ed. London and New York: Routledge.
Bendi, Merouan (2019) 'Hybrid Humour as Cultural Translation: The Example of Beur Humour', *European Journal of Humour Research*, 7: 2: 87–99.
Bosseaux, Charlotte (2018) 'Translating Voices in Crime Fiction', in Jean Boase-Beier, Lina Fisher and Hiroko Furukawa (eds) *The Palgrave Handbook of Literary Translation*, London: Palgrave, 125–144.
Catford, John C. (1965) *A Linguistic Theory of Translation*. Oxford: Oxford University Press.
Cohen, John Michael (1962) *English Translators and Translations*. London: Longmans, Green & Co.
Cragie, Stella and Ann Pattison (2018) *Thinking English Translation: Analysing and Translating English Source Texts*. London & New York: Routledge.
Culpeper, Jonathan (2011) *Impoliteness: Using Language to Cause Offence*, Cambridge: Cambridge University Press.

Culpeper, Jonathan (2019) 'Taboo Language and Impoliteness', in Keith Allan (ed) *Oxford Handbook of Taboo Words and Language*. New York: Oxford University Press, 28–40.

Delabastita, Dirk (ed) (1996) *Wordplay and Translation*. Manchester: St. Jerome.

Eelen, G. (2001) *A Critique of Politeness Theories*. Manchester: St. Jerome Publishing.

Ekman, Stefan and Audrey Isabel Taylor (2016) 'Notes Toward a Critical Approach to Worlds and World-Building', *Fafnir – Nordic Journal of Science Fiction and Fantasy Research*, 3: 7–18.

Fawcett, Peter D. (1997) *Translation and Language: Linguistic Theories Explained*. Manchester: St Jerome.

Grutman, Rainier (2006) 'Refraction and Recognition. Literary Multilingualism in Translation', *Target* 18: 1: 17–47.

Guldin, Rainer (2016) *Translation as Metaphor*. London and New York: Routledge.

Hale, Sandra, Natalie Martschuck, Jane Goodman-Delahunty, Mustapha Taibi and Han Xu (2020) 'Interpreting Profanity in Police Interviews', *Multilingua* 39: 4: 369–393.

Hatim, Basil and Ian Mason (1990) *Discourse and the Translator*. Harlow, Essex: Longman.

Hatim, Basil and Ian Mason (1997/2000) 'Politeness in Screen Translating', in Lawrence Venuti (ed) *The Translation Studies Reader*, London and New York: Routledge, 430–445.

Haywood, Louise M., Mike Thompson and Sándor Hervey (2009) *Thinking Spanish Translation. A Course in Translation Method: Spanish to English*. London and New York: Routledge.

Israel, Hephzibah (2020) 'Sacred Texts', in Mona Baker and Gabriela Saldaha (eds) *Routledge Encyclopedia of Translation Studies*, 3rd ed. London and New York: Routledge, 505–510.

Jay, Timothy (2009) 'The Utility and Ubiquity of Taboo Words', *Perspectives on Psychological Science*, 4: 2, 153–161.

Johnson, Penelope (2018) 'Border Writing in Translation: The Spanish Translations of Woman Hollering Creek by the Chicana Writer Sandra Cisneros', in Jean Boase-Beier, Lina Fisher and Hiroko Furukawa (eds) *Palgrave Handbook of Literary Translation*. London: Palgrave.

Kasper, Gabriele (1990) 'Linguistic politeness: Current Research Issues', *Journal of Pragmatics* 14: 2: 193–218.

Kecskes, Istvan (2015). 'Intercultural Impoliteness', *Journal of Pragmatics*, 86: 43–47.

Lung, Rachel (2003) 'Translating Sensitive Texts', *Perspectives: Studies in Translatology*, 11: 4: 255–268.

Lane-Mercier, Gillian (1997) 'Translating the Untranslatable: The Translator's Aesthetic, Ideological and Political Responsibility', *Target* 9: 1: 43–68.

Mapson, Rachel (2019) 'Im/politeness and interpreting', in Rebecca Tipton and Louisa Desilla (eds) *The Routledge Handbook of Translation and Pragmatics*. London: Routledge, 27–50.

Meylaerts, Reine (ed) (2006) *Literary Heteroglossia in/and Translation*, special issue of *Target* 18: 1.

Newmark, Peter (1988) *A Textbook of Translation*. Hemel Hempstead: Prentice Hall.

Nida, Eugene A. (1964) *Toward a Science of Translating*. Leiden: E. J. Brill.

Nida, Eugene A. (2000). 'Principles of Correspondence', in Lawrence Venuti (ed) *The Translation Studies Reader*. London and New York: Routledge, 126–140.

Mironciuc, Elena (2013) *Forging a New Russian Hero: Post-Soviet Science Fiction and Its Moral Objectives* [Honours Thesis. Wellesley College]. CORE.

Munday, Jeremy (2012) *Introducing Translation Studies: Theories and Applications*. London and New York: Routledge.

Nord, Christiane (1997/2014) *Translating as a Purposeful Activity*. Manchester: St Jerome.

Nord, Christiane (2003) 'Proper Names in Translations for Children: Alice in Wonderland as a Case in Point', *Meta*, 48: 1–2: 182–196.

Nord, Christiane (2005) *Text Analysis in Translation: Theory, Methodology, and Didactic Application of a Model for Translation-oriented Text Analysis*, 2nd ed. Amsterdam and New York: Rodopi.

Palaposki, Outi and Oittinen, Riita (1998) 'The Domesticated Foreign', in Andrew Chesterman et al. (eds) *Translation in Context*. Amsterdam and Philadelphia: Benjamins, 373–390.

Pattison, Ann, and Stella Cragie (2022) *Translating Change*. London and New York: Routledge.

Podleśny, Damian (2021) 'Of Dragons, Wizards, and Distant … Rugs: Proper Names in Terry Pratchett's Juvenile Stories in Polish Translation', in Joanna Dybiec-Gajer and Agnieszka Gicala (eds) *Mediating Practices in Translating Children's Literature: Tackling Controversial Topics*. Berlin: Peter Lang, 96–108.

Pym, Anthony (1996) 'Venuti's Visibility', *Target*, 8: 1: 165–177.

Robinson, Douglas (1997) *Translation and Empire: Postcolonial Theories Explained*. Manchester: St. Jerome.

Schäffner, Christina (2004) 'Metaphor and Translation: Some Implications of a Cognitive Approach', *Journal of Pragmatics*, 36: 1253–1269.

Schäffner, Christina (2012) 'Functionalist Approaches', in MonaBaker and Gabriela Saldanha (eds) *Routledge Encyclopedia of Translation Studies*, 2nd ed. London and New York: Routledge, 115–121.

Shih, Claire Yi-yi (2018) 'Translation Commentary Re-examined in the Eyes of Translator Educators at British Universities', *The Journal of Specialised Translation*, 30: 291–311.

Sidiropoulou, Maria (2021) *Understanding Im/politeness Through Translation. The English-Greek Paradigm*. Edinburgh: Springer.

Simms, Karl (ed) (1997) *Translating Sensitive Texts: Linguistic Aspects*. Amsterdam: Rodopi.

St. André, James (ed) (2010) *Thinking through Translation with Metaphors*. Manchester: St. Jerome Publishing.

Tymoczko, Maria (1999) *Translation in a Postcolonial Context*. Manchester: St. Jerome.

Tymoczko, Maria (2000) 'Translation and Political Engagement: Activism, Social Change and the Role of Translation in Geopolitical Shifts', *The Translator*, 6: 1: 23–47.

Valdeón, Roberto A. (2015) 'The (Ab)use of Taboo Lexis in Audiovisual Translation: Raising Awareness of Pragmatic Variation in English-Spanish', *Intercultural Pragmatics*, 12: 3: 363–385.

Vandaele, Jeroen (2002a) '"Funny Fictions": Francoist Translation Censorship of Two Billy Wilder Films', *The Translator*, 8: 2: 267–302.

Vandaele, Jeroen (2002b) (ed) *Translating Humour*, Special Issue, *The Translator*, 8: 2.

Venuti, Lawrence (1995/2017) *The Translator's Invisibility: A History of Translation*. London and New York: Routledge.

Vinay, Jean-Paul and Jean Jean Darbelnet (1958/1995) *Comparative Stylistics of French and English: A Methodology for Translation*, translated and edited by Juan Sager and Marie-Jo Hamel. Amsterdam and Philadelphia: John Benjamins.

Williams, Kate and Jude Carroll (2009) *Referencing and Understanding Plagiarism*. London: Palgrave.

Zabalbeascoa, Patrick (2005) 'Humor and Translation - An Interdiscipline', *Humor*, 18: 2: 185–207.

5 Writing your commentary in practice

Key concepts

- Types of assignment.
- Formative and summative assignments.
- Criteria for selecting your ST.
- Obligatory vs optional translation choices.
- Managing your time.
- Preparing for a supervision session.

5.1 Introduction

Once you have gone through the different stages described so far in this book and done the source text (ST) analysis, formulated your statement of translation strategy and your translation priorities, and created a databank of the translation challenges you have encountered so that you can select illustrative examples, you will now need to put everything together.

All these stages will be worth going through, particularly when you are learning or being trained. You might get the impression that the time has not been invested particularly efficiently, as you might only be able to use 10% of the notes you have written for each stage (in a shorter commentary). This might be more so, because students and less experienced translators might actually write much more detail than needed.

However, the time invested will not be wasted at all. It will train you to think in a particular way, appraising and weighing up alternatives, which is a skill that you will need to be a good, informed translator. Like learning any other skill or being trained for any other profession, time needs to be invested, particularly at the beginning. This type of analysis will become second nature and you will be able to go through it more quickly as you will know what to look for. It will also be useful once you are a professional translator or project manager, as it will allow you to look at the ST, plan the translation strategy from various angles, and make your decisions at the microlevel in an informed and confident way. This will, in turn, enable you to justify these decisions to your clients or your line managers in a translation company.

DOI: 10.4324/9781003273790-8

The rest of the chapter will first discuss different types of commentary assignments and will provide advice on ST selection (when required), time management, and preparation for supervision. It then provides tasks where you will be assessing excerpts from sample commentaries, following the criteria presented in Chapter 3.

5.2 Practical aspects of a translation commentary

Task 5.1

In groups, discuss the following:

1. What types of assignments, which include a translation commentary, are there in your institution? Specify the word count and format.
2. If you had to choose a ST for an assignment, what criteria would you use to select it?
3. What is the difference between summative and formative assignments?
4. What questions would you ask your supervisor about commentary writing?

5.2.1 Types of assignment

There are various types of translation commentary assignments. They can go from a list of footnotes or annotated translation, or a short paragraph to briefly indicate your translation strategy, to a substantial piece of 5000 words or longer that focuses on a particular issue (such as for example the translation of humour). They might count towards the mark of the assignment or not. Sometimes the commentary consists of justifying a revision of a published translation. At other times, you may be required to find a ST that has not been translated into the target language (TL) and write your commentary on your own translation. Some commentaries may be more directed or prescriptive; that is, you are told exactly what you need to include. Others are supervised or semi-supervised, which means that you will be guided along the way, but the writing of the commentary will be mostly self-directed. In some assignments you will be given a particular ST, while in others you will need to choose your own ST.

5.2.1.1 Formative and summative assignments

'Summative assessment is sometimes referred to as assessment *of* learning, and formative assessment, as assessment *for* learning' (Looney 2011: 7). In other words, summative assignments may include the end-of-term or end-of-year examinations or assignments, which will count towards the mark of a particular module. Whereas formative assignments might be shorter, more frequent, and interactive. Assessment through formative assignments 'emphasises the importance of actively engaging students in their own learning processes' (Looney 2011: 5).

Therefore, formative assignments allow you to explore and take risks, to try out what works and what does not work. The issue with formative assignments is that you might often be able to redo them and change them according to the feedback you get from your teacher. Even if you are not able to redo them, you will be able to use the feedback you got and apply it to the next assignment regardless of whether this assignment is formative or summative.

Some institutions might not have a formative commentary assignment, but they might have done some shorter assignments either for homework, lesson preparation, or in class. Even if this is not the case, you will be able to use the tasks in this textbook to gain some practice before submitting your summative translation commentary.

Previously, we mentioned different translation commentary assignments that vary in length, which, typically, might range from 1000 to 5000 words or more. In fact, translation commentaries could be shorter than 1000 words, even as short as 75 words. However, these shorter types of commentaries usually do not count towards the mark of the assignment and tend to just require you to specify the skopos and intended reader of the target text (TT) and, perhaps, any other issues that might need to be explained, to aid with the assessment of the accompanying translation. At the other end of the spectrum, a translation commentary may be much longer than 5000 words, like in the case of PhDs that are comprised of a translation and a commentary.

5.2.1.2 *Commentary on a revised published translation*

This is the type of translation commentary which is discussed in Sewell (2002). It entails looking at published translations of a particular ST and then offering a revised and, ideally, improved translation into the TL in question and a justification of the changes made. It could consist of a commentary of just one published translation or a comparative study of more than one translation. Sometimes you might be able to compare your revisions, with the techniques used, in translations into other languages. This type of commentary of a revised published translation might be fairly common in some contexts, as it might be difficult to find a suitable ST that has not been translated into the TL.

Even with this type of translation commentary, you will still need to do a ST analysis and, to some extent, when you justify your changes from the published translation(s) you will need to articulate a translation strategy and translation priorities in terms of skopos, intended reader, text type, medium of publication, etc. You might also be required to integrate secondary sources into your commentary (please check the requirements of your institution).

Finally, you will also need to select relevant illustrative examples, as in all likelihood you will not be able to discuss all of the changes you have made. As mentioned in Chapter 4, it would be best to categorise these changes and then select the most representative ones to illustrate the reasons why you chose a particular option.

5.2.1.3 *Prescriptive translation commentaries*

By 'prescriptive translation commentaries,' we mean those assignments where you are told exactly what aspects to include in it. You might be provided with a translation brief (discussed in Chapter 1), which might include the medium of publication, the intended reader, and even the skopos. As with the other types of assignments, you could still follow the stages discussed in Chapters 1–3. That is, taking notes on your ST analysis, formulating your statement of translation strategy following the stages proposed in Chapter 2, and then categorising your examples as suggested in Chapter 3, will give you a bank of material to select from, while still following the instructions of what you need to include in your translation commentary. The difference here is that the instructions you are given might give you a specific direction on what material you will need to gather.

5.2.1.4 *Supervised commentaries*

Those translation commentaries that are longer than 1000 words, usually 2500, 5000, or even longer, tend to be part of projects to accompany a substantial translation of 5000 to 10000 words or more. They tend to be the final assignments of an undergraduate or postgraduate degree. In many institutions, they might take place after all the teaching has finished (for example, in taught MA programmes). However, as mentioned above, it is also possible to do a commentary as part of a PhD.

The longer translation commentaries are usually supervised or semi-supervised. This means that, although the commentary would be mostly self-planned and initiated by you, you will also have a mentor or a tutor that will guide you through the process of both translating and writing your commentary. In section 5.2 we will discuss how best to prepare for the supervision sections.

Short translation commentaries, of 1000 words or less, usually accompany short translation assignments such as STs that are no longer than 1000 words, and they are carried out during term time. These short commentaries are usually not supervised and, although sometimes you might be able to produce a draft to get feedback from your teachers as a formative assignment, at other times you will have to submit your assignment without getting any feedback while you are writing it. Often, you might have to do more than one of these assignments throughout the year and, therefore, you can use the feedback you got on the earlier assignments to improve the latter ones. Your teachers should, therefore, provide you with what is called 'feed-forward' and offer some suggestions for improvement. If, however, you have to do a commentary without getting any feedback beforehand or supervision while you are writing it, the advice that has been given throughout this text-book will come in useful. Basically, remember the following:

- Use one-third of the commentary to write your ST analysis (including relevant background information), formulate your translation strategy and indicate your translation priorities. For a 1000-word commentary, it should be no longer than around 330 words.
- Select examples from two of the most relevant matrices to justify your decisions by also making references to your translation strategy. Try not to use more than 550 words, divided more or less equally between the two matrices.
- You will have around 120 words to write a conclusion where you evaluate your translation in light of the translation strategy.
- If you need to include theoretical sources, please check section 4.3.

5.2.1.5 Selecting the ST for your project (when required to do so)

Usually, for the shorter commentaries of 1000 words or less, you will be provided with a particular ST, although you might often be given a choice of several alternatives of different text types. For the longer assignments, however, you will probably have to choose your own ST and the only instructions you might be given about this is the number of words the ST needs to be. Sometimes, but not always, you might also need to choose a particular text type. In any case, the ST will usually have to be approved by your supervisor.

In order to choose a ST, you will need to play to your strengths and interests. For example, if you plan to gather a portfolio with samples of the work you did during your studies or training and you want to include technical translation, but you are more interested in literary translation, you can choose a book of fiction that combines both. For instance, you could choose a forensic crime scene with a good amount of medical terminology in a novel or a trial scene in a play with legal terminology, etc. If you are interested in discussing how the TT's intended readership has affected your translation, you might be able to select two or three different STs about the same topic but intended for different readerships. Then, you can discuss in your commentary how the different intended readers informed the translation decisions you took at the microlevel. However, you will need to check beforehand whether your institution allows you to choose more than one text for the same assignment.

Finally, if you are interested in pursuing a particular topic you might want to select your ST accordingly. For example, if you want to discuss the translation of humour you could select a text that is considered humorous in the SC. Or you might be interested in the translation of cultural references, so you could choose to translate some kind of touristic or promotional text.

Apart from playing to your own strengths and interests, you need to make sure that the ST is appropriate, particularly in terms of difficulty and complexity. If you chose something fairly straightforward for your particular language combination, you might not find enough issues to discuss in your commentary, as, in most likelihood, most of the decisions you need to take will have an obvious answer. That is, you might not have to choose between equally valid alternatives, or you might not have to preserve some aspects of the ST at the expense of sacrificing others.

On the other hand, the situation is not optimal either if the text is too complex or particularly challenging to complete in the allotted time. This might be due, for example, to the complexity of the ST's style, which might render it difficult to understand fully. Another feature that might render the ST too complex for the allotted time is the presence of footnotes or endnotes, which were discussed in Chapters 1 and 2.

You need to look at whether the grammar, syntax, register, and lexis of the ST are challenging to translate into the TL and judge the level of difficulty for doing so; you need to ascertain whether you will be able to replicate the style, tone, and effect, how much background and contextual knowledge the TT intended reader will need to have to understand the cultural references, etc. A way to gauge the level of difficulty of the ST, as well as to ascertain the challenging issues that might be worth discussing in the commentary, is to translate at least 300 words or so of any potential ST you have in mind.

The next section will discuss how to prepare for your supervision sessions.

5.2.2 Commentary supervision

As mentioned above, for most of the longer assignments, such as, for example, 2500 words long or more, you will be allocated a supervisor. The role of this supervisor is simply to guide you and facilitate your learning. That is, they are not there to do the work for you, but to help you discover and develop your ideas. Most of the time, although not always, you will have the same supervisor for both the translation assignment and the commentary. When this is the case, the emphasis often tends to be on the translation itself.

Task 5.2

Brainstorm in groups how you usually manage your time when you have an assignment. You can discuss any assignment if you have never had a translation and commentary assignment.

5.2.2.1 How to manage your time

A long commentary normally accompanies a fairly long translation, generally double the number of words or slightly longer. For example, a 5000-word translation might be accompanied by a 2500-word commentary.

Before you start translating, you would ideally do the ST analysis as set out in Chapter 1 and start articulating your statement of translation strategy and priorities. However, as the commentary is recursive, it is advisable to just do this in a rough draft form or even just notes rather than a coherent narrative. This is because, as you translate, you may actually find some issues that force you to change your translation strategy accordingly. In fact, what you could actually do, as mentioned previously, is to roughly translate 300 words of several possible STs, so that you can decide which one to select. Then, once you have identified the most appropriate ST, you should do the ST analysis, the statement of translation strategy, and set up your priorities, in rough notes. Then, you could start translating and taking notes of the challenges you find as you do it. Make sure you keep a record of these challenges, either in a translation journal, a spreadsheet, or something similar. Do not forget to also categorise these challenges by, for example, using the *Thinking Translation* matrices and colour-coding or annotating them, or using the table in Appendix 1, as mentioned in Chapter 3.

As you are doing the above, you need to do some background theoretical reading to decide what translation theories and concepts will be relevant for your commentary (check section 4.3), if this is what your assignment requires you to do. After that, you need to decide how you are going to structure your commentary (see Chapter 4) and select what you will include in it. Remember to use the space you have in a balanced way: a third of the word count for the ST analysis and statement of translation strategy, which will leave you the rest to discuss your translation decisions at the microlevel.

These assignments often take place after most of the other modules in the programme have finished. For example, in many European countries this type of assignment is called 'end of year project' or something to that effect and takes place during the summer months. This might, obviously, be different in countries in the Southern Hemisphere or in programmes that have end-of-term projects. Regardless of when the longer supervised projects take place, it would be a good idea to create a timeline or chronogram with milestones of when you plan to have a particular work done. In fact, your supervisor might ask you to write one up as part of the assignment.

5.2.2.2 *How to prepare for a supervision session*

You are likely to only have a limited number of hours of supervision. You might have something like one hour of supervision per 2000-word translation and 1000-word commentary. So, for example, for a 10000-word translation accompanied by a 5000-word commentary, you will have five hours in total. Therefore, it is advisable for you to prepare well for these sessions, so that you can make the most effective use of the time available. Obviously, this will vary from institution to institution. These might take place face-to-face or online, but you might be allowed to ask questions via email, which might not necessarily be counted as part of the supervision allocation. In any case, you will need to confirm this with your supervisor.

Most of the time, your supervisor will need to approve the ST you have chosen. Therefore, unless you already have a particular text in mind, it might be advisable to have an initial meeting to discuss your interest in, for example, particular genres, but also, perhaps, certain issues you would like to explore in your commentary. This will allow your supervisor to advise you and give you suggestions on what ST you could select.

Before the next supervisory session, you can send a timeline as well as a plan for your commentary. Make sure you include an estimate of the number of words you will write in every section, so your supervisor can advise you better and suggest changes to your structure. Sometimes this is the only advice that supervisors may be able to specifically give you about your commentary, although in very long commentaries, of 5000 words or more, they might also be able to look at a sample. If this is the case, make sure that you select those segments where you really need help and advice.

Obviously, in most sessions you will also discuss your translation. Often, you will send a sample before the session. Again, as in the case of the sample from the commentary, you should choose those particular places in your translation that you found challenging, or passages where you need some advice on weighing up the options you have or some suggestions on how to find solutions to a translation problem. You need to bear in mind, however, that most supervisors will only be able to look at a part of your translation. This could be a fourth or even a third of the complete translation, but not more. So, again, when you select the sample, it might be better not to just do the first 1000 words, for example, but to select a few paragraphs from different parts of your translation. Your supervisor will be able to advise you on this. Depending on the institution, you might be able to submit a second revised version of your sample, which makes the first sample a formative exercise. However, this is not always the case.

Even though, as mentioned above, your supervisor might not be able to give you further advice on your commentary itself, you might be able to get advice on whether the challenging translation issues you discussed in the sessions are worth discussing in your commentary or not, and also from what angle or theoretical perspective (including suggestions of relevant translation theories and concepts) this could be done. In fact, sometimes, this might be included in the written feedback you get from the translation sample.

5.2.2.3 Examples of usual questions you can ask your supervisor

You can ask your supervisor for the following advice:

- What ST to choose according to your interests and how to go about it.
- Feedback on the proposed structure.

- What contextual or background information about the ST would be relevant for your commentary and suggestions on how to find it.
- What you should cut down from your ST analysis or statement of translation strategy if you have used too many words in writing it.
- What the profile of the TT's intended reader could be from a range of possibilities you have identified.
- What solution, among a range of solutions, would be more appropriate for a particular translation challenge, taking into account your strategy.
- What set of examples from a range of possible examples would be more interesting to discuss.

Some of these questions might be too specific for your supervisor to answer, as this should be your work and you should be able to find the answers yourself. This is a form of active learning which is much more effective than when you are given the answers. Hence, what you could do before meeting your supervisor, is to find the answers to the questions above and then in the session you could ask for their thoughts on these.

Task 5.3

Select a translation you have done and think about other possible questions you could ask your supervisor that have not been included above.

5.3 Assessment criteria for commentaries

In this section, we will look at sample criteria that could be used to assess a translation commentary. The list below is by no means intended to be exhaustive. That is, not all of the criteria might be used in your institution and/or they might use other criteria.

5.3.1 Structure, style, and presentation

Your commentary should have a clear structure, regardless of whether you follow all or some of the matrices of the *Thinking Translation* series, or whether you focus on a particular issue, such as, for example, the translation of profanity, the translation of politeness, etc. You should avoid an anecdotal tone (see 3.2.1) and the style and referencing should be consistent throughout.

5.3.1.1 Structure

The strongest commentaries will be coherent and have a logical structure where it is clear when you are discussing the ST or the TT. The space available will be dedicated to the different issues in a balanced way. There will be an effective use of signposting to guide the reader. The conclusion will sum up the most important points and make a link between the techniques used at the microlevel and the translation strategy. The issues and illustrative examples selected for discussion will clearly support the line of argument. The transition between sections will be fluent and coherent.

The weaker commentaries may lack coherence, the ideas may not be ordered logically, and some issues may take much more space than others for no obvious reason. There may also be a lack of signposting to guide the reader and, often, there may be no conclusion. In addition, too many issues may have been selected for discussion, which may then render it too brief and superficial. The transition between the sections may be not fluent. Also, there may not be an explicit link between the techniques used at the microlevel and the translation strategy.

5.3.1.2 *Use of appropriate terminology*

The strongest commentaries will be concise because of using relevant terminology in an accurate, precise, and consistent manner.

The weakest commentaries may paraphrase or use descriptions rather than the relevant terminology, thus making the commentary very wordy and cumbersome. When specific terminology is used it may often have been done inaccurately, hence showing that the concept has either been misunderstood or not understood completely. Sometimes it might be used in the wrong context, which might be misleading or create ambiguities. The choice of terminology may be eclectic, originating from different sources, resulting in the same issue being referred to with different terms. One example of inconsistency in the use of terminology is using the expressions 'dynamic equivalence,' 'communicative translation,' and 'domesticating technique' in the same commentary, to refer to a TL-biased translation technique. An example of using a longwinded expression or paraphrase rather than a specific term is, for instance, to say something like 'the currency was translated by the TL term so that the reader might understand it without any further explanation,' or something to that effect. This would not be the best or most effective way of using the space available, particularly if we have to do it every time we discuss a cultural reference.

5.3.1.3 *Integration of secondary and theoretical sources*

The stronger commentaries will mention theories relevant to the issues discussed. They will be linked to the examples and will also be properly integrated as an essential part of the narrative. The referencing will be consistent throughout.

The weaker commentaries may mention the most typical citations by a particular scholar and either do not refer to them again, or the citation in question may contradict the actual translation decisions taken. That is, the theories may be superimposed rather than integrated into the commentary, simply for the sake of being there, but they are never revisited, and they are not illustrated by examples. In other words, there is not enough engagement with the theories. In addition, some clearly relevant theories may not have been mentioned. As for the referencing, it may be inconsistent and some of the sources may not have been acknowledged properly or not at all.

5.3.1.4 Presentation

This is also linked to the structure, coherence, and the effective use of signposting in your commentary. The strongest commentaries will have a clear and consistent use of headings and subheadings, an accurate use of punctuation, and the examples will be provided in a consistent and effective way, including back translations when necessary.

The weaker commentaries may either not use headings and subheadings or, when they do, it may be done in an inconsistent and confusing way. The use of punctuation may be inaccurate. The examples may be presented in an inconsistent and unclear way and back translations may be provided hardly ever or not at all.

Task 5.4

Read the sample commentary at the end of this chapter and also the sample rubric with descriptors in Appendix 2. In groups assess this commentary in terms of its structure, use of appropriate terminology, integration of secondary sources, and its presentation, including referencing (see 4.3).

5.3.2 Macrolevel analysis

As mentioned previously, this part of the commentary should be roughly around one-third of the total word count. Therefore, we would typically have the following number of words to write it: around 1500 for a 5000-word commentary; 700 words for a 2500-word commentary; and around 300 words for a 1000-word commentary. This would mean that in the shorter commentaries you will need to be much more precise and concise, so that you can still provide the relevant information. Remember that you will, ideally, still include this section in a thematically structured commentary.

5.3.2.1 ST analysis

The stronger commentaries will include some relevant background and contextual information about the ST author and the SC, as well as the ST's genre or text type, its skopos, intended readership and medium of publication. They might also mention something about the ST's salient features, such as its particular effect or tone, which will be referred to when formulating the translation strategy and setting up the translation priorities.

The weaker commentaries either do not discuss some of the issues above and/or spend too long on one particular aspect at the expense of others. They might also include issues that are not clearly relevant to the discussion.

5.3.2.2 Formulation of the translation strategy

The stronger commentaries will explicitly mention the following: TT genre or text type, its skopos, intended readership and medium of publication. The longer commentaries will usually include a rather detailed profile of the TT's intended readership and medium of publication.

The weaker commentaries may either miss some of the information above or they might not discuss it in an explicit manner. It may also be hard to tell when the discussion is about the ST or the TT. As was the case with the ST analysis, some of the issues may be discussed in too much detail at the expense of others.

5.3.2.3 Setting up of translation priorities

The stronger commentaries will explicitly set up the translation priorities in a clear and concise manner, cross referencing them with the translation strategy and the salient features of the ST identified in the analysis. These priorities are linked to the translation strategy and the ST's salient features.

The weaker commentaries may not have formulated any translation priorities explicitly. If they have been formulated, they might not be consistent with the translation strategy, or the salient features of the ST identified in the analysis. They might also formulate them in a vague or inaccurate manner (for example, 'my priority is to translate the ST communicatively'), or they might be inconsistent with the translation techniques used in the TT.

Task 5.5

Read the sample commentary at the end of this chapter and also the sample rubric with descriptors in Appendix 2. In groups assess it in terms of the ST analysis, the formulation of the translation strategy and the setting up of the translation priorities.

5.3.3 Microlevel analysis

This part of the commentary would ideally be roughly just under two-thirds of the total word count. Therefore, we would typically have the following number of words at our disposal: around 3000 for a 5000-word commentary; 1500 words for a 2500-word commentary; and around 600 words for a 1000-word commentary. This would mean that, as was the case with the macrolevel analysis, in the shorter commentaries you will need to be much more precise and concise, so that you can still provide the relevant information. Remember that you will still need to select illustrative examples for a thematically structured commentary. Your job will be made easier by keeping a translation journal, spreadsheet, or any other way you have built your databank of categorised examples from which you can make your selection.

5.3.3.1 Selection of illustrative examples

The stronger commentaries will select just enough examples to illustrate a particular point. This allows for enough space to develop the justification for a particular decision and integrate the examples fully within the narrative.

The weaker commentaries might have too many examples without really discussing how they link to any part of the commentary. Or there might not be enough examples at all. Some of the examples might have been chosen from inaccurate translation decisions.

5.3.3.2 Integration of illustrative examples

The stronger commentaries will explore the examples fully by cross-referring them to the translation strategy and priorities to justify the techniques used. They will be properly referenced (by using, for example, line numbers) to be easily found. In a thematically structured commentary, there will be both a clear engagement with theoretical concepts and examples to justify the decisions taken.

The weaker commentaries may present a list of examples in a descriptive manner without offering an adequate justification for the decisions taken to translate that example in a particular way. They may not follow a particular structure, theme, or category to discuss the translation decisions, such as, for example, following the matrices or using a thematic structure. The weaker commentaries may also just put the line numbers instead of writing out the examples, which makes it hard for the reader to find them.

5.3.3.3 Relevance of illustrative examples

The stronger commentaries will have selected examples that are relevant for the discussion or are important to explore because of either being too controversial and going against the intended TT readers' expectations, or because they contradict other translation techniques used in the same text. They might also select those instances where there is some kind of loss or gain and justify why a particular translation solution was chosen.

The weaker commentaries may choose examples that are not particularly representative of the overall translation strategy taken, when there were alternatives that were obviously better choices.

Task 5.6

Read the sample commentary at the end of this chapter and also the sample rubric with descriptors in Appendix 2. In groups, assess it in terms of the selection, integration, and relevance of the illustrative examples.

5.4 Conclusion

It goes without saying that you need to prepare well for your supervision sessions, so you make the most effective use of them. This means that you should try to find the answers to your possible questions beforehand and select for discussion those questions you could not find the answer to, or where you are not happy with the answer you found. In any case, even if you have used all of your supervision sessions or you are doing an assignment that is not being supervised, you can still use the assessment rubric in Appendix 2 in combination with the checklist below to be able to improve your commentary (you can find a printable version of this checklist in Appendix 3):

Structure, style, and presentation

1. Is the structure logical?
2. Is it clear where you are discussing the ST and the TT?
3. Is the signposting effective?
4. Is the transition between the sections fluent and coherent?
5. Have you dedicated the allocated word count to the different parts of the commentary in an effective and balanced way?
6. Does the conclusion sum up the most important points?
7. Is the appropriate terminology used accurately and consistently?
8. Are the secondary and theoretical sources relevant to the issues discussed?
9. Are the secondary and theoretical sources linked to examples and are they properly integrated as an essential part of the narrative?
10. Is the referencing consistent?
11. Is the use of punctuation accurate and consistent?

Macrolevel analysis

1. Have you included some relevant background and contextual information about the ST, the ST's author, and the SC?
2. Have you included information on the ST's genre or text type, skopos, intended readership, and medium of publication?
3. Have you discussed the ST's salient features?
4. Have you discussed explicitly the TT's genre or text type, skopos, intended readership, and medium of publication?
5. Have you set up your translation priorities in a clear, explicit, and concise manner?
6. Have you linked your translation priorities to your translation strategy and the ST's salient features?

Microlevel analysis

1. Do the examples you selected deal with optional rather than obligatory decisions you had to make?
2. Have you selected the appropriate number of examples to discuss a particular point?
3. Do the illustrative examples support the line of argument of the commentary? Are they relevant?
4. Have the translation techniques used in the examples selected been linked to the translation strategy and translation priorities?
5. Is there a clear engagement with both theoretical concepts and illustrative examples to justify the decisions you have taken?

Apart from preparing for the supervision sessions, you need to manage your time effectively. In order to do this, it is advisable to do a timeline or chronogram where you could insert the main milestones to be reached and by when (5.2.2.1). You should also write extensive notes, without worrying about word count, when doing the ST analysis and formulating your translation strategy. Remember to make notes or keep some type of journal to keep examples of the translation challenges you find as you translate and to categorise them by, for example, using the *Thinking Translation* matrices or the table in Appendix 1. You will then be able to select from all of these notes and databank the most relevant and important points to include on your commentary, regardless of its length. Even though it might feel very time consuming, you will save time in the long run. You will also be practising and acquiring skills not just to get a good mark, but for your own learning and professional development as a translator.

5.5 Summary

In this chapter, we looked at different types of translation commentary assignments and provided suggestions on selecting the ST for your project when the assignment requires you to do so. Then, we provided advice on how to manage your time and how best to prepare for the sessions with your supervisor, when applicable. The chapter finished with the assessment criteria in terms of structure, style, and presentation; macrolevel analysis (ST analysis, formulation of a translation strategy, and setting up translation priorities); and microlevel analysis (selection of illustrative examples, integration of illustrative examples, and relevance of illustrative examples). Chapters 6 and 7, which form Part III, *Beyond the written word*, will look at writing a reflective report in interpreting, audiovisual translation, localisation, and transcreation.

Further reading

Cottrell, Stella (2019) *The Study Skills Handbook*, 5th ed. London: Bloomsbury Academic.

List of references

Cottrell, Stella (2019) *The Study Skills Handbook*, 5th ed. London: Bloomsbury Academic.
Looney, Janet (2011) 'Integrating Formative and Summative Assessment: Progress Toward a Seamless System?', *OECD Education Working Papers*, No. 58. Paris: OECD Publishing.
Sewell, Penelope (2002) *Translation Commentary: The Art Revisited*. Dublin: Philomel.

Please use the commentary below to carry out the tasks in this chapter
Sample commentary to accompany a translation into Russian

1. INTRODUCTION

The source text (ST) is an extract from the book Young Mungo by Douglas Stuart. Douglas Stuart won the Booker prize for his first novel Shuggie Bain and Young Mungo is his second novel and was published in April 2022. The book was written in the genre of fiction and is set in 1980's Glasgow and follows the style used by other modern Scottish writers such as Irvine Welsh in incorporating a very high level of regional dialect into the text, with sentences being written exactly as they would be spoken.

Young Mungo tells the story about a young gay, Protestant boy, Mungo, who becomes friends with a Catholic neighbour called James. Mungo has a brother, Hamish, who is a local gang leader, and a sister Jodie who is bright and ambitious. They live with their alcoholic mother who disappears for weeks at a time in a deprived, violently sectarian working-class part of Glasgow where there was no way for Mungo to be queer and safe. The narration also talks about the struggle of women and their fate being controlled by men. Douglas Stuart's first novel Shuggie Bain is considered autobiographical, and Young Mungo can be presumed also to be at least partially autobiographical as the book characters are set in the same world and live on a housing estate as that experienced by Stuart in his childhood (BBC Radio 4 This Cultural Life Podcast with Douglas Stuart).

This book is primarily aimed at both people in the LGBTIQA+ community and those who do not identify themselves as part of such community but want to be informed and educated about LGBTIQA+ issues. This piece of literature is also targeted at anyone who is interested in contemporary literature fiction and learning about life in working class Glasgow in the late 20th century.

The excerpts from Young Mungo were chosen for the extended final project because they depict the harsh cultural and political situation in Glasgow over the timeline described in the book. Furthermore, there are significant linguistic forms that are representative of the city as well as the fact that the author writes in a mix of Standard English and Glaswegian dialect, a variety of Scots, which would be a challenging task to translate into Russian. Also, I thought that those parts of the ST were especially emotionally charged (i.e., recorded the author's personal experience) which helps reflect the messages of the book.

2. A MACRO-TEXTUAL LEVEL AND THE USE OF THEORY

The Skopos theory was chosen to guide decision making when performing the translation of the literary text into the target language (TL) at a macro-textual level. The skopos of the TT is to transmit the author's intentions of expressive function of language and hence the ST can be classified as an expressive text type. The scholars Reiß and Vermeer define the aim of an expressive text type is to 'convey artistically organised content, consciously verbalising the content according to aesthetic criteria' (Reiß, Vermeer 2013: 182). In the specific case of the translation of literature, 'the style of the ST author is a priority' (Munday 2013: 114). Therefore, when using the Skopos theory in the translation of fiction, the function of translator is to identify and transfer the specific way the author of the ST expresses the message of the ST and to convert this all into the target text (TT). The 'identifying' translation method was used as the main translation strategy to take on the author's perspective (Ibid., 114).

Looking at the notion of translation, Nida defines the nature of translating 'in reproducing in the receptor language the closest natural equivalent of the source-language message, first in terms of meaning and secondly in terms of style' (Nida 2021: 12). As well as translation is not only considered as a process of rendering a message via equivalence from one language into another but the production of a text for another culture. It is noteworthy to mention, therefore, how the contact between the author and the target reader – literary communication – can work across cultural and linguistic boundaries. As per Nord, the sender (the author of the ST) 'intends to produce a certain effect on the receivers and the translator tries to verbalise that intention' in the translated literature (Nord 2014: 84).

In the view of this situation, Nord stresses that 'what is actually translated is not the sender's intention but the translator's interpretation of the sender's intention' (Ibid., 85). Firstly, the translator must think of the target audience and be aware of the readers' world and cultural knowledge, their understanding of societies and cultures in the context of the book characters, and the language they use. With all this in mind, the translator must be able to provide the same effect intended by the author of the ST on to the TT readers. Secondly, the translator has to have an individual understanding of the ST and to be able to produce a good translation they must be able to interpret linguistic and stylistic markers as well as the geographical, cultural, and social features of the ST.

This, however, can present the translator with a serious challenge due to the presence of sociocultural references in a literary ST. 'The sociocultural gap between the amount of information presupposed with respect to the ST receivers and the actual cultural knowledge of the TT addressees can be sometimes bridged by additional information or adaptations introduced by a translator' (Ibid., 86). Considering the importance of the meaning of the ST content as well as the role of style and register is similarly significant, Equivalence theory was determined as the most appropriate solution to achieve a natural reproducing of the author's message in the TT (See Nida 2021: 12-33, Pym 2014: 33-63). Consequently, the function of the TT as a literary text can be achieved via adding changes at a micro-level that the TT readers will use to establish coherence between the information given in the text and their prior knowledge.

3. TRANSLATING YOUNG MUNGO.
A MICRO-TEXTUAL LEVEL

3.1 THE FORMAL LEVEL

At the formal level, many adaptations of selected excerpts from Young Mungo were made to satisfy the function of the expressive text type of the TT. The formatting of paragraphs was altered to achieve adequate translation and coherent communication between the author and the readers. Other alterations were made to reflect the fact that punctuation rules are different in English and Russian languages. In the ST, direct speech is reproduced in speech marks (quotation marks), when in the TT a dash in dialogue is used instead and each character's speech begins with a new line. Moreover, the punctuation that follows before or after the direct speech was also taken into consideration according to the syntactic structure of sentences.

At the syntactic level, changes to grammatical structures and word order were made to maintain the theme and rheme of the ST in the TL. Moreover, one of the strategies used was to join sentences together via additional conjunctions, for example, 'иначе' (TT154) to make the flow of the text more coherent. The opposite strategy was to split one sentence into two via changing the syntax for a greater clarity, and this was used in TT637-641.

3.2 TRANSLATION OF CHARACTERS AND FOREIGN NAMES AT THE CULTURAL LEVEL

To render the characters' names or other foreign names as well as the names of places, the Library of Congress system (LoC 2012) was used to transliterate them into Russian: "Джоди Хэмильтон" (TT106), "Кэмпбелл" (TT123), "бар Бэйрдс" (TT386), "Дроверс Инн" (TT864), "Пэрейд"(TT660), "Сайтхилл" (TT683), "Кардован" (TT872), except where established spelling was found such as "Мунго" (TT4) (https://academic.ru), "Святой Кентигерн" (TT79-80) (https://pravoslavie.ru). Terms that describe a particular geographical location were formatted via using the transposition technique of shifting the noun category into the adjective category without altering the meaning of the text. Lexical equivalence was achieved by adding the suffix -ск and ending -ие since the particular items are plural which, however, will also be varied depending on case, for example, "эрискейских пони" in Genitive case, plural (TT321) and "бригтунские парни Билли" in Nominative case, plural (TT329). Of note, Brigton or Brigtoun is the Scots form of Bridgeton, a district in Glasgow. Therefore, the Glaswegian pronunciation was considered.

In translation of literary text, the meaning of a particular communication is often implicit within the context and, therefore, the ST has to be analysed not only semantically but pragmatically. In particular, choices were made neither to translate nor transliterate the following Gaelic terms into Russian: "uisge beatha" (TT875) and "ceilidhs" (TT862). The use of cultural specific forms that may cause difficulties to pronounce for anyone of both source language (SL) and TL and who is not familiar with such cultural features, shows the author's intention to indicate the book characters' belonging to a certain group of people and their authenticity phonetically and lexically.

3.3 TRANSLATION BY CULTURAL SUBSTITUTION

Where necessary, an application of equivalent existing loan words in Russian is considered to fulfil the skopos of the TT. Examples of this are "Сиерра" (TT246), "Рейнджерс" (TT373), "Селтик" (TT377), "у ниверситет Глазго" (TT828), "фольксвагены" (TT846), "мерседессы" (TT846), "Рэбби Бэрнс" (TT862). Translators can face challenges of non-equivalence at the word level which 'means that the target language has no direct equivalent for a word which occurs in the source text' (Baker 1992: 20). I considered the strategy of translation by cultural substitution in the TT to replace a culture-specific word or phrase. The first examples are "a Sooty puppet" (ST399) translated as "кукла-петрушка" (TT464), and "a peepin' Tom" (ST546) as "извращенец" (TT634). Such strategy gives the reader 'a concept with which they can identify, something familiar and appealing' (Ibid., 31). Brand names such as "Avon" (TT518) and "Barbour" (TT731) are connotative and, therefore, were not translated into the TT as it is presumed that the target readers are familiar with these items. The title of the song (TT290) was conveyed in the TT by transferring its original form and preserving the pronunciation.

However, other items can be considered more culturally specialised and known only to those target readers with a higher level of cultural knowledge. Such specialised terms could be food ("Selkirk bannock" (ST151), "a plate of mince" (ST165) which refers to a traditional Scottish dish mince and tatties, "smoked Scottish salmon" (ST752)), drinks ("whisky and pints" (ST396), "uisge beatha" (ST753)), and cultural attributes ("the local Orange marching" (ST236), "Tam-o'-Shanters" (ST239), "the Lambeg drum" (TT242), "the Orange song" (ST281), 'the Old Firm game' (ST320), "lambswool" (ST742), "Rabbie Burns" (ST744), "ceilidhs" (ST744), "bagpipes" (ST744), "walks around Loch Voil" (745)).

The following approaches were applied to ensure an adequate translation and to make the TT accessible to the target audience. Firstly, this can be achieved by Newmark's suggested descriptive equivalence (Newmark 1988: 83), a technique of integration of descriptive words to help to explain to the readers their meaning but without affecting the perception of the main text, for example, "в четырёхэтажном муниципальном многоквартирнике из песчанника" (TT161-162), "кусок лепёшки селки рского бэннока" (TT180), "судостроительная фирма «Ярроу Шипбилд инг»" (TT183), "пункте базирования Фаслейн" (TT213), "береты тамо-шэнтеры" (TT285), "консервированный пирог с мясом и почками продукции «Фрэй Бентос»" (TT601), "у моей двери толпились папаши от района Гована до Гарнгада" (TT796). Such solution helps not to overload the body of the TT with metatext but rather to perceive the author's message which match the text's skopos as an expressive text type at the cultural level.

At some point, however, interventions in form of extratextual gloss such as footnotes to the text are necessary in order to compensate the cultural markers of the foreign text. Footnotes as the second approach were added to the TT for the terms "Proddy" (TT168), "Thatcher" (TT185), "John Major" (TT216), "Fenians" (TT256), "the Orange marching band" (TT281-282), "The Sash My Father Wore" (TT290), "the Billy Boys" (TT326), "the Old Firm" (TT373), "minstrel dollies" (TT867). These examples of where footnotes were used to 'warn readers that they are about to encounter a different view of the world. Readers' background knowledge can be challenged without affecting the coherence of a text' (Baker 1992: 249).

Were the whole book to be translated rather than an excerpt, an initiative could be proposed such as a translator's foreword to bridge the cultural gap between the ST and a Russian-speaking audience. This helps to acquaint the target audience with the political and cultural context that represents the city of Glasgow and its citizens as the book's storyline is set in the 1980s. These are working-class people whose employment was destroyed by policies enacted by the British government and, as a result, there were generations of families left without work and income and having to exist on benefits. It was also a key cultural feature of the groups covered in the book that men were viewed as the main income provider. Moreover, alcohol became a part of daily life for both men and women. In addition, children often grew up in single parent-families, while suffering neglect, living in terror of drunken family members and being involved in fighting gangs.

The use of such explanatory text allows the translator to be 'a cross-cultural mediator by revealing the features of linguistic culture through historical, cultural, linguistic information' (Tonkopeeva 2017: 72). Since the body of the translation does not allow the translator to explain to the audience the elements of a linguistic relativity (See the Whorf Thesis adapted in Brown and Lennenberg 1954: 454–462), tools such as translator's foreword helps to achieve the intended by the author semantic and pragmatic features in the TL.

3.4 SCOTTISH CULTURE AND CREATION OF
LINGUACULTURAL TYPE OF 'GLASWEGIAN'

The author intends to represent the book characters' identity to Scotland and Scottish culture in the ST and this was done via several methods. Firstly, by extralinguistic aspects such as highlighting Scottishness via a negative attitude towards England, English culture, and English attitudes. Examples in the ST include "the English government had been frustrated" (ST184-185), "tired of subsidizing Scotland" (ST185), "they got laid off by some suit-wearing snobs in Westminster who couldnae find Glasgow on a map, who didnae give a flyin' fuck if the men had families to feed" (ST477-479), "uppity ginger bitch decides that's the end of them" (ST481). A second approach used was for the characters to have a strong sense of belonging to their neighbourhood and no choice or possibility of leaving it. Examples of this in the ST include "He wandered along familiar streets, winding back and forth" (ST228), "He had spent his whole life on these streets and some days it could make him feel like a mouse in a maze" (ST232-233), "To Jodie, the university was another city altogether, one whose postcode was a moat that kept East End middens like her out" (ST715-717), "university life was not available to her. It was not for Glaswegians like her" (ST755). As per the chosen Nida's equivalence translation approach, the message of the ST was conveyed via 'tailoring' lexical and grammatical adjustments in the TT.

A sociolinguistic approach used to represent the language variety that is specific to the geographical area. *Young Mungo* is a book that operates a dual narrative and is written in Standard English and Glaswegian dialect. Glaswegian dialect is a result of 'the mixture of two dialect systems: the local vernacular, a variety of Scots, and Standard English' (Macafee 1983: 7). This indicates the origin of the author himself and his life experience and represents the working class in a realistic way. The author employs Glaswegian dialect and accent via grammatical, lexical and phonological markers to identify the characters' belonging to a certain geographical place, culture, class, and social status as well as the complex sociological factors described in the section 3.3. which are involved in the workingclass or underclass characters' linguistic choices. To compare, according to Corbett and Stuart-Smith, Scottish Standard English is usually assumed to be spoken by middle-class speakers (Corbett, Stuart-Smith in Hickey (Ed.), 2012: 76).

There are a few examples that represent 'the point of Glasgow' (Macafee 1983: 44) at the varietal level: a name for the police 'polis' (ST16, ST616), a colloquial term 'gallus' (ST117, ST142, ST346), the use of the intensifier "dead" ("очень" (TT127, TT697)) that is functionally and semantically similar to really (ST106, ST600) has 'more impact on the speech of the working class in Glasgow' (Macaulay 2005: 112–128). Some dialect-lexical items are associated with a particular geographical community, in this case Glasgow. Glaswegian dialect is also rich with the frequent usage of idioms, slang and swearwords, 'non-standard forms which have a wide urban-distribution in Glasgow' (Macafee 1983: 43). Such language can, therefore, be associated with a particular social class or social group or referred to sociolect and indicative of 'people's social positions influenced by education, income, place of residence, and such factors influence the way people speak' (Wardhaugh and Fuller 2015: 42).

As noted by Wardhaugh an Fuller, 'register, a level of language use which is related to the degree of formality and choice of vocabulary, is closely connected with the notion of a sociolect' (Ibid., 53). The usage of colloquial words both in third-person narrative and dialogue is used by the author for their realism and to denote a disadvantaged and deprived area of Glasgow. A few examples of the informal/ colloquial lexes in the ST are "c'mon" (ST83), "spazzes out" (ST84), "ned" (ST97), "fanny around" (ST112), "telly" (ST115), "gallus" (ST117), "spunks" (ST205), "racket" (ST376), "bevvy" (ST379), "wittering" (ST470), "the winching" (ST678). The dialogue of the characters includes several swearwords and vulgar words: "shite" (ST87), "fuckcuntfannybaws" (ST116), "getitupyeyahairypuss" (ST117), "cunt" (ST178), "bastard" (ST201), "flabby-arsed" (ST202), "poofter" (ST305). "Fuck" is the most frequently used swear word and functions as either a phatic phrase, a verb, or as an adjective. The large number of lexical choices in speech acts of sociolect was taken as a major theme. Thus, translation into the TL was done either via finding naturally equivalent words or changing syntax which increased emotional intensity and emphasis and also gave a certain impression of everyday communication in working-class Glasgow.

Moreover, the author of the ST shows how these different groups of people within one culture shift the language they speak appropriate to a specific situation even though all characters of the novel are Glaswegian and from one social class. There is a pattern of codeswitching, 'a switching between language varieties, or even between languages for social camouflage, persuasive purposes via different registers sociolects and dialects' (Hervey, Higgins 2002: 168). Even though, the characters speak the vernacular, Mungo uses Standard English switching into dialect when needed. This points out the author's idea of Mungo as a person who doesn't belong to this community. Another example of codeswitching is the use of Queen's English. In the TT, the strategy of keeping the original language was used to show the differences between language varieties and to convey the same effect it has in the

ST (TT354-355). Variation within these registers in the text is great and the functional style of literary text type was identified to choose between 'bookish' or informal/ colloquial stylistic levels when undertaking the translation.

As an example, in the situation when Mungo is worried about his mother's disappearance, the informal and emotive language was used when describing his inner thoughts. However, in dialogue with his sister, the literary word "умерла" (TT10,13) was used in the translation to convey the respect and love Mungo has to his mother. The author's message of attachment to mother is crucial and the meaning of it must be transferred in the TT, part of the TT skopos.

3.5 TRANSLATING THE GLASWEGIAN DIALECT

The author of *Young Mungo* renders the Glaswegian accent of his characters phonetically via phonetic spelling -in (or -in') instead of the standard -ing. Examples of this in the ST are: darlin (ST426), nothin (ST452), flyin' (ST479), haudin' (ST480), cookin' (ST485). Other phoneticised displays of the accent in the ST are mea (me (ST163)), ma (my (ST165)), hame (home (ST302)), ya (ye) (Scots), you (Standard English) (ST305)), whit (what (ST341)).

The Dictionaries of the Scots Language (DSL)/ Dictionars o the Scots Leid (https://dsl.ac.uk) and Scottish Corpus of Texts & Speech (https://www.scottishcorpus.ac.uk) were used to identify and classify the following examples of Glaswegian dialect:

- nouns ("fella" fellow (ST659), "wean" child (ST251), "lassie" girl (ST413), "heid" head (ST451)),
- verbs ("gonnae" gonna (ST40), "wisnae" was not (ST106) 'didnae' did not (ST302), "havnae" have not (ST351), "gie" give (ST363)),
- contractions: "couldnae" could not (ST478), "cannae" cannot (ST553), "doesnae" does not (ST674)),
- pronouns ("ah" I (ST654), "ye" you (ST654), "youse" you (usually more than one person) (ST203), "yer" your (ST379)),
- adjectives ("wee" little, small (ST73), "bonny" beautiful, pretty (ST77)),
- adverbs ("mibbe" maybe (ST392), "the gether" together (ST614)),
- prepositions ("wi" with (ST625), "tae" to (ST398), "afore" before (ST399), "frae" from (ST399)),
- and interjection "aye" yes (ST469), "naw" no (ST199).

As we can see, the dialect of the characters carries a huge semantic load, so the importance of its correct transfer in translation is crucial. One of the main tasks in order to achieve this transfer is to try to preserve style and register of the ST and attributes of working-class Glasgow dialect at the varietal level. Initially, Vyatsky dialect, a variety of Russian northern dialect, was considered for the translation of Glaswegian dialect. However, according to Obvintseva, it is 'not recommended to transfer the dialect of the ST into one of dialects of the TL because they are not equivalent' (Obvintseva 2020: 260–266). The Glaswegian dialect and sociolect was formed in certain historical geographical and sociopolitical environments and, therefore, the cultures of the ST and TT are different and unique to one another.

To convey Glaswegian dialect and to create a linguacultural type of a Glaswegian in the TT, the translation solutions defined by Vinay and Darbelnet were used as more suitable option (translated and adapted in Pym 2014: 58). Examples of how these were used in the translation of text from Young Mungo are shown below.

- Adaptation:

| 1 | "Oh! Mungo son, what did ye wash this wi'?" "Just shampoo, Missus Campbell." (ST148-149) | - О, Мунго, сынок! Чем ты помыл пол?
- Шампунем, миссюс Кэмпбелл. (TT177-178). |
| 2 | "Wummin don't know what nonsense to be up to these days. Too much choice. No doubt she'll show up when she dries out." (ST169-170) | «Женсчины не знают, какой ерундой заняться в эти дни. Слишком много выбора. Конечно, она появится, как только просохнет» (TT203-204) |

The adaptation solution was used when something specific to SL is expressed but totally different in the TL. The characters have Glaswegian accent and in order to transfer this difference with standard norms of language, a technique of breaking lexical and phonetical norms of Russian language was used to achieve such effect.

Transliteration: "Aye" (ST168) as "Ай" (TT202).

This solution was applied to transliterate Scottish dialectic word which will be recognisable to a target reader who is familiar with Scottish or British culture. Moreover, it indicates the presence of the dialect and retains the intended effect of the original in the TT.

- Complex transformation:

Ah was gonnae batter the little shit-stabber, but ye should've heard what he said tae me next. Gen up. Ah had tae get away frae him afore he tried tae stick a haun up my arsehole. Ah'm no a Sooty puppet. Dirty fuckin' reprobate. (ST397-400)	«Я собирался отлупить этого мелкого говнюка, но вы бы слышали, чё он говрил мне дальше. Мне пришлося удрать от него, пока он не попытался засунуть руку в мою задницу. Я ему не пальчиковая кукла. Грязный гребённый развратник!» (TT462-465)

Complex transformation includes several techniques such as literary translation and adaptation. Literary translation helps to translate the message of the ST via conveying lexical choice and syntax close to the original and to create an idiomatic text. In addition, adaptation carried out the effect of non-standard norms of speech by shortening the morphemes of a word "говрил" or adding extra vowels "пришлося".

- Complex transformation with compensation:

1	"Here now, what a good-looking wee boy ye've got there." (ST73-74)	- Посмотри, какой хорошенький махонький мальчуган. (TT88)
2	"Ye've had yer bevvy. Ye've had yer fun. It's yer bed yer needing now."	- Ты надринькался, навеселился. Теперь те надо пойти в кровать.
	"Who the fu-"	- Ты кто, бл…?
	"Don't come the wide-o wi' me." The bachelor cut him short. "Ye don't frighten me, Graham. I was raised by a wife beater." "S'at so?"	- Не блякай мне тут. – Неженатик оборвал его на полуслове. – Я тя не боюсь, Грэхем. Я вырос в доме, где отец колотил мать.
	"Aye. I have pent-up aggression. Dr Doak telt me so. Ye want to help me feel better?" (ST379-385)	- Да ты чё?
		- Ай. У меня накопилось много агрессии. Так доктор Доак говрит. Ты хочешь помочь мне почувствовать себя лучше? (TT440-446)

3   "And whut did they get for aw their troubles, eh? They got laid off by some suit-wearing snobs in Westminster who couldnae find Glasgow on a map, who didnae give a flyin' fuck if the men had families to feed. They get telt that they're the problem wi' this country, that they're haudin' back progress because they're no afraid of hard work. Then some uppity ginger bitch decides that's the end of them with a stroke of her fountain pen. Done, finito, kaput." (ST477-482)

И чё они получают взамен за их-то беды, а? Уволены снобами в деловых костюмах из Вестминстера, которые даже не знают, где находится Глазго на карте и которых не колышит, есть ли у мужиков семьи, которые надо кормить. Им говрят, что они являются проблемой этой страны и тормозят прогресс, потому что не боятся засучить рукава. Потом некая рыжая сучка решает взмахом перьевой ручки, что с них хватит. Всё кончено! Финито! Капут! (ТТ557-562)

As discussed in section 3.4., the ST dialectal features are associated with other features of language variety, as per Hervey and Higgins it was possible to use sociolect and register 'to help compensate for the loss of connotations carried by the ST dialect' (Hervey, Higgins 2002: 167). In example 1, colloquial words were used to compensate colloquial dialectal speech. In example 2, there are a few complex transformations were made to achieve the same effect of the ST in the TT. The word "надринькался", in this case, is a jargon and transliteration of English "drink" that has already widespread in Russian informal language. Swear words carry out the function of building up an image of working-class Glasgow for the target readers, thus, match the skopos of expressive text type. The interrogative pronoun "чё" is seldom used in formal writing and literary texts in Russian and in this case, it represents the expressive spoken language of the ST. Adaptation technique carried out the function of 'broken' Russian. Similar solutions were applied in example 3 including the lexical change "мужиков" rather than "мужчин" to maintain colloquial/ low style. As well as the original sentence (ST482) was split into three separate ones with additional exclamation marks to reproduce strong emotion of the ST in the TT.

The author presents a notorious voice of the community through the sound of a chant that was sang by gangs of the Protestants and that is also to become an anthem for fans of Glasgow Rangers Football Club (ST276-279). To translate such a song, and transfer the melody of it into the TL can be challenging to the translator because of the rhyme and rhythm differences among Russian and English languages. As per Sullivan, it is recommended to read it out load as 'sound helps to determine form and to establish meaning' (Sullivan in Washbourne, Wyke (Eds.), 2018: 271). Consequently, the choice of lexis in ST was considered to transfer the message of the chant into the TT by using natural equivalent words: "парни Билли", "шуму", "По колено мы в фенианской крови – сдавайся или умри". Additional exclamation marks intensify the emotional being expressed (TT326-329). These elements convey the meaning of the ST and create the same effect of fear and pride. It is noteworthy to mention a clear presence of Glaswegian dialect in lexes such as "hallo" (ST276), "ye" (ST277), "Brigton" (ST279). The transfer of the dialect was achieved phonetically via changing the morpheme in "хею-хей" (TT326) and keeping the Glaswegian pronunciation "бригтунские" (TT329). The modulation technique was used to recreate the lines (TT356-357) of the ST by modulating grammatical choices where the sentence gets a new clause "мы намутили" (TT327) and the second half of the next line becomes impersonal "сдавайся или умри" (TT328). The coma was substituted with a dash to create a pause between two parts of the sentence (TT328). The syntactic changes were made to create poetic metre where it interacts with lexes of the text to create alliteration, rhyme and rhythm. The latter, for its part, creates dynamic of the text.

Not only the sound creates the aesthetical function of the expressive text type but the greater number of metaphors. The metaphors' meaning and close connection to the text is be conveyed by 'sticking very closely to ST lexis and syntax' (Newmark adapted in Munday, 70) but at the same time, different cultural elements can cause imbalance in the TT. The techniques described by Newmark were used to convey a metaphor in literary translation into the TL:

- the metaphoric image of the nicknames "Зырик Огилви" (TT281), "Бедняга Цыпочка" (TT437) were preserved and expressed and it is understandable in the TL,
- a translation of the metaphor "его сжатые кулаки походили на твёрдые копыта" (TT4449-450) is closed to the original and represent the author's message,
- the metaphor is translated by comparison "мистер Кэмпбелл попятился в квартиру словно назойливая кукушка" (TT501-502),
- "Левая рука миссис Кэмпбелл выглядела онемевшей, и по тому, как её нижняя часть была согнута в кармане фартука словно сломанное крыло" (TT473-474) where the equivalence was achieved by paraphrase.

The use of several translation solutions in the process of recreating the cultural type of 'Glaswegian' and rendering the Glaswegian dialect seems to be justified, since it provides the translator with greater number of techniques to convey the author's message in the TT.

4. CONCLUSION

To sum up, it was important for the translator to familiarise with the author's perspective and intention of the usage of non-standard English in the ST. The translator can distinguish between Standard English and Scots, particularly, Glaswegian accent and dialect and look at the socio-cultural viewpoint of the narrative. This was helpful in decision-making because the culture and language varieties differ from the TL and target culture as they are unique to Scotland and Glasgow. Consulting secondary sources helped to understand the author's message and reproduce the emotional charge of the original. Several adaptations to the formatting were made to fulfil the TT's skopos as a coherence expressive text. Applied equivalence theory was used to convey the ST style and keep the author's communication with the readers by minimising the socio-cultural gap between the ST and the target audience which makes the result of translation comprehensive and accurate.

References

Baker, M. (1992) *In Other Words: A Coursebook on Translation*. London and New York: Routledge, 20, 31, 249.

BBC Radio 4 This Cultural Life Podcast www.bbc.co.uk, 11 December 2021. Accessed on 18 July 2022. https://www.bbc.co.uk/programmes/m0012fdp.

Brown, R. W. and E. H. Lenneberg (1954) 'A Study in Language and Cognition', *The Journal of Abnormal and Social Psychology*, 49: 3: 454–462. https://psycnet.apa.org. Accessed on 19 August 2022. https://psycnet.apa.org/record/1955-03957-001.

Corbett, J. and Stuart-Smith, J. (2012) 'Standard English in Scotland' in R. Hickey (ed) *Standards of English: Codified Standards Around the World (Studies in English language)*. Cambridge: Cambridge University Press, 72–95.

Hervey, S. and I. Higgins (2002) *Thinking French Translation: A Course in Translation Method: French to English*. London and New York: Taylor & Francis Group, 167, 168.

Hickey, R. (ed) (2012) *Standards of English: Codified Varieties Around the World (Studies in English Language)*. Cambridge: Cambridge University Press, 76.

https://academic.ru 'Святой Мунго'. Accessed on 10 July 2022. https://dic.academic.ru/dic.nsf/ruwiki/1519502.

https://pravoslavie.ru 'Святой Кентигерн'. Accessed on 25 July 2022. https://pravoslavie.ru/67872.html. 8. https://www.scottishcorpus.ac.uk.

Macafee, C. (1983) *Glasgow*. Amsterdam/Philadelphia: John Benjamins Publishing Company, 44.

Macaulay, Ronald K. S. (2005) 'Adverbs and Social Class', in *Talk That Counts: Age, Gender, and Social Class Differences in Discourse.* New York, 2005; online edn, Oxford Academic, 1 September 2007. https://doi.org/10.1093/acprof:oso /9780195173819.003.0010: 112–128. Accessed on 23 August 2022.

Munday, J. (2013) *Introducing Translation Studies: Theories and Applications*, 3rd ed. London and New York: Routledge, 70, 114.

Newmark, P. (1988) *A Textbook of Translation.* New York: Prentice Hall, 83.

Nida, E. and C. Taber (2021) *The Theory and Practice of Translation.* Leiden, The Netherlands: Brill. Accessed on 20 August 2022: 12, 12–33. https://doi-org .ezphost.dur.ac.uk/10.1163/9789004496330.

Nord, C. (2014) *Translating as a Purposeful Activity: Functionalist Approaches Explained.* London and New York: Routledge, 84.

Obvintseva, O. M. (2020) 'Sposoby Peredachy Dialekta Pri Perevode Hudozhestvennogo Proizvedeniya (Na Promere Knig Terry Pratchetta)', *The Journal of the Annual Conference.* Chelyabinks: State Chelyabinsk University: elibrary.ru. Accessed on 25 July 2022.

Pym, A. (2014) *Exploring Translation Theories*, 2nd ed. London and New York: Routledge, 33–63.

Reiss, K. and H. J. Vermeer (2013) *Towards a General Theory of Translational Action: Skopos Theory Explained*, 1st ed., trans. C. Nord. London and New York: Routledge, 182.

Scottish Corpus of Texts & Speech. https://www.scottishcorpus.ac.uk.

Stuart, D. (2022) *Young Mungo.* London: Picador. ISBN: 978-1-5290-6876-4.

Sullivan, C. (2018) 'Poetry', in K. Washbourne and B. V. Wyke (eds) *The Routledge Handbook of Literary Translation*, 1st ed. London: Routledge. https://doiorg .ezphost.dur.ac.uk/10.4324/9781315517131: 271.

The Dictionaries of the Scots Language (DSL)/ Dictionars o the Scots Leid. https:// dsl.ac.uk.

The Library of Congress. (2012) 'Russian', Loc.gov. Accessed on 20 July 2022. https://www.loc.gov/catdir/cpso/romanization/russian.pdf.

Tonkopeeva, M. D. (2017) *Lingvokulturniy Tipazh Shotlandtsa v Britanskoy Prose (V Aspekte Perevoda).* Saint Petersburg State University: St. Petersburg. https:// dspace.spbu.ru. Accessed on 08 July 2022. https://dspace.spbu.ru/bitstream/11701 /7590/1/Tonkopeeva_dissertaciya.pdf.

Wardhaugh, R. and J. M. Fuller (2015) *An Introduction to Sociolinguistics*, 7th ed. Oxford: Wiley-Blackwell, First published in 1986, 42.

Part III
Beyond the written word

6 Writing a reflective report for interpreting

Key concepts

- Interpreting vs translation.
- Skills for interpreting.
- Interpreting assessment and accreditation.
- Professionalisation of interpreting.
- The role of reflective reports in learning and assessing interpreting.

6.1 Introduction

In the first edition of Pöchhacker (2022) *Introducing Interpreting Studies*, published in 2004, he talks about 'the young discipline of interpreting studies, which has yet to reach maturity' (2004: 1). The epithet 'young' was not deemed necessary in subsequent editions. One can safely say that, nowadays, Interpreting Studies is considered to be a discipline in its own right, despite being seen for a long time as a branch of Translation Studies – which has sometimes even been qualified as the 'parent discipline' of Interpreting Studies (Pöchhacker and Shlesinger 2002: 2). The two disciplines share similarities but there are also many differences between them.

Even though traditionally interpreting has been described as *oral translation*, a more precise definition of the discipline takes into account its immediacy. In other words, 'in principle, interpreting is performed "here and now" for the benefit of people who want to engage in communication across barriers of language and culture' Pöchhacker (2022: 10). This focus on its immediacy as a unique characteristic that distinguishes interpreting from other types of language mediation allows for the inclusion, within the discipline, of other activities that are not strictly oral, such as sign language interpreting, or sight translation, for example (Pöchhacker 2022). However, it is precisely this immediacy – that is, the fact that you cannot go back and edit your performance – which makes an interpreting reflective report rather different from the translation commentary. Nevertheless, there are certain aspects that are shared by both activities and therefore, much of what has been said in Chapters 1–5 of this textbook can, to a certain extent, be applied to interpreting reflective reports.

DOI: 10.4324/9781003273790-10

This chapter is not about interpreting per se. The main focus is on using self-reflection to improve your interpreting skills and to demonstrate that you have reached the skills required to be a professional interpreter. Hence, this reflective report can be used as both assessment by trainers, teachers and assessors and also as self-assessment by both students and professional interpreters. The next section looks at the relationship between interpreting and translation, including differences and similarities between both disciplines.

Task 6.1

In groups, write a list of different types of interpreting that would fit with the definition above.

6.2 Interpreting vs translation

Task 6.2

1. Brainstorm what you think the main differences between translation and interpreting are.
2. Focus on the set of skills necessary for each of them (some of these might be shared between both disciplines).
3. Brainstorm what, in your opinion, are the greatest similarities between both disciplines, particularly with regard to the training necessary to become a professional.

Referring back to the definition of interpreting given above, it is the sense of immediacy that differentiates interpreting from other types of linguistic mediation. This means that, while in written translation we can take our time in finding the right expression or word and we can also make revisions, this is not possible in the case of interpreting. We need to think on our feet and be able to recall the particular words that we need to render the source language (SL) speech into the target language (TL).

Bowker (2023: 168) points out that interpreting and translation attract people with different personalities. Interpreters 'need to be able to multitask, work under intense pressure, and work well with others,' while translators tend to be 'patient, detail-oriented and content to working largely independently' (2023: 168). This takes us back to the concept of immediacy. It is precisely this immediacy that requires the interpreter to be able to multitask and work under pressure.

Apart from attracting different personalities, translation and interpreting require a different set of skills. The International Association of Conference Interpreters (AIIC) lists the following key skills on their website:

- An in-depth knowledge of their working languages and the cultures related to them.
- The ability to listen and concentrate.
- A good memory.
- Mental dexterity.
- Speed of thought.
- A broad general knowledge.
- Analytical skills.
- A pleasant voice.
- The ability to keep cool under pressure.
- The poise required to perform before a large audience.
- Respect for professional confidentiality.

To this we can also add a few more key skills listed by Bowker (2023: 177–179): such as 'shorthand or structured note-taking,' 'an ability to multitask,' and 'clear enunciation.' She also adds that interpreters need to 'refrain from editorializing.' Even though these skills refer to Conference Interpreters, most of them are also applicable to other types of interpreting.

The key skills from the list above that are shared by a professional translator are 'fluency in the source and target language,' 'cultural awareness,' and 'a broad general culture,' the rest of the skills are not particularly relevant to translation. This means that to become a professional in either of the disciplines you would ideally undergo different training, teaching, and assessment.

Many interpreter programmes at universities, whether at undergraduate or postgraduate level, include the teaching of translation. Often, these programmes require that the students pass translation modules as a pre-requisite to doing an interpreting module. However, as Sawyer (2004) points out, 'with the demand for specializations rising in the language industry, it would seem self-evident that a future interpreter does not need to complete a full course of study in translation before beginning to study interpretation' (2004: 210). That is, there is no reason why the interpreting modules could not be taken at the same time as a translation module. In fact, there are interpreter training programmes that do not include written translation training at all.

Nevertheless, there are some institutions and certifying bodies that include a written translation in their assessment. For example, the Chartered Institute of Linguists (CIOL) exam to gain the Diploma in Public Service Interpreting in the UK has two translations in both directions of the language combination in question.

Regardless of whether interpreter programmes include written translation training or not, this chapter focuses on the use of reflective reports to learn, teach, and assess interpreting skills. In the next section, we will look at general issues of learning, teaching, and assessing interpreting.

6.3 Interpreting

Task 6.3

1. Before reading the next section, write a list of as many different types of interpreting you can think of.
2. Discuss the differences between them.

6.3.1 Types of interpreting

Following our consideration of immediacy as a defining characteristic of interpreting that distinguishes it from other types of language mediation, below is a list that includes some of the main types of interpreting:

- *Bilateral or liaison interpreting.* A variation of *consecutive interpreting* where the interpreter works in both language directions (Bowker 2023: 170).
- *Consecutive interpreting.* In this type of interpreting, the interpreter takes notes while the speaker is talking and then he or she will render the SL discourse into the TL by making use of the notes (Bowker 2023: 170).
- *Courtroom interpreting.* A variation of *legal interpreting*, a service which is offered in oral judicial proceedings when one or more of the participants has hearing impairments or does not understand the language of the court (Morris 2015: 91).
- *Dialogue interpreting.* Also known as *community interpreting, public service interpreting, service interpreting,* and *social interpreting* (Turner 2015: 390). This usually takes place to 'enable an individual or a group who does not speak the dominant language of the community to access government or central services' (Bowker 2023: 173). This type of interpreting can be *bilateral* (working in both directions), *whispering,* or *sight translation* (Bowker 2023: 173).
- *Healthcare interpreting* or *medical interpreting.* Similar to *dialogue interpreting,* which takes place in healthcare contexts (Hsieh 2015: 177).
- *Relay interpreting.* In this type of interpreting, the SL discourse is rendered in the TL via a third language because there is no interpreter available to do it directly between the language pair (Čeňková 2015a: 339–340).
- *Remote interpreting.* In this type of interpreting, the interpreter might be in a different room or a different country and the interpreting is done by phone or videoconferencing (Braun 2015: 346).

- *Sight translation.* In this type of interpreting, the interpreter renders a written source text (ST) into an oral or signed target text (TT) (Čeňková 2015b: 374).
- *Signed language interpreting* or *deaf interpreting.* In this type of interpreting, the interpreter works either between two different signed languages or between a spoken and a signed language (Napier and Leeson 2015: 376).
- *Simultaneous consecutive interpreting.* A variation of *simultaneous interpreting* in which a rendering of the source speech is produced simultaneously from a playback of a digital recording (Pöchhacker 2015: 381).
- *Simultaneous interpreting.* In this type of interpreting, the interpretation into the TL of the speaker's utterance is given no more than a few seconds after it has been spoken. This means that the interpreter is listening and interpreting at the same time (Bowker 2023: 170–171).
- *Simultaneous interpreting with text.* Another variation of *simultaneous interpreting* in which there is a rendering of a ST which is being read out loud by the speaker. Usually, the interpreter has access to the ST, which makes this type of interpreting similar to *sight translation* (Setton 2015: 385).
- *Speech to text interpreting* or *Respeaking.* In this type of interpreting, a *respeaker* produces simultaneous subtitles of a live SL discourse by using speech recognition software, also including punctuation marks and other features (such as colour changes for different speakers) for the deaf and hard of hearing (Romero-Fresco 2015: 350).
- *Whispered interpreting* (*Chuchotage*). A variation of *simultaneous interpreting* which takes place without a booth and for only a few listeners. The interpreter sits or stands close to the client or group of clients to render the SL discourse in the TL (Diriker 2015: 383).

The training necessary for all of these different types of interpreting is varied; however, it is the feature of immediacy that characterises all of them and makes a reflective report very different from a translation commentary. Before we discuss the reflective report per se (see section 6.4), we will first look at the most common learning objectives of interpreter training, then at the training and teaching of the discipline, and finally at assessing an accreditation.

6.3.2 Learning objectives

Linked to the key skills listed in 6.2, the most common learning objectives of the interpreter training programmes are as follows:

- Developing fluency and clear enunciation in both SL and TL.
- Developing note-taking skills.
- Developing active listening skills, such as anticipation, inferencing, and knowledge mobilization.

- Developing short-term memories.
- Developing skills in pre-interpreting preparation.
- Developing cultural awareness, such as diplomatic protocols (Bowker 2023: 178).
- Developing the ability to multitask.

6.3.3 Teaching and training

Interpreters might work between more than two languages which are called 'active languages,' [A] languages, [B] languages, and [C] languages. The AIIC gives the following definitions of the languages an interpreter works with:

- *Active languages* are the languages the interpreter works into.
- *[A] Language* is the interpreter's native language or the main active language.
- *[B] Language* is not the interpreter's native language, but it is one of their main languages.
- *[C] Language* is a language that the interpreter understands perfectly but it is not an active language, as they do not interpret into it.

Depending on the institution, you might achieve the learning objectives above by being taught in different modules. For example, to develop fluency and clear enunciation in your active languages, you might be taught in separate language classes or in written translation classes of the language combination in question. The active listening skills might also be taught in a separate language class. According to Pöchhacker (2022: 207), most institutions tend to separate the teaching into three sections, sometimes separated into different modules and other times being part of the same module: one section focusing on note-taking for consecutive interpreting, one on simultaneous interpreting, and the other one on community interpreting.

Typical activities used in interpreter training are note-taking exercises (particularly for consecutive interpreting), sight translation, shadowing (i.e. repeating exactly what you hear in a podcast, recording, or video with the delay of a few seconds), oral summaries of recordings or podcasts, liaison interpreting simulations, and practice on segmenting or 'chunking' and reorganising speeches.

You might also be taught techniques on how to deal with the SL speech complexity caused, for example, by sentence length, specialised terminology, numbers, proper nouns, false cognates, etc., and also the added difficulty that emerges when the SL and TL have very different syntactical structures. Some of these techniques include anticipation, waiting, lagging, and chunking (i.e. dividing the SL segment into smaller units to make it easier to remember). Another skill taught is the use of condensation, compression, and adaptation to communicate the content of the SL discourse.

Internships and work placements are also important to acquire and develop the key skills mentioned above. Albl-Mikasa (2013: 32) points out that interpreters gain and develop the necessary interpreting competences and key skills 'on the job,' 'before the job,' and 'over time.' As it is argued in 6.4, a reflective report, either as part of the assessment for your modules, for an internship, or for a work placement, will help you in gaining experience and learning from previous actions – not only from mistakes but also from accurate behaviour (i.e. the things we do well).

Despite the above overview, many countries do not have a systematised interpreter training, which inevitably 'leads to a lack of an accreditation system and to subsequent credentials, thus hindering the formation of a profession' (Rudvin 2015: 438). One issue that has been pointed out by García-Beyaert (2015: 57), but which is beyond this textbook, is the need to 'educate' the clients of the interpreting service, which usually have certain expectations that are often impossible to comply with due to the complexity of the discipline. Often, they are not really aware of the difference between translation and interpreting (Gile 2009: 7).

We will discuss the professionalisation and academisation of the discipline in 6.4, after looking at the assessment and accreditation necessary for becoming a professional interpreter in 6.3.3.

6.3.4 Assessment and accreditation

In 1997, Hatim and Mason pointed out that there was not much literature on interpreting assessment. Five years later, Campbell and Hale (2003: 211–212) claimed that most of the literature was about entry tests for conference interpreting training courses and certification examinations to become community interpreters. The following year, Sawyer (2004) published his monograph on interpreting assessment, which included several types of interpreting. He was one of the first scholars to propose the use of a portfolio which included a self-evaluative or reflective statement as part of interpreting assessment.

Often, there are strict measures to become a certified interpreter. This might include evidence of training, testing, prior experience, on-the-job performance assessment, etc., which is the case with the China Accreditation Test for Translators and Interpreters (CATTI) and the membership policy of the AIIC. Nevertheless, Pöchhacker (2022: 173) and Turner (2015: 390) found that, in many cases, you only need a test-based assessment to be certified as an interpreter, regardless of whether you have had prior training or professional experience. This state of affairs, once again, has a detrimental effect on the professionalisation and academisation of the discipline.

We will now look at the assessment criteria and also at three types of assessment typically used: formative, summative, and ipsative.

6.3.4.1 Assessment criteria

The assessment criteria that are generally used in interpreting training are usually linked to the competences listed above (6.1), such as the knowledge of the working languages and relevant cultures, the ability to listen and concentrate, a good memory, mental dexterity, speed of thought, a broad general knowledge, analytical skills, a pleasant voice, the ability to keep cool under pressure, the poise required to perform before a large audience, and a respect for professional confidentiality.

Collados Aís et al. (2007: 215) proposed the following criteria, which was organised in four blocks:

1. Sense consistency and cohesion.
2. Completeness, terminology, and fluency.
3. Diction, style, and grammatical usage.
4. Intonation, voice, and accent.

Here, we can see that both content and performance are being assessed, moving beyond simply error counting, which is seen as problematic (Pöchhacker 2022: 214; Bartlomiejczyk 2007: 248). As Pöchhacker (2022) pointed out, '[t]here is a widespread agreement that performance must be assessed for both content (i.e. source-target correspondence) and target-language presentation (i.e. expression and delivery)' (2022: 214). Bartlomiejczyk (2007: 248) also suggests assigning different weighting to different aspects of the interpreting performance, which will move away from simply focusing on the errors and allow the assessors to consider the delivery and public speaking skills (Kalina 2002: 126).

6.3.4.2 Types of assessment

Usually, in higher education establishments the concepts of formative and summative forms of assessment (defined below) are frequently used in documents, such as, for example, module descriptions. We have also mentioned them in 5.2.1.1. Sawyer (2004: 106) includes a third type, ipsative assessment, which is particularly relevant for self-assessment or for a reflective report, as we will see in 6.4.

6.3.4.2.1 FORMATIVE

Formative assessment is the assessment carried out during the course of a module. It has the objective of generating feedback to enhance not only the learning but also the teaching (Dawrant and Han 2021: 258). Some types of feedback could also be considered to be feedforward, as they are supposed to help you improve.

6.3.4.2.2 SUMMATIVE

Summative assessment usually takes place at the end of a module or at the end of the academic year. Its main objective is to provide evidence that the learning outcomes of the module or programme have been met (Dawrant and Han 2021: 258). As mentioned above, there are credentialling bodies (such as the CIOL in the UK) that offer summative certification tests, which you can take without having had any training. Both formative and summative assessment could include different tasks, such as 'shadowing, cloze tests (both oral and written), written translation, sight translation, memory tests, and interviews' (Campbell and Hale 2003: 212).

6.3.4.2.3 IPSATIVE

Ipsative assessment normally takes place throughout the course of the module or teaching unit. It typically takes the form of a survey where students do a self-evaluation exercise by answering multiple-choice or true or false questions that include statements such as, 'I was able to identify most of the errors I have made,' 'I am able understand why I have made those errors by referring to the relevant theoretical sources,' 'I am able to formulate a plan on how not to make the same errors in the future,' etc. Ipsative assessment can be used as part of both formative and summative assessment.

The reflective report we are discussing in this chapter is more relevant for university training programmes than for other types of professional or vocational training. Ideally, this reflective report will be part of all three types of interpreting assessment: formative, summative, and ipsative. Therefore, its role would be to complement the 'one shot' test, which might not accurately reflect the students' acquired abilities and skills (Sawyer 2004: 126).

6.4 Using a reflective report for learning and assessing interpreting

In section 6.1, we discussed immediacy as one of the main features that distinguishes interpreting from other types of language mediation. It is, in fact, this feature of immediacy that makes writing an interpreting reflective report a different activity to writing a translation commentary. This is mainly due to the fact that this reflective report can only be written retrospectively and only if the interpreting session has been recorded. In this section, we will first provide a rationale for writing an interpreting reflective report as part of the assessment to be accredited as a professional interpreter. After that, we will look at types of reflective reports (section 6.4.2) and then we will provide advice on how to write the report.

6.4.1 Rationale for an interpreting reflective report

In some institutions, a reflective report forms part of a portfolio where you would select different samples of your work such as: a statement of personal goals; video- and audiotapes of student work; instructor's feedback; journal or other reflective statements; self-assessment statements; peer review statements; action research paper, etc. (Sawyer 2004: 127). Hence, the self-assessment statements, the journal or other reflective statements, and, to a certain extent, the action paper research could all be considered to be different types of reflective reports.

According to Sawyer (2004: 16), a portfolio assessment has been explored as a means to provide alternative forms of assessment. He believes that '[t]he use of portfolio assessment is a means to gather a greater range and depth of sample performances and facilitate both process- and product-oriented assessment as complementary approaches' (2004: 94). That is, it would provide a multiplicity of points to calculate the mark of a student, rather than just using a one-shot exam (2004: 126).

However, there have also been some institutions that were not in favour of using portfolios for interpreting assessment. Russell and Malcolm (2009: 349–350) found that in 2002, the Association of Visual Language Interpreters of Canada rejected the use of a portfolio-based assessment system for being time consuming and not an effective use of the assessor's or instructor's time. They also found them problematic, as many of the assessors would be uncertain about what they were assessing. Another issue pointed out was that in certain contexts, such as medical, mental health, or legal settings, it might not be possible to record the samples. It was believed that, rather than being used for summative assessment, the portfolio should be used either as coursework or for students to show the learning they had achieved.

In answer to these criticisms, it could be said that, for example, the assessor's uncertainty could be dealt with by providing proper training and clear and comprehensive assessment criteria and rubrics. As for the lack of efficiency timewise, it would be up to each training institution to allocate sufficient time to each tutor or assessor to carry out the task. Moreover, having clear assessment criteria and rubrics will clearly make portfolios more time-efficient to assess. Finally, with regard to the fact that it would be impossible to record interpreting performance in certain settings, this could be easily dealt with by setting out in-class mock simulations of these settings, so that they can be recorded for future use by both students and teachers.

Apart from Sawyer (2004), there has not been much research carried out about the use of reflective reports in interpreting assessment, possibly because not many training institutions do it. Nevertheless, assessment and accreditation are crucial for the development of a discipline, and it is our contention that reflective reports could play an important role here.

According to Pöchhacker (2022: 28), professionalisation and an academic infrastructure, as well as academic research, are important for the development of a discipline. However, despite all the advances in interpreter training, people still become interpreters by unconventional means, such as bilinguals, without having specific training (Boéri 2015: 39; Gile 2009: 6). This clearly has had a damaging effect on the professionalisation of interpreting.

The professionalisation and academisation of the discipline was boosted by the university training programmes that started in the 1940s and 1950s, which mainly focused on conference interpreter training (Dam and Gentile 2021: 278). This university level certification enhanced the conference interpreters' prestige (Dam and Gentile 2021: 278) and also helped in raising the professional standards of the discipline as well as the social status of the interpreting professionals (Gile 2009: 7).

Nevertheless, due to the fact that these programmes inevitably have an emphasis on practical training, it is still important to include, as a part of the assessment, a more theoretical and research-based task. This task would enable students to pursue a research path, if they so wished, and, in turn it would aid in the academisation of the discipline. This is particularly relevant in those programmes from highly research-oriented universities. This task could consist of a reflective report which is effectively underpinned by the relevant theories. According to Gile (2009: 24), certain theoretical issues in interpreter and translation training can help students in their 'understanding of phenomena, difficulties, strategies and tactics,' hence helping them to develop both during and after their training in their professional lives.

Nevertheless, in his research about interpreter training programmes, Pöchhacker (2022: 202) found that '[m]ajor differences exist in the relative weight given to professional vs academic course content and the requirements for a graduation thesis.' It could be argued that a reflective report, particularly if it is part of a portfolio showing samples of a student's work, is useful both in a professional and academic environment. It is the point where both the theory and practice would converge and allow for the gathering of a greater and more in-depth range of samples of the students' performance (Sawyer 2004: 16) for tutors, assessors, and potential employers.

In her study, Albl-Mikasa (2013: 27) found that, according to the interpreters she interviewed, what made a professional interpreter was 'all about performing better at what they do and about doing each individual assignment to the best of their abilities under the circumstances.' Hence, getting used to engaging in self-assessment during your training and carrying on using it in your professional life would be a way of honing your skills in continuous professional development. Writing reflective reports as part of lifelong and lifewide learning (Washbourne 2022: 10) will help you improve and to do the best you can well into your professional life.

Apart from the above, integrating self-assessment in interpreter training allows students to actively participate in their learning (thus being more motivating). It also provides opportunities and guidelines to improve their skills progressively, as well as opportunities to adopt the point of view of the user (Postigo Pinazo 2008: 186–187).

6.4.2 Types of reflective report

Due to its immediacy, the only way to make an interpreting reflective report is to have your performance recorded, either by yourself, your peers, or your teacher. This recording can then be used by your teacher to assess you, by your peers to provide peer assessment, or by yourself to use in your reflective report. In fact, in some institutions the teacher records all class productions and keeps them for future use (Postigo Pinazo 2008: 189).

A reflective report may take many forms. Here we are going to focus on three types: a reflective report which is part of a portfolio; a standalone reflective report; and a thematically structured reflective report. The latter shares many similarities with the thematically structured translation commentary discussed in Chapter 4.

6.4.2.1 A reflective report as part of a portfolio

Task 6.4

Brainstorm what could be included in a portfolio, apart from the reflective report or self-assessment statements. Think of specific examples, if possible.

In a portfolio you need to gather evidence to show your learning and progress. Sometimes, it might be used to prove that you have achieved the learning outcomes of the module as part of the summative assessment. This portfolio can also be used to show samples of your work to prospective employers. As mentioned in 6.3.1, some of these samples could include: a statement of personal goals; video- and audiotapes of student work; instructor's feedback; journal or other reflective statements; self-assessment statements; peer review statements; action research paper, etc. (Sawyer 2004: 127). In other words, the portfolio functions as a reflective tool for self-assessment and as evidence of the level you have reached (Arumí Ribas 2010: 57). However, it is the self-assessment part of the portfolio that makes it self-regulatory and where you as a student take charge of your own learning (Arumí Ribas 2010: 57).

In some institutions, these self-assessment statements or reflective reports might take place three times during the course of a module: at the start, at some point midway through, and at the end of the module. This may vary to just once at the end of the course; or twice, once midway and once at the end of the course.

• The self-assessment statement or reflective report at the start of the course functions as a diagnostic exercise were both you and your teacher will become aware of your actual level and find your strong points and the areas you need to work on.

- The midway self-assessment statement or reflective report could either be formative assessment, with feedforward comments from your teacher, so that you can improve, or it might be part of what is called *continuous assessment*, in which case it will have some weighting towards the final mark of the report (which might typically vary from 10% to 25% of the mark). Even as part of the continuous assessment, it will still have some formative and feedforward aspects from the teacher, which you could still take into account to improve for the end-of-course assessment.
- The self-assessment statements or reflective report at the end of the course are usually summative and therefore there is no feedforward. It has usually some weighting towards the final mark of the interpreting module in question, which might vary between 10% to 50% of the whole mark.

Depending on your institution, you might be required to integrate theoretical concepts and sources within the report. The integration of theoretical sources will be discussed in section 6.5. You might also be asked to comment on the samples included in your portfolio. If there is a word restriction, this may prove slightly complex, as you might not have enough space to discuss any issues in great depth.

If you need to include more than one reflective report in the portfolio, you might be asked to reflect on previous reports and discuss the extent to which there has been progression and learning gain.

6.4.2.2 A standalone reflective report

Task 6.5

Discuss in groups how a standalone reflective report differs from a report that is part of a portfolio. Would they deal with the same issues?

In practical terms, there is not much difference between a reflective report that is part of a portfolio and one that is not. The main difference is the fact that a standalone reflective report will only include an audio or video recording of you interpreting of a SL segment or segments and then your discussion of this interpretation. It might also be more focused than a report that is part of a portfolio, as you would not have any other samples or pieces of work to comment on. You might also need to integrate theoretical concepts and sources (discussed in 6.4), perhaps even more so than with reports that are part of a portfolio.

Some institutions may require you to submit a standalone reflective report up to three times in the course of a module: at the start, midway, and at the end. Therefore, if you need to submit more than one report, you might also be required to comment on the progression and learning gain that has taken place since your previous reports.

6.4.2.3 A thematically structured reflective report

Task 6.6

1. Discuss in groups the difference and similarities between a thematically structured reflective report and the other two types discussed above.
2. Make a list of possible topics that could be discussed in a thematically structured reflective report.

A thematically structured reflective report is rather different from the previous two reports. It clearly shares some things in common with the thematically structured translation commentary. However, the immediacy of interpreting needs to be factored in within the discussion, as it plays an important role in the rendering of the SL segment into the TL. The report will still be based on an audio or video recording and your interpreting performance of the SL segment. You will likely be expected to include relevant theoretical sources, and the tone will need to be formal and academic; more so, in fact, than the other two types of report.

The important thing to do when writing this reflective report is to select a recording of an SL segment that includes one or more of the following issues in the list below. Please take note that this is not intended to be an exhaustive list of the issues you can research.

- Interpreting politeness (Mapson 2019); for example, face-saving strategies (Alexieva 2002), which deal with how people from different cultures manage conflict and disagreements; or hedging (Pöchhacker 2022: 143), that is the way people from different cultures express certainty or uncertainty (see 4.1.2.7).
- Interpreting profanity (Allan and Burridge 2006; Culpeper 2019; Hale et al. 2020), also linked to impoliteness, what is considered profanity or taboo in the source culture (SC) might not be considered so in the target culture (TC) and vice versa (see 4.1.2.9).
- Interpreting humour (Culpeper 2019; Zabalbeascoa 2005; also see 4.1.2.2). It is particularly culturally bound and sometimes it is based on taboo language.

- Orality/literacy of the SL segment (Alexieva 2002). This involves the 'degree of planning' which affects the choice of lexis and grammatical structures, as well as references to culture-specific items (Alexieva 2002: 227–228).
- Interpreting culture-specific items (Alexieva 2002; also see 4.1.2.3).
- The concept of *conduit*, according to which interpreters are to remain neutral, detached, and faithful to the original (Guldin 2020), vs *footing*, i.e. the interpreter's alignment to a particular utterance (Angelelli and Jacobson 2009; Hsieh 2003: 12; Pöchhacker 2022: 144, 151–153).
- Interpreting sensitive texts (Baker 1997; Lung 2003; also see 4.1.2.8).
- Interpreting non-verbal features (Pöchhacker 2022: 148; Poyatos 1987/2002), such as intonation, demeanour, gesticulation, etc.

This type of reflective report could actually turn into an *action research* paper. Action research refers to when research is conducted while taking action. An example of action research in interpreting is conducting your research on your own interpreting by critical reflection. An action research paper is one of the items Sawyer (2004: 127) suggested to be included in a portfolio, an undergraduate or MA dissertation, or even a PhD thesis.

6.5 How to write an interpreting reflective report

Task 6.7

Discuss in groups what the main differences and/or similarities are between an interpreting reflective report and a translation commentary.

Some of the major differences between an interpreting reflective report and a translation commentary have to do with the immediacy of interpreting. This means that, as mentioned before, you will need to watch or listen to a recording of your performance to write the report. Therefore, most of the time, rather than analysing the ST and then making a decision on how best to translate a particular SL segment, you will analyse both the SL discourse and your performance, retrospectively.

Sometimes, error detection is one of the criteria for assessment. Therefore, you might be required to write a comprehensive report where you provide a list of all the errors you have made, an error analysis, and solutions to prevent reoccurrence. Sometimes, but not always, you might be required to underpin your discussion with theoretical sources. This report might be part of a portfolio, or it might be a standalone report, but a thematically structured report would not be the appropriate format for this type of comprehensive report, where you have to discuss all the errors you detect.

You might, however, be required to write a report where you discuss and analyse both good renderings and errors and also integrate theoretical sources. This type of report could be any of the three types discussed in 6.3.2; that is, it might be part of a portfolio, a standalone report, or a thematically structured report.

Apart from the above, in most cases you will be given a particular recording of your interpreting performance to analyse which has been recorded by your teacher. However, sometimes, particularly in those cases where all of the lessons are recorded, you might be allowed to make a choice between several recordings, or you might even be asked to organise the recording yourself.

6.5.1 *How to write an interpreting reflective report which is error-focused*

Your institution might provide you with a grid that you would fill in, going segment by segment through the recording, in a linear way. In other institutions, you might be provided with a document with several questions that you need to answer. Often, these questions are divided into three groups, depending on the type of error: understanding of the ST, TL rendering of the SL segment, and delivery.

If you have not been provided with any such document, you could use Arumí Ribas' (2010: 54) first five categories below to organise the type of errors you observe in your performance: understanding, content, reproduction, sense and coherence, and expression. Even if you have been provided with one of these documents, you could still use these categories to organise the errors you detect. Arumí Rivas' (2010: 54) final category, 'techniques and strategies,' will be useful for both explaining why the error took place and for providing plans to prevent reoccurrence.

Below is Arumí Ribas' (2010: 54) list of categories, which is normally used for simultaneous interpreting but could also be used for other types of interpreting:

- Understanding of the original discourse (problems with understanding due to lexis, syntax, subject matter, speed of the discourse, accent of speaker, etc.).
- Content and information (omissions, additions, and changes).
- Reproduction of the discourse (pace, pronunciation, intonation, etc.).
- Sense and coherence (use of connectors, presence of ambiguities, sentence fragments, etc.).
- Expression (appropriate register, idiomaticity, range of vocabulary, accuracy, precision, transmission of figures, proper nouns and cultural references, etc.).
- Techniques and strategies (coordination of listening and analysis, use of redundancy in the discourse to recover information, anticipation, summarising, and condensation).

Regardless of whether your reflective report is part of a portfolio or a standalone report, or whether you need to complete a particular document provided by your institution or not, you should really take extensive notes and follow several stages of analysis which are similar to the translation commentary stages. This would not only allow you to write a good reflective report but would also help develop your critical and analytical thinking skills, which, in turn, will help you develop as a professional.

You will first need to watch or listen to the recording to analyse the SL discourse, in terms of its complexity including word frequency, lexical variability, specialised terminology, proper names, numbers, false cognates, nonstandard language, culture-specific language, humorous language, sentence and word length, etc. (Pöchhacker 2022: 130).

Then, you will need to focus on your TL rendering of the SL discourse, detect all of the errors you have made, and organise them by, for example, using Arumí Ribas' (2010: 54) categories discussed above, or by using any other categories you might find useful. You will also need to indicate what you consider the level of seriousness of these errors to be. You would then explain the reason why these errors occurred by making reference to your analysis of the SL discourse. If you are required to integrate theories and theoretical concepts, this would be a good place to do it, although you should aim to do so throughout the whole report (see 6.6.3).

Finally, in most instances, you will be required to discuss your plans to prevent error reoccurrence. Here, you can use the final category of Arumí Ribas' (2010: 54) above, and also integrate other theories, if you are required to do so. You may also need to refer to your analysis of the SL discourse.

If you are required to do a linear report – that is, if you are required to discuss the errors made in chronological order – you will need to be careful not to repeat yourself too much. There will inevitably be repetitions, because some of the errors may be recurrent, or they might belong to the same category and, therefore, the reasons why they occurred would be similar or the same.

If the report you need to write is not linear, then you could first write a few lines about your analysis of the SL discourse, as discussed above. Then, you could group the errors in different categories and dedicate different sections to this, for example, understanding of the ST, TL rendering of the SL segment, delivery, etc. You could even categorise them further according to the level of seriousness of the error. Finally, you would include your plans to prevent the reoccurrence of these errors, basing yourself in theoretical sources and concepts. In fact, if you are required to integrate theoretical sources, then it would be advisable to do so throughout the whole report (see 6.5.3).

6.5.2 How to write an interpreting reflective report which includes both good renderings and errors

If you are required to include in your report not just the errors, but also what you consider to be good renderings, many of the suggestions given above will still be applicable. Even in this type of report, one of the assessment criteria might be error detection, in which case you would have to explain all of the errors you have made, but also include comments on good renderings. This report may be part of a portfolio, a standalone report, or you may be able to choose to write a thematically structured report. You might also be provided with a grid or a document with questions to answer, as in the previous type of report.

However, regardless of what format the report you are required to write has, it will still be advisable to follow the stages recommended in 6.6.1. The only difference is that when you analyse your TL rendering of the SL discourse you would also focus on identifying good renderings rather than just errors.

Again, regardless of whether this report is part of a portfolio, a standalone report, or a thematically structured report, you will still need to write substantial notes on your analysis of the SL discourse, of your TL rendering, and of your plans for improvement. As with the type of reports described above, you might be expected to go through your interpreting performance in a linear way. If this is the case, you again need to be careful not to repeat yourself too much.

For non-linear reports, where error counting is not a criterion for assessment, as well as for a thematically structured reflective report, you will ideally have gathered a pool of examples of your interpreting performance from which you can make your selection to include in the report for discussion. This pool should contain both errors and good renderings as well as your explanation of them, into which, ideally, you would have already integrated theoretical sources.

6.5.3 How to integrate the relevant theories into a reflective interpreting report

Often, you might be required to integrate theoretical sources into your report. As is the case with the translation commentary, it might be easier to integrate concepts and theories in a thematically structured report. However, you can also integrate them in reports with other structures.

In a linear report, you can integrate theories in the explanation of the errors and of the good renderings. For example, if the SL discourse is humorous, you can integrate theories on the translation of humour to explain either your error or your good rendering. In a non-linear report, you can integrate the relevant theories throughout: when you write your analysis of the SL discourse, when you explain both good renderings and errors, and when you discuss your plans for improvement.

However, as pointed out in 4.3, you need to be careful not to apply theories inaccurately by not linking them to examples; or by mentioning a claim by a particular scholar, for the sake of including secondary references, and then not referring back to it at all for the rest of the report. In other words, it is important to make sure that the theories are relevant to the point under discussion.

6.6 Assessment criteria for an interpreting reflective report

---

Task 6.8

In groups, write a list of the most important criteria in assessing an interpreting reflective report.

As mentioned above, interpreting assessment criteria tends to focus on both content and delivery (Pöchhacker 2022: 214). That is, it focuses on how much correspondence there is between the SL and the TL segments in terms of completeness and coherence, and also on whether the intonation, accent, diction and style, body language, etc., are appropriate.

When it comes to the reflective report, some institutions use, as marking criteria, three main points: detection of errors (often divided into errors of understanding of the SL segment, rendering in the TL, and delivery), explanation of why the errors have taken place, and solutions to prevent reoccurrence of these errors. Some, but not all institutions, require the integration of theoretical sources both to support the explanation of why the error was made, and to provide a rationale for the effectiveness of the plans to prevent reoccurrence. Please see the sample assessment rubric for this type of error counting assignment in Appendix 4.

Despite the fact that, as mentioned above, there has been a call to move beyond error counting in interpreting assessment (Pöchhacker 2022: 214; Bartlomiejczyk 2007: 248), this error counting or detection might play a role in reflective reports or self-assessment exercises, as their main objective is for you as a student to self-regulate and take charge of your own learning. Identifying your own errors, considering why they happened, and thinking of solutions as to how to avoid making them again in the future might actually be a very effective way to learn and to develop professionally. Particularly when you are asked to identify the seriousness of the errors and when you receive feedback from your teacher on how comprehensive and accurate your error analysis was. In fact, the feedback that your teacher will provide on your reflective reports creates a 'feedback loop' (Washbourne 2014: 243), which will help you identify where you need improvement and the way to do it.

Nevertheless, your institution might want you to discuss in your reflective report not just the errors you have made, but also what you consider good renderings and the reasons why you consider them so. This would mean that, depending on the word count you have available, you might need to select examples of both errors and good renderings, rather than discuss them all.

Below, you can see sample criteria that could be used to assess an interpreting reflective report. The list is by no means intended to be exhaustive. You can also find a sample assessment rubric for this type of interpreting reflective report (i.e. which requires the analysis of good renderings, errors, and engagement with theoretical sources) in Appendix 4.

6.6.1 Structure, style, and presentation

Your reflective report should have a clear structure, regardless of whether it is part of portfolio, a standalone report, or a thematically structured report. You should avoid an anecdotal tone (see 3.1.1), and the style and referencing should be consistent throughout.

6.6.1.1 Structure

The stronger reflective reports will be coherent and have a logical structure by, for example, starting with ascertaining the ST complexity – in terms of word frequency, specialised terminology, proper names and numbers, sentence length, etc. (Pöchhacker 2022: 130) – followed up by analysis of good renderings and errors. The space available will be dedicated to the different issues in a balanced way. There will be an effective use of signposting to guide the reader. The conclusion will sum up the most important points. The issues and examples selected for discussion will clearly support the line of argument. The transition between sections will be fluent and coherent.

The weaker reflective reports may lack coherence, the ideas may not be ordered logically, and some issues may take much more space than others for no obvious reason. There may also be a lack of signposting to guide the reader and, often, there may be no conclusion. In addition, too many issues may have been selected for discussion, which may then render it too brief and superficial. The transition between the sections may be not fluent.

6.6.1.2 Use of appropriate terminology

The stronger reflective reports will be concise because of using relevant terminology in an accurate, precise, and consistent manner.

The weaker reflective reports may paraphrase or use descriptions rather than the relevant terminology, thus making the report very wordy and cumbersome. When specific terminology is used, it may often have been done inaccurately, hence showing that the concept has either been misunderstood or not understood completely. Sometimes, the terminology might be used in the wrong context, which might be misleading or create ambiguities. The choice of terminology may be eclectic, originating from different sources, resulting in the same point or issue being referred to with different terms.

6.6.1.3 *Integration of secondary and theoretical sources*

The stronger reflective reports will mention theories relevant to the issues discussed. They will be linked to the examples and will also be properly integrated as an essential part of the narrative. The referencing will be consistent throughout.

The weaker reflective reports may mention the most typical citations by a particular scholar and not refer to them again. Sometimes, the citation in question may contradict the actual decisions taken. That is, the theories may be superimposed rather than integrated into the report, simply for the sake of being there, without ever being revisited, and without being illustrated by examples. In other words, there may not be enough engagement with the theories. In addition, some clearly relevant theories may not have been mentioned. As for the referencing, it may be inconsistent and some of the sources may have been acknowledged improperly or not at all.

6.6.1.4 *Presentation*

The stronger reflective reports will have a clear and consistent use of headings and subheadings, an accurate use of punctuation, and the examples will be provided in a consistent and effective way, including back translations when necessary.

The weaker reflective reports may either not use headings and subheadings or, when they do, it may be done in an inconsistent and confusing way. The use of punctuation may be inaccurate. The examples may be presented in an inconsistent and unclear way and back translations may be provided hardly ever or not at all.

6.6.2 *Analysis of good renderings*

As mentioned above, you might be asked to only discuss and analyse the errors you have made, rather than good renderings. If this is the case, this criterion will not be applicable, but you might still want to analyse your good renderings for your own self-assessment and self-improvement.

6.6.2.1 *Selection, integration, and relevance of examples*

This criterion will only apply to those cases where you are not required to discuss all of the interpreting segment in a systematic way.

The stronger reflective reports will select just enough examples to illustrate a particular point. They will explore them fully by cross referring them with other parts of the report and will reference them properly to be easily found. In a thematically structured report, there will be a clear engagement with both theoretical concepts and examples to justify the decisions taken. The examples selected will either be relevant for the discussion or important to explore because of either being controversial and going against the TL audience's expectations, or because they contradict other interpreting techniques used in the same SL discourse. They might also select those instances where there is some kind of loss or gain and justify why a particular interpreting solution was chosen.

The weaker reflective reports might either have too many examples or not enough. Some of the examples might have been chosen from inaccurate interpreting decisions. There may also be a list of examples presented in a descriptive manner without offering an adequate justification or explanation, often without a theoretical underpinning, for the decisions taken to interpret that example in a particular way. They may contain examples that are not particularly representative of the overall interpretation approach taken, when other examples would have been a better choice.

6.6.2.2 Explanation

The stronger reflective reports will explain why the examples selected are considered to be particularly good solutions by engaging with the relevant theories.

The weaker reflective reports may lack an explanation of why the examples selected are considered to be good solutions and/or there may be no theoretical engagement when explaining these solutions. The examples chosen may be inaccurate renderings of the SL discourse.

6.6.3 Error analysis

Please take note that the criteria presented below is not applicable to an error-counting assignment, as the selection and relevance of examples is one of the assessment criteria used for this type of assignment.

6.6.3.1 Selection, integration, and relevance of examples

The stronger reflective reports will select just enough examples of errors, preferably from each type (ST understanding, TL rendering, and delivery). They will explore them fully and reference them properly, so that they are easily found. The examples selected will be relevant for the discussion. All of the serious errors will have been selected for discussion.

The weaker reflective reports might either have too many examples or too few. They may be presented as a list of examples in a descriptive manner without offering an adequate explanation and will often have no theoretical underpinning for the reasons why the errors were committed. They may contain examples that are not particularly representative of the type of error made, when other examples were obviously better choices. Some serious errors may not have been discussed, either from a lack of appropriate selection criteria or because they were not detected.

6.6.3.2 Explanation and categorisation

The stronger reflective reports will categorise the errors accurately according to their level of seriousness (for example, in terms of substantially changing the meaning of the ST, TL, the content not being rendered in full, grammatical or lexical errors that impede the understanding, wrong use of register, wrong intonation, etc.). There will be a clear engagement with both theoretical concepts and examples to explain why the errors were made.

The weaker reflective reports may not attempt to categorise the errors according to their level of seriousness and, when they do, they may do it inaccurately by misjudging how serious the error is. There may be either no engagement or very little engagement with theoretical concepts to explain why the errors were made. When there is engagement, the theories chosen may be either not relevant or inconsistent with the point under discussion. There might also be no evidence of awareness of the reason why the error was made.

6.6.3.3 Solutions to prevent reoccurrence

The stronger reflective reports will provide plans and approaches based on engagement with theoretical sources to prevent error reoccurrence.

In the weaker commentaries, there may be either no plans or solutions to prevent reoccurrence, or when there are, they may not be effectively based on theoretical sources.

Task 6.9

1. Observe an interpreting recording of your peers and assess it.
2. Record yourself while interpreting and write a reflective report.

6.7 Conclusion

As we have seen, being a professional interpreter requires different skills than those required for being a professional translator, such as, for example, being able to listen and concentrate, have mental dexterity, being able to work under pressure, being able to multitask, etc. The main difference between interpreting and other types of language mediation is its sense of immediacy. Due to this sense of immediacy, an interpreting reflective report is different from the translation commentaries we have discussed in Chapters 1–5. This is because the only way to write it is retrospectively, by listening and watching a recording of your interpreting performance.

Not all institutions require you to write a reflective report, but it would be advisable for you to do it regardless, as it is a useful learning tool both during your training and in your professional life. You might be provided with some supervision sessions on how to write your report, but whether this is the case or not, you can still use the assessment rubric in Appendix 5 together with the checklist below (you can find a printable version of this checklist in Appendix 6) to help you write it:

Structure, style, and presentation

1. Is the structure logical and coherent?
2. Have you included an analysis of the complexity of the SL discourse?
3. Is the signposting effective (including the use of headings and subheadings)?
4. Is the transition between the sections and paragraphs fluent and coherent?
5. Have you dedicated the allocated word count to the different parts of the reflective report in an effective and balanced way?
6. Does the conclusion sum up the most important points?
7. Is the appropriate terminology used accurately and consistently?
8. Are the secondary and theoretical sources relevant to the issues discussed?
9. Are the secondary and theoretical sources linked to examples and are they properly integrated as an essential part of the narrative?
10. Is the referencing consistent?
11. Is the use of punctuation accurate and consistent?

Analysis of good renderings

1. Have you selected the appropriate number of examples to discuss a particular point?
2. Do the illustrative examples support the line of argument of the reflective report? Are they relevant?
3. Have you effectively explained why you consider your examples to be particularly good renderings?
4. Is there a clear engagement with both theoretical concepts and illustrative examples to justify the decisions you have taken?

Error analysis

1. Have you selected the appropriate number of examples to discuss a particular point?
2. Have you selected all of the serious errors you have detected?
3. Have you categorised the errors according to their level of seriousness?

4. Do the illustrative examples support the line of argument of the reflective report? Are they relevant?
5. Have you effectively explained why you consider your examples to be particularly good renderings?
6. Is there a clear engagement with both theoretical concepts and illustrative examples to justify the decisions you have taken?
7. Have you provided effective plans to prevent error reoccurrence which have a firm underpinning with theoretical sources?

This checklist is more relevant to non-linear and non-error counting reflective reports, but you can adapt it to the format you are required to use.

6.8 Summary

In this chapter, we have looked at the different types of interpreting reflective reports and provided advice on how to write a reflective report which is error-focused, which contains good renderings and errors, or which is thematically structured. It also provided advice on how best to structure the report, how to integrate both good renderings and errors within the discussion, how best to explain them and categorise them, and how to provide plans for future improvement, while integrating theoretical sources all the way through. Chapter 7 will look at writing a reflective report in audiovisual translation, localisation, and transcreation.

Further reading

Mikkelson, Holly and Renée Jourdenais (eds) (2015) *The Routledge Handbook of Interpreting*. London and New York: Routledge.
Pöchhacker, Franz (ed) (2015) *Routledge Encyclopedia of Interpreting Studies*. London and New York: Routledge.
Pöchhacker, Franz (2022) *Introducing Interpreting Studies*, 3rd ed. London and New York: Routledge.
Pöchhacker, Franz and Miriam Shlesinger (eds) (2002) *The Interpreting Studies Reader*. London and New York: Routledge.

List of references

AIIC (International Association of Conference Interpreters) https://aiic.org/site/world/conference/whatittakes (retrieved 30/4/2023).
Albl-Mikasa, Michaela (2013) 'Developing and Cultivating Expert Interpreter Competence', *Interpreters Newsletter*, 18: 17–34.
Allan, Keith and Kate Burridge (2006) *Forbidden Words*. Cambridge: Cambridge UP.
Alexieva, Bistra (1997/2002) 'A Typology of Interpreter-Mediated Events', in Franz Pöchhacker and Miriam Shlesinger (eds) *The Interpreting Studies Reader*. London and New York: Routledge, 218–233.

Angelelli, Claudia V. and Holly E. Jacobson (2009) 'Introduction', in V. Claudia Angelelli and Holly E. Jacobson (eds) *Testing and Assessment in Translation and Interpreting Studies: A Call for Dialogue between Research and Practice*. Amsterdam and Philadelphia: John Benjamins Publishing Company, 1–10.

Arumí Ribas, Marta (2010) 'Redefinir la Enseñanza-Aprendizaje de la Interpretación en el Marco del EEES: Propuestas en un Contexto de Cambio', *Redit*, 4: 42–62.

Baker, Mona (1997) 'Non-Cognitive Constraints and Interpreter Strategies in Political Interviews' in Karl Simms, (ed.) *Translating Sensitive Texts*. Amsterdam: Rodopi, 111–130.

Bartlomiejczyk, Magdalena (2007) 'Interpreting Quality as Perceived by Trainee Interpreters', *The Interpreter and Translator Trainer*, 1: 247–67.

Boéri, Julie (2015) 'Key Internal Players in the Development of the Interpreting Profession', in Holly Mikkelson and Renée Jourdenais (eds) *The Routledge Handbook of Interpreting*. London and New York: Routledge, 29–44.

Bowker, Lynne (2023) *De-mystifying Translation: Introducing Translation to Non-translators*. London and New York: Routledge.

Braun, Sabine (2015) 'Remote Interpreting', in Franz Pöchhacker (ed) *Routledge Encyclopedia of Interpreting Studies*. London and New York: Routledge, 346–348.

Campbell, Stuart and Sandra Hale (2003) 'Translation and Interpreting Assessment in the Context of Educational Measurement', in Gunilla Anderman and Margaret Rogers (eds) *Translation Today. Trends and Perspectives*. Clevedon: Multilingual Matters, 205–224.

Čeňková, Ivana (2015a) 'Relay Interpreting' in Franz Pöchhacker (ed) *Routledge Encyclopedia of Interpreting Studies*. London and New York: Routledge, 339–341.

Čeňková, Ivana (2015b) 'Sight Interpreting/Translation', in Franz Pöchhacker (ed) *Routledge Encyclopedia of Interpreting Studies*. London and New York: Routledge, 374–375.

Collados Aís, A, A. M. Pradas Macías, E. Stévaux. and O. García Becerra. (eds) (2007) *Evaluación de la Calidad en interpretación Simultánea: Parámetros de Incidencia*. Granada: Comares.

Culpeper, Jonathan (2019) 'Taboo Language and Impoliteness', in Keith Allan (ed) *Oxford Handbook of Taboo Words and Language*. New York: Oxford University Press, 28–40.

Dam Helle V. and Paola Gentile (2021) 'Status and Profession(alization) of Conference Interpreters', in Michaela Albl-Mikasa and Elisabet Tiselius (eds) *The Routledge Handbook of Conference Interpreting*. London and New York: Routledge, 275–289.

Dawrant, Andrew C. and Chao Han (2021) 'Testing for Professional Qualification in Conference Interpreters', in Michaela Albl-Mikasa and Elisabet Tiselius (eds) *The Routledge Handbook of Conference Interpreting*. London and New York: Routledge, 258–274.

Diriker, Ebru (2015) 'Simultaneous Interpreting', in Franz Pöchhacker (ed) *Routledge Encyclopedia of Interpreting Studies*. London and New York: Routledge, 382–385.

García-Beyaert, Sofía (2015) 'Key External Players in the Development of the Interpreting Profession', in Holly Mikkelson and Renée Jourdenais (eds) *The Routledge Handbook of Interpreting*. London and New York: Routledge, 45–61.

Gile, Daniel (2009) *Basic Concepts and Models for Interpreter and Translator Training*, Revised Edition. Amsterdam: John Benjamins.

Guldin, Rainer (2020) 'Metaphorics', in Baker, Mona and Saldanha, Gabriela (eds) *Routledge Encyclopaedia of Translation Studies*, 3rd ed. London and New York: Routledge, 325–329.

Hale, Sandra, Natalie Martschuck, Jane Goodman-Delahunty, Mustapha Taibi and Han Xu (2020) 'Interpreting Profanity in Police Interviews', *Multilingua* 39: 4: 369–393.

Hsieh, Elaine (2003) 'The Importance of Liaison Interpreting in the Theoretical Development of Translation Studies', 翻譯學研究集刊 *Fan I Hsueh Yen Chiu Chi K'an [Studies of Translation and Interpretation]*, 8: 283–322.

Hsieh, Elaine (2015) 'Healthcare Interpreting', in Franz Pöchhacker (ed) *Routledge Encyclopedia of Interpreting Studies*. London and New York: Routledge, 177–182.

Kalina Sylvia (2002) 'Quality in interpreting and Its prerequisites – A Framework for a Comprehensive View', in G. Garzone and M. Viezzi (eds) *Interpreting in the 21st Century: Challenges and Opportunities*. Amsterdam, Benjamins, 121–130.

Lung, Rachel (2003) 'Translating Sensitive Texts', *Perspectives: Studies in Translatology*, 11: 4: 255–268.

Mapson, Rachel (2019) 'Im/politeness and Interpreting', in Rebecca Tipton and Louisa Desilla (eds) *The Routledge Handbook of Translation and Pragmatics*. London: Routledge, 27–50.

Morris, Ruth (2015) 'Courtroom Interpreting', in Franz Pöchhacker (ed) *Routledge Encyclopedia of Interpreting Studies*. London and New York: Routledge, 91–93.

Napier, Jemima and Lorraine Leeson (2015) 'Signed Language Interpreting', in Franz Pöchhacker (ed) *Routledge Encyclopedia of Interpreting Studies*. London and New York: Routledge, 376–381.

Pöchhacker, Franz (2004) *Introducing Interpreting Studies*. London and New York: Routledge.

Pöchhacker, Franz (ed) (2015) *Routledge Encyclopedia of Interpreting Studies*. London and New York: Routledge.

Pöchhacker, Franz (2022) *Introducing Interpreting Studies*, 3rd ed. London and New York: Routledge.

Pöchhacker, Franz and Miriam Shlesinger(eds) (2002) *The Interpreting Studies Reader*. London and New York: Routledge.

Pöchhacker, Franz and Miriam Shlesinger (2002) 'Introduction', in Franz Pöchhacker and Miriam Shlesinger (eds) *The Interpreting Studies Reader*. London and New York: Routledge, 1–12.

Postigo Pinazo, Encarnación (2008) 'Self-Assessment in Teaching Interpreting', *TTR*, 21: 1: 173–209.

Poyatos, Fernando (1987/2002) 'Nonverbal Communication in Simultaneous and Consecutive Interpertation: A Theoretical Model and New Perspectives', in Franz Pöchhacker and Miriam Shlesinger (eds) *The Interpreting Studies Reader*. London and New York: Routledge, 234–246.

Romero-Fresco, Pablo (2015) 'Respeaking', in Franz Pöchhacker (ed) *Routledge Encyclopedia of Interpreting Studies*. London and New York: Routledge, 376–381.

Rudvin, Mette (2015) 'Interpreting and Professional Identity', in Holly Mikkelson and Renée Jourdenais (eds) *The Routledge Handbook of Interpreting*. London and New York: Routledge, 432–446.

Russell, Debra and Karen Malcolm (2009) 'Assessing ASL-English Interpreters: The Canadian Model of National Certification', in V. Claudia Angelelli and Holly E.

Jacobson (eds) *Testing and Assessment in Translation and Interpreting Studies: A Call for Dialogue Between Research and Practice*. Amsterdam and Philadelphia: John Benjamins Publishing Company, 331–376.

Sawyer, David B. (2004) *Fundamental Aspects of Interpreter Education*. Amsterdam and Philadelphia: John Benjamins Publishing Company.

Setton, Robin (2015) 'Simultaneous with Text', in Franz Pöchhacker (ed) *Routledge Encyclopedia of Interpreting Studies*. London and New York: Routledge, 385–386.

Turner, Jean (2015) 'Assessment', in Holly Mikkelson and Renée Jourdenais (eds) *The Routledge Handbook of Interpreting*. London and New York: Routledge, 384–399.

Washbourne, Kelly (2014) 'Beyond Error Marking: Written Corrective Feedback for A Dialogic Pedagogy in Translator Training', *The Interpreter and Translator Trainer*, 8: 240–256.

Washbourne, Kelly (2022) 'Introduction', in Cristiano Mazzei and Laurence Jay-Rayon Ibrahim Aibo (eds) *The Routledge Guide to Teaching Translation and Interpreting Online*. London and New York: Routledge, 1–13.

Zabalbeascoa, Patrick (2005) 'Humor and Translation - An Interdiscipline', *Humor*, 18: 2: 185–207.

7 Writing a reflective report for audiovisual translation, localisation, and transcreation

Key concepts

- Audiovisual translation.
- Localisation.
- Transcreation.
- Skills for audiovisual translation, localisation, and transcreation.
- Assessment, accreditation, and professionalisation.
- Reflective reports in audiovisual translation, localisation, and transcreation.

7.1 Introduction

This chapter looks at audiovisual translation (AVT), localisation, and transcreation. All three share many aspects in common with each other as well as with translation, which is why they are being discussed together in this last chapter. In fact, localisation has often been included within AVT (Cerezo Merchán 2019: 472–473) and Gránell (2011: 199) calls it 'an exigent modality of audiovisual translation.' As for transcreation, O'Hagan (2019: 152) talks about research carried out on its applicability in game localisation, thus giving the impression that transcreation is considered to be a translation approach or technique, rather than a discipline in its own right or even a subdiscipline. This goes to show how the field of language mediation is constantly evolving with emergent disciplines becoming consolidated, while new disciplines are still appearing. This is particularly the case with those disciplines that are very closely linked to technology and technological development. In this textbook, we consider audiovisual translation, localisation, and transcreation as independent disciplines in their own right.

As we will see, certain types of AVT have some aspects in common with interpreting, such as, for example, *respeaking*, or *voice-to-text*, which is done simultaneously as the source language (SL) segment is being uttered. However, most of the types of AVT are not carried out simultaneously and, hence, what has been said about translation in the first five chapters will be applicable to all three types of language mediation discussed in this chapter. There are also some aspects mentioned in 4.2.2, such as the translation of humour, of profanity, language variety, metaphors, etc., which will also be applicable to all three types, and also to interpreting.

DOI: 10.4324/9781003273790-11

Moreover, there are also issues, such as the focus on practical experience rather than on theory and research in the teaching and training of these three modes of language mediation, which render many of the things said in Chapter 6 applicable to them as well. For example, the lack of academisation and/or professionalisation, their general absence from most curricula of tertiary education programmes or, often, being simply optional or ancillary modules, etc. However, in time, things might become more academicised and professionalised, and reflective reports may play an important role in this. Carrying out research is essential for a discipline to become established and, as mentioned in Chapter 6, writing a reflective report provides students with the necessary skills to write an action research paper or even a PhD.

7.2 Audiovisual translation

Audiovisual Translation is defined by Haywood et al. (2009: 268) as 'the translation of dialogue in films, video, television programmes and opera or theatre performances, either by means of dubbing, voiceover, or by means of subtitles or surtitles.' In this definition, they mention three of the types of audiovisual translation, which will be discussed below.

7.2.1 Types of audiovisual translation

Task 7.1

Before you read this section, discuss in small groups the following questions:

1. What do you understand audiovisual translation to be?
2. Think about examples where you have experienced audiovisual translation and discuss them.

Below is a list of the main types of audiovisual translation:

- *Subtitling.* This is a written translation, which appears generally at the bottom of the screen (and sometimes at the top), of the original dialogue of the particular programme being subtitled. It also includes other elements, such as letters, graffiti, placards, etc., and other information of the soundtrack (Díaz Cintas and Remael 2007: 8).
- *Dubbing.* This is an oral translation that replaces the original soundtrack, where the sounds and the actors' lip movements are synchronised, giving

the illusion that the actors are speaking the target language (TL) (Bowker 2023: 152).

• *Voiceover.* This is an oral translation that can be heard at the same time as the original soundtrack, which can be faintly heard in the background (Bowker 2023: 152).

• *Subtitling for the D/deaf and the hard of hearing (SDH).* Also referred to as *closed captioning (cc)*, they are subtitles aimed to give accessibility to the 'Deaf,' with capital D (referring to people who use sign language as their mother tongue), to the 'deaf,' with a lowercase d (who acquired deafness, but sign language is not their mother tongue), and to those with hearing impairments (Neves 2008: 172, n.2; Bowker 2023: 162; Díaz Cintas and Remael 2007: 245). Here, we could also include *respeaking* or *speech-to-text* or *voice-to-text*, discussed in 6.3.1, which is a type of SDH which involves a *respeaker* producing simultaneous subtitles of a SL utterance using speech recognition software. Sometimes these subtitles are also used by people learning how to read or learning an additional language (Díaz Cintas and Remael 2007: 245).

• *Surtitling.* This is used in live stage performances such as opera. The captions of translated lyrics or dialogues may appear above or to the side of the stage. Theatres may also be equipped with the technology to project the captions on screens behind the seats, often in several languages that the audience can choose from (Bowker 2023: 154; Secară 2019: 130–131). Surtitles may also be intralingual, that is, written in the SL.

• *Audio description for the blind and the partially sighted (AD).* Also referred to as *video description, described video,* and *audio captions* (Perego 2019: 114), this consists of a spoken translation of the visual elements of a performance, such as body language, facial expressions, place descriptions, etc. This translation accompanies and complements the original soundtrack, and it is usually intralingual. It can be used for films but also for other events such as museum exhibitions, public meetings, religious events, etc. It can be delivered live (in which case it has similarities with interpreting) or in a pre-recorded format (Bowker 2023: 162–163; Perego 2019: 114). It can be used not just by the blind and visually-impaired people, but also by older adults, children, and language learners (Perego 2019: 115).

To the list above, we could add the fan-based audiovisual translations, such as *fansubbing* (audiovisual content made by fans), *fandubbing* (dialogues dubbed by fans), *fan translation of games* or *romhacking* (translations of videogames by fans), and *scanlation* (translations of scanned comics and manga made by fans) (Vazquez-Calvo et al. 2019: 194).

Task 7.2

In small groups, discuss the following:

1. Are there any types of audiovisual translation listed above that you have not come across before?
2. Do you have any preference for a particular type of audiovisual translation? Why?

As we have seen when we discussed the different types of interpreting, the training necessary for all these different types of audiovisual translation is also varied and, although they all share things in common with translation and, some of them, with interpreting, there are some skills that are particularly relevant to audiovisual translation, such as, for example, the skill to condense or summarise the source text (ST). We will next look at the learning objectives of audiovisual translation training.

7.2.2 Learning objectives in audiovisual translation

As we saw in 7.2.1, there are many types of audiovisual translation, some of which require different skill sets and therefore have different training needs. However, apart from the fact that, as with any type of language mediation, they all require an ability to transfer content between two or more different languages, all the types of audiovisual translation require you to have well-developed technical skills. (Kajzer-Wietrzny and Tymczyńska 2015: 344). In fact, as Díaz Cintas (2008a: 7) points out, both trainees and also trainers in audiovisual translation need not only to be versed in Information and Communications Technology (ICT), but to be prepared to keep up to date with new developments of programmes and specifications.

With regard to subtitling, Imhauser (2000), mentioned by Kruger (2008: 81), divides the required skills into technical, linguistic, project management and interpersonal, and general. Even though the focus is just on subtitling, many of these skills are applicable to other types of audiovisual translation:

- Technical
  - Sensitivity to image and sound – including the ability to 'identify and exploit the interaction between image, sound and text' (Kruger 2008: 81).
  - Ability to 'adapt to the rhythm and speed of dialogue' (Kruger 2008: 81).
  - Ability to manage the constraints on time and space. This means that it is essential for a subtitler to have excellent condensation skills, discussed below.

- Linguistic
  - Condensation skills.
  - Adaptation and reformulation skills.
  - Proofreading skills.
  - Aural comprehension skills.
- Project management skills and interpersonal skills.
- General
  - Text analysis skills (see Chapters 1 and 3 of this textbook).
  - Visual literacy.
  - Computer literacy.
  - Knowledge of film production.
  - Knowledge of the film and television industry.
  - Knowledge of language policy.

In what follows, we will look at some of the skills necessary for *subtitling, dubbing, voiceover, subtitling for the D/deaf and the hard of hearing, surtitling*, and *audiodescription*. Between them, they also cover the skills that will be required for the rest of the audiovisual translation types that appear on the list in 7.2.1.

7.2.2.1 Subtitling

Díaz Cintas and Remael (2007: 29) pointed out that a 'translator has to be multi-talented, but a subtitler also has to be a verbal acrobat – a language virtuoso who can work within the confines of a postage stamp.' This is why, apart from having technical skills, learning to summarise and condense the SL message is essential for subtitling.

In addition to the skills listed above, what is particularly relevant to subtitling with regard to technical skills is the ability to manage the constraints on time and space in subtitles. For example, a subtitler needs to be able to identify the best place 'to break a line or split a subtitle' (Bowker 2023: 155); subtitles need to be short, as the recommended maximum exposure time is of roughly six seconds (Díaz Cintas 2008b: 95; Bowker 2023: 155–156); regarding space restriction, a subtitle needs to be roughly no more than '32 to 41 characters per line in a maximum of two lines,' including spaces (Díaz Cintas and Remael 2007: 9).

You also need to be able to carry out *cueing* or *spotting*; that is, indicating the 'in and out times of each individual subtitle' (Díaz Cintas 2008b: 95; Díaz Cintas and Remael 2007: 30). Subtitles need to keep *temporal synchrony*; that is, appear or disappear when the person starts and stops talking (Díaz Cintas 2008b: 95). They also need to be consistent and coherent with what is happening on the screen. For example, nodding should be accompanied by a positive statement in the subtitle rather than a negative (Bowker 2023: 156). Here, we also need to be aware of the different meanings that non-verbal language, such as, for example, gestures, might have in different cultures. The subtitling of non-verbal communication might be a topic for a thematically-structured reflective report (see 7.5.1.).

7.2.2.2 Dubbing

According to Chaume (2008: 129), dubbing 'is a well-known example of the invisibility of translation,' as the aim of dubbing is to provide the illusion that the persons on the screen are talking in the TL. This is why the skill of synchronisation is considered to be the most important feature of dubbing. Although, according to Chaume (2008: 130), 'emulating oral discourse' is just as important.

There are three types of synchronisation:

- *Lip sync,* also known as *phonetic synchrony* or *lip synchrony* (Chaume 2008: 135). The absence of lip sync is referred to as *lip flap* (Bowker 2023: 157).
- *Kinetic synchrony,* when the movements of the actors are synchronised with the TL dialogue (Bowker 2023: 157).
- *Isochrony,* when the TL dialogue fits within the time when the actor opens and closes his mouth (Bowker 2023: 158; Chaume 2008: 134).

An ability to carry out all three types of synchronisation is essential to become a professional.

7.2.2.3 Voiceover

Even though voiceover does not need the same type of synchronisations as dubbing, you still need what is called *voiceover synchrony.* That is, you will need to fit in the TL discourse a few seconds after the beginning of the SL segment and a few seconds after it ends (Matamala 2008: 117–118). This means that you still need condensation skills. You will also need to maintain the same register as the ST, and as your text will be read by a voice artist, it needs to be able to be easily read (Matamala 2008, 120–121; Kajzer-Wietrzny and Tymczyńska 2015: 344).

7.2.2.4 Subtitling for the D/deaf and the hard of hearing (SDH)

This form of subtitling gives access to what is happening on the screen (such as sound effects, contextual information, music, etc.) to the D/deaf and the hard of hearing (De Higes Andino and Cerezo Merchán 2018: 70); in other words, making the sound visible (Neves 2008: 177). This means that you need to be *sound literate,* and be able to interpret sound, understand its value within the narrative, determine how relevant it is, and then convey it in your subtitles. Being sound literate will enable you to select from the sounds you hear and decide what will need to be included in the subtitles and what not (Neves 2008: 177). The selection of the sounds for inclusion in the subtitles could be the main topic of a thematically-structured reflective report.

7.2.2.5 Surtitling

One of the differences between mainstream TV subtitles and surtitles is that, rather than being on the screen for as little time as possible, surtitles need to stay above the heads of the audience for longer, without too much text, in order to aid comprehension (Orero and Matamala 2008: 265). This means that being able to reduce and condense the content of the message is a skill which is still particularly important for this form of subtitling.

7.2.2.6 Audio description

Audio description gives access to different products to the blind and visually-impaired persons. The language used needs to have visual intensity and be vivid, imaginative, and concise. The syntax should be plain, and the organisation of the information should be logical. The style should be consistent throughout a film or series, and coherent with the programme's style, tone, and pace, and also with the scene and event being described (Perego 2019: 120).

As for the skills required to be a professional audio descriptor, apart from being able to analyse and understand the ST (Perego 2019: 119), also needed for other types of language mediation, you will also need to have: observation skills (Snyder 2008: 194–195); editing skills, to select the most salient visual elements and make the right choice of words (Perego 2019: 119; Snyder 2008: 194–195); language skills; and vocal skills (Snyder 2008: 195–196), that is, to be able to create meaning with your intonation, pauses, etc.

Apart from the above, as is the case with other forms of audiovisual translation, to be a professional audio descriptor you need to be able to summarise. To develop this ability, rather than focusing on the individual words, you need to focus on the overall message and be able to discern what is essential in constructing the meaning of the ST and what is not. However, you need to keep a balance between conciseness and clarity. That is, it would not be acceptable to summarise your ST too much and make it incomprehensible (Bowker 2023: 144–145).

7.2.3 Teaching and training

It was not until the 1990s that audiovisual translation was incorporated into tertiary education, as the industry often preferred to provide the training for their new employees in-house (Kruger 2008: 72–73; Cerezo Merchán 2019: 468). Other reasons why it has taken this long to be incorporated could be down to the technological requirements and their cost, as well as a lack of trainers with the necessary expertise (Díaz Cintas and Remael 2007: 41). Currently, even though many universities are offering teaching and training in audiovisual translation, it is often done as parts of a module, extra seminars, intensive courses, etc., thus 'making it difficult to go beyond the introductory states' (Díaz Cintas and Remael 2007: 41).

7.2.4 Assessment and accreditation

Not much attention has been given to either the teaching or the assessment of audiovisual translation (Cerezo Merchán 2019: 468). One of the main issues is likely to be that industry and academia have very different conceptions of quality when it comes to evaluating audiovisual translation (De Higes Andino and Cerezo Merchán 2018: 69). Whereas universities might have a 50% or even 40% pass mark, most working environments have almost a zero tolerance for errors (Kruger 2008: 84; Kajzer-Wietrzny and Tymczyńska 2015: 343).

According to Cerezo Merchán (2019: 477), there are not many types of assessment of audiovisual translation that go beyond the evaluation of translations, and many of the evaluations are based on error-counting. However, this type of assessment does not show the process you have followed, your ability to detect and solve errors, whether you have understood and internalised relevant theories, etc. (Galán-Mañas and Hurtado Albir 2015: 69). In fact, Kajzer-Wietrzny and Tymczyńska (2015: 352) propose the possibility of rewarding particularly good translation solutions with extra points. This would be more in line with holistic assessment.

Kajzer-Wietrzny and Tymczyńska (2015), Granell (2011), and Kelly (2010) believed that formative assessment should be used for the evaluation of translation competence, which could also be applicable in assessing audiovisual translation competence. In their view, summative assessment should be comprised not of just a one-shot exam but several projects throughout the course (Cerezo Merchán 2019: 477). These projects could also include reflective reports.

The use of a reflective report for assessing audiovisual translation is hardly mentioned in the literature, with the exception of Galán-Mañas and Hurtado Albir (2015) and De Higes Andino and Cerezo Merchán (2018). They advocate a holistic method of assessment which uses different assessment tools, such as reflective diaries, reports, questionnaires, etc., to assess the learning process and not just the final product (Cerezo Merchán 2019: 478).

7.3 Localisation

As mentioned above, localisation has been considered part of audiovisual translation (Cerezo Merchán 2019: 472–473; Gránell 2011: 199); however, in this textbook we believe it to be an independent discipline. Jimenez-Crespo (2013: 20) proposes what he calls a 'holistic definition' of localisation as

> a complex communicative, cognitive, textual and technological process by which interactive digital texts are modified to be used in different linguistic and sociocultural contexts, guided by the expectations of the target audience and the specifications and degree requested by initiators.

Among these interactive digital texts, we find websites, videogames, software, mobile apps, virtual assistants, etc. Therefore, due to the characteristics of these texts, localisers need to not only change the language but to also adapt the visual content, layout, etc. to the target culture (TC) (Bowker 2023: 114). Apart from that, localisers also need to deal with the non-linearity of digital texts because of their hypertextual features (Jimenez-Crespo 2013: 2).

The localisation sector has adopted the acronym GILT, which stands for *Globalisation, Internationalisation, Localisation, and Translation*, because of the realisation that it is much more efficient and cost effective to consider localisation from the development phase of a product and have translation in mind from the start (O'Hagan 2019: 149).

As Bowker (2023: 112) points out, internationalisation and localisation are two crucial steps for a successful globalisation. In localisation, we first have to produce an internationalised version, whereby the ST is made as culturally neutral as possible (Jimenez-Crespo 2013: 31), before it gets localised. Apart from the internationalised version, the localiser is usually also provided with a *localisation pack* (also known as a *localisation kit*) that includes general instructions on how to go about the translation; information about the particular digital text and previous instalments, when relevant; a glossary of terms; and files for the translation memory tool (Bernal-Merino 2008: 142).

Another characteristic of localisation is that it is usually a collaborative process that involves not only the localisers, but also localisation engineers, project managers, terminologists, QA operators, etc. (Jimenez-Crespo 2013: 9, 31).

Task 7.3

Select a website and create an internationalised version by making it as culturally neutral as possible. Then, discuss in groups what aspects you have neutralised and why you have done it.

7.3.1 Types of localisation

As Jimenez-Crespo (2013: 27) points out, in the 2000s, several types of localisation emerged and consolidated into different categories. However, as further modalities carry on emerging, these first categories are becoming more hybrid and the differences between them less clear. He proposes the following localisation types: web, videogames, software, small device, and multimedia (2013: 28), to which we can add mobile apps, virtual reality, and virtual assistants (Bowker 2023: 116).

One type of localisation that has received particular attention is the videogame localisation, possibly due to the fact that it has become 'a global multi-billion pound industry that covers all genres and targets all age groups' (Bernal-Merino 2008: 155). A distinguishing feature of game localisation from other types of localisation is that it has user engagement and the user's affective responses as its main aim (O'Hagan 2019: 145). In addition, because of being an interactive media product, all the different components play an important role in the experience (Bernal-Merino 2008: 143). Game localisers also need to take into account issues about age suitability and cultural sensitivity, which may vary in different regions. Apart from the above, some games require subject-specific terminology to be localised; for example, games that include military combat scenarios, sports, music, etc. Others, such as role-playing games, may require literary skills to localise the narrative or the characters' dialogue, etc. (O'Hagan 2019: 151).

7.3.2 Learning objectives in localisation

Apart from having general translation competences (such as communicative and cultural competence in both the SL and TL), expert localisers are expected to also have general knowledge, specialised knowledge in copywriting (e.g. legal, technical and advertising), and technological skills (Jimenez-Crespo 2013: 168–170). In game localisation, they also need to be familiar with popular gaming culture and be proficient in using translation memory tools (Bernal-Merino 2008: 144)

7.3.3 Teaching and training in localisation

Since the 1980s, technological innovation created a demand for professional localisation services. Most of the localisers were translators and multilingual developers, who were usually trained on the job, rather than at universities (Jimenez-Crespo 2013: 163). As pointed out by Jimenez-Crespo (2013: 162), localisation training appears to be polarised, with the industry on the one hand and academia on the other. Industry approaches focus on 'knowledge of tools, technological processes and workflow management,' whereas at universities, rather than focusing on small technological components, they believe that modules in localisation should cover a wider range of translation technology (Jimenez-Crespo 2013: 162–163). However, despite the growing demand for qualified professional localisers, universities are having difficulties in offering modules or courses in localisation. The problem is that it is not easy to find trainers that are qualified or have the right expertise (Bernal-Merino 2008: 146), and that there is also a lack of research on localisation training. In addition, as was the case with audiovisual translation, educational institutions may be reluctant to invest in acquiring the necessary technology. As for game localisation training, there is also an added problem of having difficulties in accessing real materials, due mainly to copyright issues. This has a real impact when creating materials for both teaching and assessment (Bernal-Merino 2008: 142–143).

7.3.4 Assessment and accreditation in localisation

In industry, localisation quality assessment is divided into three processes carried out by different evaluators or even machines: linguistic testing (which focuses on the textual segments), cosmetic testing (which focuses on the visual aspects), and functionality testing (which checks for functionality problems). In industry, functionality testing takes priority over the other two (Jimenez-Crespo 2013: 105).

The Localisation Industry Standards Association (LISA) Quality Assurance (QA) model is an error-based system, covering language, formatting, and errors of functionality (Jimenez-Crespo 2013: 110). However, as is the case with interpreting (Chapter 6), error-based approaches to assessment are generally considered to be problematic, because they do not provide a comprehensive quality evaluation due to focusing too much on the microlevel. Thus, errors of a pragmatic or communicative nature that might have occurred at the macrolevel are likely to be missed (Jimenez-Crespo 2013: 116).

An alternative to error-based approaches to assessment is a holistic evaluation which is based on functionalist or skopos theories. This holistic approach takes into account several aspects to evaluate the target text (TT), such as functional and textual adequacy, use of TT, specialised content and terminology, etc. (Jimenez-Crespo 2013: 120). Jimenez-Crespo (2013: 127) proposes a framework divided into three dimensions: 'intratextual' (subdivided into linguistic criteria and discourse-based criteria), 'extratextual' (subdivided into functional criteria, web usability, communicative issues, and non-verbal elements), and 'relationship to source text' (evaluated according to the localisation brief and the grade of localisation requested).

As for game localisation, the range of genres being produced means that it is necessary to think case by case for the most appropriate translation approach rather than using one common approach (O'Hagan 2019: 151), which makes the formulation of assessment criteria particularly hard. This is exacerbated by the fact that in game localisation QA, 'even major translation blunders can be tolerated … as long as the core game experience is maintained in the eyes of the end users' (O'Hagan 2019: 153). This is particularly interesting when we compare it with the zero tolerance for errors that the audivisual translation industry has. Here, a reflective report might prove to be a more effective type of evidence to demonstrate that you have reached the learning outcomes of the module or course, because you need to provide a rationale for the decisions taken.

7.4 Transcreation

Benetello (2018: 28) points out that, despite what many may think, transcreation is not a synonym for 'creative translation.' The term is believed to have originated in India and it was an approach often used in the translation of sacred texts (Munday 2016: 280; Pedersen 2014: 57). Language service providers were enthusiastic about the word when it first began to circulate in the early 2000s (Gaballo 2012: 95), and, according to Bernal Merino (2006: 32), they started to use it in order 'to distance themselves from traditional translation firms.' However, translators and translation scholars saw it just as re-branding for what translators already do, particularly literary translators (Katan 2021: 221).

As for what makes transcreation different from other types of language mediation, Gaballo (2012) believes that it is not just creativity, because there is an element of creativity involved in varying degrees in all types of translations, but the 'generation of new words and meanings' (2012: 95).

When we compare translation with transcreation, we can see that, for example, in the case of advertising or marketing materials, the important thing is to cause an effect on the audience and make an emotional connection, rather than simply transfer the message (Bowker 2023: 127–128). This type of persuasive texts often contains devices such as puns, wordplays, alliterations, etc., which require a process of transcreation (Pedersen 2014: 59). Another difference between translation and transcreation is that the ST is subordinated to the *creative brief* or *transcreation brief*, which includes the client's most important specifications to be considered both when the marketing is being developed and when creating copywriting content (Morón and Elisa 2018: 129–130). This is in line with skopos theory's premises, discussed in Chapters 1–3 (Morón and Elisa 2018: 130).

Apart from the above, another difference in the transcreation process is the fact that clients very often require that the transcreator sends a report with several alternatives for translating challenging segments, accompanied by an explanation for each alternative, which provides the 'inspiration or rationale behind each idea' (Morón and Elisa 2018: 131). Then, the client is able to make a choice between the different options and, sometimes, they even provide their own suggestions, which is what makes transcreation a particularly collaborative process. As Benetello (2018: 41–42) points out, whereas a translator might communicate with the editor if there are some issues once the translation has been completed, the process of transcreation entails continuous back-and-forth negotiations with the client before, during, and after the work is carried out, as is also the case with copywriting projects. This is particularly relevant for a transcreation reflective report, which could take the form of a mock report to a client, where several possible translations for challenging issues are included and accompanied by a comprehensive rationale for each of the options. This reflective report is particularly different from a translation commentary, as, in the latter, it is the translator that ultimately selects one of the options and then has to explain and justify his or her choice.

As for localisation, as mentioned above, some scholars believe that transcreation is a translation technique or approach used in localisation (Mangiron and O'Hagan 2006; and O'Hagan 2019). Nevertheless, others consider localisation and transcreation to be separate practices because, while localisation usually deals with software and videogames, transcreation focuses on advertising and creative campaigns (Pym 2014; Rike 2013; Pedersen 2014).

7.4.1 Types of transcreation

As mentioned above, most instances of transcreation are in marketing or advertising contexts. In the literature, there is not much written about the different types of transcreation, possibly because of it being a relatively young discipline. Nevertheless, Gaballo (2012: 105–108) mentions various contexts that go beyond marketing and advertising. Hence, transcreators are also 'word creators' or '*ante-litteram* transcreators,' who create neologisms when new technology, artefacts, concepts, etc., enter a culture, such as, for example, when translating legal concepts. Transcreation is also used in poetry, such as, for instance, nonsense poetry such as Lewis Carroll's (1871) 'The Jabberwocky.' This poem contains many words that were invented by Carroll without any clear meaning, but with sounds that evoke different feelings and emotions in the reader.

7.4.2 Learning objectives in transcreation

Benetello (2018) believes that 'transcreation is a different service, which requires a specific skillset that makes the transcreation professional more of a consultant than a language service provider' (2018: 42). Some of the skills that a professional transcreator needs are shared by other types of language mediation, such as, for example, language skills and cultural sensitivity. However, transcreators also need to be aware of the target market and have copywriting skills (Benetello 2018: 28; Bowker 2023: 136). Cultural sensitivity is perhaps particularly relevant to transcreation, as we need to be aware of what is acceptable in the TC and what is not. You also need to research the images and wording that competing brands use in the TC to make sure that the options you propose are original (Bowker 2023: 134).

Gaballo (2012: 111) points out that transcreation 'can be looked at as a strategy to overcome the limits of "untranslatability" but in fact it is a holistic approach in which all possible strategies, methods and techniques can be used.' According to her (2012: 111, 104), transcreation requires the ability to:

- Generate ideas and meaningful responses.
- Repurpose and develop ideas.
- Produce rare and novel ideas.
- Conceive new words.
- Imagine new worlds.
- Think laterally.

7.4.3 Teaching and training

There is not much mentioned in the literature about transcreation teaching and training. The reason for this is likely to be because it is a young discipline. Another reason could be because it is not taught in a systematic way in educational establishments, but as part of a translation or localisation module. The translation studies theories that are particularly relevant to transcreation are skopos theories, because of the importance of the creative brief, and possibly Nida's (1964) concept of *dynamic equivalence*, because the aim is usually to replicate, in the TC, the effect that the ST had on its readers.

7.4.4 Assessment and accreditation

What is interesting in the case of transcreation assessment, which distinguishes it from other types of language mediation, is the fact that what would be considered an error in language use is likely to be what is required, such as, for example, breaking grammatical or spelling rules (Benetello 2018: 28). Therefore, an error evaluation grid is not applicable to transcreation. This is why a reflective report is a useful tool in assessing transcreation skills.

In transcreation, once you receive the creative brief from the client, where you would be told what response you need to elicit from the intended audience, you need to start brainstorming and keeping a record of the ideas you have. As Bowker (2023: 134) states, you do not usually find a solution to a challenge straightaway, as transcreation is an iterative process and you need to try out, revise, and improve the ideas that you have. In fact, as we have seen, the client usually participates in the decision process. In addition, transcreators are often asked to ascertain whether a particular brand name has negative connotations in the TC and also to check for brand names and concepts already used by competitors (Benetello 2018: 41).

Therefore, a transcreation reflective report will not only give you the chance to present the rationale for the different options presented, but it will also simulate what actually happens in a real work situation, where you need to provide the client with a report that includes several alternatives to translate challenging segments and your explanation for each one of these options.

Task 7.4

Think of a particular object, brand, or service. Formulate a creative brief for a transcreator into one of the languages you work with. Include the following information, which is based on a sample brief provided by Morón and Elisa (2018: 137):

- Company, brand: description of the product.
- When, how, and where the translation is going to be used.
- Target audience: age and sex.
- What reaction is expected from the target audience.
- Tone and style.
- Way of addressing the target audience: formal and informal.
- Reference material.
- Target language and country.

7.5 How to write a reflective report

There is not much literature about audiovisual translation, localisation, and transcreation assessment, and even less, if any, about the use of a reflective report or portfolio as a way of assessing these modes of language mediation. However, much of what has been said so far in this textbook could be applicable to all three modes. De Higes Andino and Cerzo Merchán (2018) are some of the few scholars that propose the use of reflective reports or portfolios. They provide arguments that are similar to those made by Sawyer (2004) for the use of portfolios in interpreting assessment.

Due to the fact that, with perhaps the exception of respeaking or voice-to-text in audiovisual translation, all three disciplines – audiovisual translation, localisation and transcreation – are not characterised by a sense of immediacy, the error-counting method of assessment would not be particularly useful here, as there is time to think about and consider how best to translate a particular SL segment. Therefore, the reflective reports would be more similar to a translation commentary, where you would analyse the ST and have a statement of strategy and translation priorities. You would also need to select illustrative examples and integrate them within the narrative along with the relevant theories. Some of these relevant theories may come from Translation Studies, or from any of these three disciplines. A thematically-structured reflective report may be more relevant in a reflective report for these three modes of language mediation, due to the fact that many of the restrictions or factors that affect them lend themselves to be explored fully in a thematically-structured report.

7.5.1 How to write an audiovisual translation reflective report

7.5.1.1 Linear reflective reports

Some audiovisual assessment tasks may require you to also write a commentary or reflective report. Therefore, you could take similar steps to the translation commentary described in Chapters 1–5. You would start by carrying out an ST analysis. Then, even though your teacher might give you a fairly comprehensive brief, you might still need to add further details, particularly in terms of intended audience and skopos (see Chapter 2). Please take note that compliance with the translation brief and addressee might be one of the assessment criteria for both your translation and your reflective report (De Higes Andino and Cerezo Merchán 2018: 83). Therefore, if this is the case, it is important that you discuss explicitly in the report how you achieved this. In addition, the *Thinking Translation* matrices discussed in Chapter 3 (cultural, formal, semantic, varietal, and intertextual) might be useful to categorise your examples before selecting them for inclusion in your reflective report.

Other issues more specifically related to audiovisual translation that you might need to discuss are: the summarising techniques used due to restrictions of space and time; and the presentation of the subtitles on the screen: form, positioning, reading speed, duration, synchronisation, overlapping, and also character identification. In addition, with regard to the translation for the D/deaf and the hard of hearing, you will need to discuss how you dealt with the sound effects, the required contextual information, and the plot and background music (De Higes Andino and Cerezo Merchán 2018: 79). Obviously, due to the number of varieties of audiovisual translation (see 7.2.1), you will need to focus on the specific type in question, as some of the points suggested above may not be relevant.

7.5.1.2 Thematically-structured reflective report

Task 7.5

Before reading the section below, discuss in groups the following:

1. Which topics could you include in a thematically-structured audiovisual translation report?
2. What issues or restrictions that characterise audiovisual translation do you need to take into account when carrying out an audiovisual translation?

Here is a list of possible topics, which is by no means intended to be exhaustive (please check 4.2.2 and 6.4.2.3 for further discussion and recommended theoretical sources; also see the relevant further reading section):

- Translation of profanity (Bowker 2023: 154).
- Translation of language variety, particularly conveying different accents (Bowker 2023: 154–156; Kruger 2008: 81).
- Translation of intonation and pauses (Bowker 2023: 154–156), by, for example, using a larger font or punctuation.
- Translation of kinesic signs (Chaume 2008: 131). These are non-verbal messages communicated with posture, gestures, facial expressions, eye contact, etc. These non-verbal messages might have different meanings in different cultures. Also, you may need to carry out explicitation by providing an explanation or contextual information about the meaning of the kinesic sign in question.
- Use of explicitation, amplification, and/or reduction in audiovisual translation (Chaume 2008: 134). You will need to refer to relevance theory (Gutt 2000) and also to comment on any differences regarding conventions of use of these techniques in the cultures and languages you work with.
- Use of phonetic equivalence in dubbing (Chaume 2008: 136), which, because of having to lip sync, takes priority over semantic or pragmatic equivalence.
- Translation of culture-bound terms.
- Translation of slang and colloquialisms.
- Translation of puns.
- Translation of humour.
- Translation of songs.

7.5.2 How to write a localisation reflective report

7.5.2.1 Linear reflective reports

You may be asked to provide a reflective report to accompany a localisation project. Many of the issues mentioned in 7.5.1.1 about audiovisual linear reflective reports are applicable here. You could follow steps taken when writing a translation commentary discussed in Chapters 1–5. That is, you would start by carrying out a ST analysis. Your teacher might provide you with a brief, and one of the assessment criteria for the report might be the extent to which you have complied with it. Therefore, it is important to mention it explicitly in your report. The *Thinking Translation* matrices discussed in Chapter 3 might be useful to categorise your examples before selecting them for inclusion in your reflective report.

7.5.2.2 Thematically-structured

Task 7.6

Before reading the next section, discuss in groups some of the topics that could be discussed in a thematically-structured localisation reflective report

---

Here is a list of possible topics, which is by no means intended to be exhaustive (please check 4.2.2 and 6.4.2.3 for further discussion and recommended theoretical sources; also see the relevant further reading section):

- Non-linear texts in localisation (Jimenez-Crespo 2013: 2), due to their hypertextual features. Here, you could look into issues of coherence and cohesion.
- ST internationalisation, achieved by neutralising culture-specific features.
- The role of users' expectations in game localisation. These will be more or less relevant depending on the genre of the game, and also whether it is based on an existing popular creation, such as films, comic books, TV shows, and children's literature. An example of this is the *Harry Potter* franchise (Bernal-Merino 2008: 142).
- User engagement in game localisation (Bernal-Merino 2008).
- Age suitability of content in game localisation (O'Hagan 2019: 148), which may vary from culture to culture (O'Hagan 2019: 148).
- Cultural sensitivity in game localisation (O'Hagan 2019: 148), which again, may vary from culture to culture. Here, you may include violence, sexual innuendo, nudity, and religious references, etc.
- Subject-specific terminology in game localisation, for example, in 'sports, music, cooking or military combat scenarios' (O'Hagan 2019: 151).
- Register and style in game localisation (O'Hagan 2019: 151), for example, in some role-playing games you may need literary translation skills to localise the narrative. You might also need to use a particular register and style for the dialogues.
- Humour in game localisation (O'Hagan 2019: 152).
- Skopos theory and game localisation (O'Hagan 2019: 153).

7.5.3 How to write a transcreation reflective report

As mentioned above, professional transcreators are usually asked by the client to provide a report which includes several options for translating the ST's challenging segments and also an explanation for each one of these options (Benetello 2018: 42). This is so that the client can either make a choice or suggest a different option (Morón and Elisa 2018: 130). Therefore, in order to simulate a real work situation, you might be asked to write this type of reflective report.

7.5.3.1 *Report for clients*

Your teacher might provide you with a creative brief. As was the case with audiovisual translation and localisation reflective reports, one of the criteria for assessment could be the extent to which you have complied with this brief. Therefore, once again, it would be important to mention this explicitly in your report. If you have not been provided with a brief, you can use Morón and Elisa's (2018: 137) categories, already mentioned in 7.4.2, to formulate your creative brief, on which to base your transcreation:

- Company, brand: description of the product.
- When, how, and where the translation is going to be used.
- Target audience: age and sex.
- What reaction is expected from the target audience.
- Tone and style.
- Way of addressing the target audience: formal and informal.
- Reference material.
- Target language and country.

It is interesting that, in the list above, the main focus is both on the function and the TT's intended audience (see sections 2.3 and 2.4). This means that skopos theories will be particularly relevant for integrating in your report if you are required to do so. Sometimes your client may not be fluent in the TL, in which case it would be advisable to include a back translation in your report.

Task 7.7

Transcreation is often used for translating brands and company names, because they tend to use puns and wordplay to be memorable and hook the audience. The problem with this is that puns and wordplay are very culturally bound, particularly if they include intertextual references, as in the examples below.

Here are the names for two fictional business: 'Curl up and dye,' the name for a hairdresser's, and 'Rough around the hedges,' the name for a gardening company. 'Curl up and dye' is pronounced the same as the idiomatic phrase 'Curl up and die,' which is used to mean to feel very ashamed and sorry. The word dye is what makes it relevant for a hairdresser's. Similarly, 'Rough around the hedges' sounds very similar to the saying 'Rough around the edges,' which is used to mean unsophisticated and unrefined. The word 'hedges' is what makes it relevant to a gardening company.

Choose one of the above fictional names and write a report for a prospective client that includes the creative brief and the rational for the options suggested.

7.5.3.2 *Thematically-structured report*

Task 7.8

Before reading this section, discuss in groups some of the topics that could be discussed in a thematically-structured transcreation reflective report

Here is a list of possible topics, which is by no means intended to be exhaustive (please check 4.2.2 and 6.4.2.3 for further discussion and recommended theoretical sources; also see the relevant further reading section):

- Transcreation of rhymes and alliteration.
- Transcreation of puns and wordplay.
- Cultural sensitivity in transcreation. For example, some brand names may have connotations which are not appropriate in the TL.
- Transcreation and humour.
- Transcreation and idioms.
- Transcreation and intertextuality.

7.6 Assessment criteria

As mentioned above, because the three disciplines – audiovisual translation, localisation, and transcreation – are not typically characterised by a sense of immediacy, an error-counting method is not particularly useful in their case. Therefore, you would not be expected to detect them or identify them in your reflective report. This means that the criteria that might be used to assess a reflective report in these three disciplines are very similar to the criteria used to assess translation commentaries. Below, we will give a summary of the main points, but please see 5.2 for further information.

7.6.1 *Structure, style, and presentation*

Your reflective report should have a clear structure, regardless of whether it is linear, thematically-structured, or a client report in the case of transcreation.

You should avoid an anecdotal tone (see 3.1.1) and the style and referencing should be consistent throughout.

7.6.1.1 *Structure*

The stronger reflective reports will be coherent and have a logical structure where it is clear when you are discussing the ST or the TT. The space available will be dedicated in a balanced way to the different issues. There will be an effective use of signposting to guide the reader. The conclusion will back up the most important points and will make a link between the techniques used at the microlevel and the translation strategy or the brief you have been provided with. The issues and illustrative examples selected for discussion will clearly support the line of argument. The transition between sections will be fluent and coherent.

The weaker reflective reports may lack coherence, the ideas may not be ordered logically, and some issues may take much more space than others. There may also be a lack of signposting to guide the reader and, often, there may be no conclusion. Too many issues may be discussed very briefly and superficially. The transition between the sections may not be fluent. There may be no explicit link made between the techniques used at the microlevel and the brief or the translation strategy.

7.6.1.2 *Use of appropriate terminology*

The stronger reflective reports will be concise because of using relevant terminology in an accurate, precise, and consistent manner.

The weaker reflective reports may paraphrase or use descriptions rather than terminology, thus making the report very wordy and not concise. When terminology is used, it may often be inaccurate, showing that the concept has either been misunderstood or not understood completely. Sometimes it may be used in the wrong context, which may be misleading or create ambiguities. The choice of terminology may often be eclectic, originating from different sources, and the same issues may be referred to by different terms.

7.6.1.3 *Integration of secondary sources*

The stronger reflective reports will mention theories relevant to the issues discussed. They will be linked to examples and properly integrated as an essential part of the narrative. The referencing will be consistent.

The weaker commentaries may mention the most typical citations from a particular scholar and either not refer to them again, or the citation in question may contradict the actual translation solutions chosen. Some clearly relevant theories may not have been mentioned. There may be no consistent referencing and sometimes the sources may either have not been acknowledged properly or not at all.

7.6.1.4 Presentation

The stronger reflective reports will have a clear and consistent use of headings and subheadings, an accurate use of punctuation, and the examples will be provided in a consistent and effective way, including back translations where necessary.

The weaker reflective reports may either not use headings and subheadings or, when they do, it may be done in an inconsistent and confusing way. The use of punctuation may be inaccurate. The examples may be presented in an inconsistent and unclear way and back translations may hardly ever be provided or not at all.

7.6.2 Macrolevel analysis

As mentioned, when discussing the translation commentary, this part of the reflective report should roughly be around one-third of the total wordcount. This would mean that in the shorter reflective reports, you will need to be much more precise and concise, so that you can still provide the relevant information. Remember that you will, ideally, still include this section in a thematically-structured reflective report.

7.6.2.1 ST analysis

The stronger reflective reports will include some relevant background and contextual information, discuss the ST's salient features, such as its effect or tone and, most importantly, its intended reader or user, which will be referred to when formulating the translation strategy and setting up the translation priorities.

The weaker reflective reports either may not discuss some of the issues above and/or may spend too long on one particular aspect at the expense of others. They might also include issues that are not clearly relevant to the discussion.

7.6.2.2 Formulation of a translation strategy

The stronger reflective reports will include a summary of the brief, when available, and provide further details on the skopos and intended readership or user.

The weaker reflective reports may either miss some of the information above or they might not discuss it in an explicit manner. Some of the issues may be discussed in too much detail at the expense of others.

7.6.2.3 Setting up translation priorities

The stronger reflective reports will explicitly set up the translation priorities in a clear and concise manner, cross-referencing them with the translation strategy or brief, if available, and the salient features of the ST identified in the analysis. These priorities are linked to the translation strategy and the ST's salient features.

The weaker reflective reports may not have formulated any translation priorities explicitly. If they have been formulated, they might not be consistent with the translation strategy or brief, or the salient features of the ST identified in the analysis. They might also be formulated in a vague or inaccurate manner, or they might be inconsistent with the translation techniques used in the TT.

7.6.3 Microlevel analysis

This part of the reflective report would ideally be roughly just under two-thirds of the total wordcount. This would mean that, as was the case with the macrolevel analysis, in the shorter reflective reports, you will need to be much more precise and concise, so that you can still provide the relevant information. Remember that you will still need to select illustrative examples for a thematically-structured commentary. Your job will be made easier by keeping a translation journal, spreadsheet, or any other way you have built your databank of categorised examples from which you can make your selection.

7.6.3.1 Selection of illustrative examples

The stronger reflective reports will select just enough examples to illustrate a particular point. This allows for enough space to develop the justification and explanation for a particular decision and integrate the examples fully within the narrative.

The weaker reflective reports might have too many examples without really discussing how they link to any part of the report. Or there might not be enough examples at all. Some of the examples might have been chosen from inaccurate translation decisions.

7.6.3.2 Integration of illustrative examples

The stronger reflective reports will explore the examples fully by cross referring them to the brief or translation strategy and priorities, to justify the techniques used. They will be properly referenced to be easily found. In a thematically-structured reflective report, there will be a clear engagement with both theoretical concepts and examples to justify the decisions taken.

The weaker reflective reports may present a list of examples in a descriptive manner without offering an adequate justification for the decisions taken in translating that example in a particular way. They may not follow a particular structure, theme, or category to discuss the translation decisions. The examples may not be properly referenced, which makes them hard to find.

7.6.3.3 *Relevance of illustrative examples*

The stronger reflective reports will have selected examples that are relevant for the discussion or are important to explore because of either being too controversial, or because they contradict other translation techniques used in the same text. They might also select those instances where there is some sort of loss or gain and justify why a particular translation solution was chosen.

The weaker reflective reports may choose examples that are not particularly representative of the overall translation strategy taken, or do not comply with the brief, where there were alternative examples that were an obviously better choice.

7.7 Conclusion

In this textbook, we consider audiovisual translation, localisation, and transcreation as independent disciplines that require different skills, training, and assessment. This is true even for the different types and subdisciplines of each one of them. In the literature, very little has been written about training and assessment in these three disciplines, and much less with regard to using a reflective report as a tool for assessment. This is likely to be because, often, they are not taught in a systematic way, particularly in the case of localisation and transcreation. This means that not many institutions will require you to write a reflective report. However, as was the case with interpreting, and since it is a useful learning tool, it might be useful for you to do it whether you have been asked to or not. In order to do that, you can use the assessment rubric in Appendix 7 in combination with the checklist below (you can find a printable version of this checklist in Appendix 8):

Structure, style, and presentation

1. Is the structure logical?
2. Is the signposting effective?
3. Is the transition between the sections fluent and coherent?
4. Have you dedicated the allocated word count to the different parts of the reflective report in an effective and balanced way?
5. Does the conclusion sum up the most important points?
6. Is the appropriate terminology used accurately and consistently?
7. Are the secondary and theoretical sources relevant to the issues discussed?
8. Are the secondary and theoretical sources linked to examples and are they properly integrated as an essential part of the narrative?
9. Is the referencing consistent?
10. Is the use of punctuation accurate and consistent?

Macrolevel analysis

1. Have you included some relevant background and contextual information?
2. Have you discussed the ST's salient features?
3. Have you discussed explicitly the TT's skopos and intended readership or user?
4. Have you set up your translation priorities in a clear, explicit, and concise manner?
5. Have you linked your translation priorities to the brief or your translation strategy and the ST's salient features?

Microlevel analysis

1. Have you selected the appropriate number of examples to discuss a particular point?
2. Do the illustrative examples support the line of argument of the commentary? Are they relevant?
3. Have the translation techniques used, in the examples selected, been linked to the brief or your translation strategy and translation priorities?
4. Is there a clear engagement with both theoretical concepts and illustrative examples to justify the decisions you have taken or, in the case of transcreation, to explain the options provided?

7.8 Summary

In this chapter, we have looked at the different types of reflective reports that may be used in audiovisual translation, localisation, and transcreation. After looking at the main issues for each one of these types of language mediation, we have provided advice on how best to structure your report. We have also looked at the assessment criteria for reflective reports and suggested several topics that would be relevant for discussion in a thematically-structured report in each of these disciplines.

Further reading

Audiovisual Translation

Díaz Cintas, Jorge and Aline Remael (2007) *Audiovisual Translation: Subtitling.* Manchester: St Jerome.

Díaz-Cintas, Jorge and Aline Remael (2021) *Subtitling.* London and New York: Routledge.

Pérez-González, Luis (ed) (2019) *The Routledge Handbook of Audiovisual Translation.* London and New York: Routledge.

Localisation

Bernal-Merino, Miguel (2014) *Translation and Localisation in Video Games.* London and New York: Routledge.

Jimenez-Crespo, Miguel (2013) *Translation and Web Localization*. London and New York: Routledge.

O'Hagan, Minako (2019) 'Game Localization: A Critical Overview and Implications for Audivisual Translation', in Luis Pérez-González (ed) *The Routledge Handbook of Audiovisual Translation*. London and New York: Routledge, 145–159.

Transcreation

Bowker, Lynne (2023) *De-mystifying Translation. Introducing Translation to Non-translators*. London and New York: Routledge.

Gaballo, Viviana (2012) 'Exploring the Boundaries of Transcreation in Specialized Translation', *ESP Across Cultures*, 9: 95–113.

Pedersen, Daniel (2014) 'Exploring the Concept of Transcreation – Transcreation as "More Than Translation"?', *Cultus. Journal of Intercultural Mediation and Communication*, 7: 57–71.

List of references

Bernal-Merino, Miguel (2006) 'On the Translation of Video Games', *JoSTrans: The Journal of Specialised Translation*, 6: 22–36.

Benetello, Claudia (2018) 'When Translation Is Not Enough: Transcreation as a Convention Defying Practice. A Practitioner's Perspective', *JosTrans*, 29: 28–44.

Bernal-Merino, Miguel (2008) 'Training Translators for the Video Game Industry', in Jorge Díaz Cintas (ed) *The Didactics of Audiovisual Translation*. Amsterdam and Philadelphia: John Benjamins Publishing, 141–155.

Bowker, Lynne (2023) *De-mystifying Translation. Introducing Translation to Non-translators*. London and New York: Routledge.

Cerezo Merchán, Beatriz (2019) 'Audivisual Translator Training', in Luis Pérez-González (ed) *The Routledge Handbook of Audiovisual Translation*. London and New York: Routledge, 468–482.

Chaume, Frederic (2008) 'Teaching Synchronisation in a Dubbing Course: Some Didactic Proposals', in Jorge Díaz Cintas (ed) *The Didactics of Audiovisual Translation*. Amsterdam and Philadelphia: John Benjamins Publishing, 129–140.

De Higes Andino, Irene and Beatriz Cerezo Merchán (2018) 'Using Evaluation Criteria and Rubrics as Learning Tools in Subtitling for the D/deaf and the Hard of Hearing', in *The Interpreter and Translator Trainer*, special issue on *New Perspectives in Assessment in Translator Training*, 12: 1: 68–88.

Díaz Cintas, Jorge and Aline Remael (2007) *Audiovisual Translation: Subtitling*. Manchester: St Jerome.

Díaz Cintas, Jorge (2008a) 'Introduction: The Didactics of Audiovisual Translation', in Jorge Díaz Cintas (ed) *The Didactics of Audiovisual Translation*. Amsterdam and Philadelphia: John Benjamins Publishing, 1–18.

Díaz Cintas, Jorge (2008b) 'Teaching and Learning to Subtitle in an Academic Environment', in Jorge Díaz Cintas (ed) *The Didactics of Audiovisual Translation*. Amsterdam and Philadelphia: John Benjamins Publishing, 89–103.

Díaz-Cintas, Jorge and Aline Remael (2021) *Subtitling*. London and New York: Routledge.

Gaballo, Viviana (2012) 'Exploring the Boundaries of Transcreation in Specialized Translation', *ESP Across Cultures*, 9: 95–113.

Galán-Mañas, A. and A. Hurtado Albir (2015) 'Competence Assessment Procedures in Translator Training', *The Interpreter and Translator Trainer*, 9: 1: 63–82.

Granell, Ximo (2011) 'Teaching Video Game Localisation in Audivisual Translation Courses at University', *JoSTrans: The Journal of Specialised Translation*, 16: 185–202.

Gutt, Ernst-August (2000) *Translation and Relevance: Cognition and Context*. Manchester: St. Jerome.

Haywood, Louise M., Mike Thompson and Sándor Hervey (2009) *Thinking Spanish Translation. A Course in Translation Method: Spanish to English*. London & New York: Routledge.

Jimenez-Crespo, Miguel (2013) *Translation and Web Localization*. London and New York: Routledge.

Kajzer-Wietrzny, Marta and Maria Tymczyńska (2015) 'Devising a Systematic Approach to Examination Marking Criteria for Audio Visual Translation: A Case Study from Poland', *The Interpreter and Translator Trainer*, 9: 3: 342–355.

Katan, David (2021) 'Transcreation', in Yves Gambier and Luc van Doorslaer (eds) *Handbook of Translation Studies*, Vol. 5. Amsterdam: John Benjamins, 221–225.

Kelly, Dorothy (2010) 'Curriculum', in Yves Gambier and Luc van Doorslaer (eds) *Handbook of Translation Studies*. Amsterdam and Philadelphia: John Benjamins, 87–93.

Kruger, Jan-Louis (2008) 'Subtitler Training as Part of a General Training Programme in the Language Professions', in Jorge Díaz Cintas (ed) *The Didactics of Audiovisual Translation*. Amsterdam and Philadelphia: John Benjamins Publishing, 71–87.

Mangiron, Carmen and Minako O'Hagan (2006) 'Game Localisation: Unleashing Imagination with "Restricted" Translation', *The Journal of Specialised Translation*, 6: 10–21.

Matamala, Anna (2008) 'Teaching Voice-over: A Practical Approach', in Jorge Díaz Cintas (ed) *The Didactics of Audiovisual Translation*. Amsterdam and Philadelphia: John Benjamins Publishing, 114–127.

Morón, Marián and Calvo Elisa (2018) 'Introducing Transcreation Skills in Translator Training Contexts: A Situated Project-based Approach', *The Journal of Specialised Translation* 29: 126–148.

Munday, Jeremy (2016) *Introducing Translation Studies. Theories and Applications*, 4th ed. London and New York: Routledge.

Neves, Josélia (2008) 'Training in Subtitling for the d/Deaf and the Hard-of-Hearing', in Jorge Díaz Cintas (ed) *The Didactics of Audiovisual Translation*. Amsterdam and Philadelphia: John Benjamins Publishing, 172–189.

Nida, Eugene A. (1964) *Toward a Science of Translating*. Leiden: E. J. Brill.

O'Hagan, Minako (2019) 'Game Localization: A Critical Overview and Implications for Audivisual Translation', in Luis Pérez-González (ed) *The Routledge Handbook of Audiovisual Translation*. London and New York: Routledge, 145–159.

Orero, Pilar and Anna Matamala (2008) 'Accessible Opera: Overcoming Linguistic and Sensorial Barriers', *Perspectives: Studies in Translatology*, 15: 4: 262–277.

Perego, Elisa (2019) 'Audio Description. Evolving Recommendations for Usable, effective and Enjoyable Practices', in Luis Pérez-González (ed) *The Routledge Handbook of Audiovisual Translation*. London and New York: Routledge, 114–129.

Pedersen, Daniel (2014) 'Exploring the Concept of Transcreation – Transcreation as "More Than Translation"?', *Cultus: Journal of Intercultural Mediation and Communication*, 7: 57–71.

Pérez-González, Luis (ed) (2019) *The Routledge Handbook of Audiovisual Translation*. London and New York: Routledge.

Pym, Anthony (2014) *Exploring Translation Theories*. London and New York: Routledge.

Rike, Sissel Marie (2013) 'Bilingual Corporate Websites – from Translation to Transcreation?', *The Journal of Specialised Translation*, 20: 68–85.

Sawyer, David B. (2004) *Fundamental Aspects of Interpreter Education*. Amsterdam and Philadelphia: John Benjamins Publishing Company.

Secară, Alina (2019) 'Surtitling and Captioning for Theatre and Opera', in Luis Pérez-González (ed) *The Routledge Handbook of Audiovisual Translation*. London and New York: Routledge, 130–144.

Snyder, Joel (2008) 'Audio Description. The Visual Made Verbal', in Jorge Díaz Cintas (ed) *The Didactics of Audiovisual Translation*. Amsterdam and Philadelphia: John Benjamins Publishing, 192–198.

Vazquez-Calvo, Boris, Liudmila Shafirova, Leticia Tian Zhang, and Daniel Cassany (2019) 'An Overview of Multimodal FanTranslation: Fansubbing, Fandubbing, Fan Translation of Games and Scanlation', in María del Mar Ogea Pozo and Francisco Rodríguez Rodríguez (eds) *Insights into Audiovisual and Comic Translation. Changing Perspectives on Films, Comics and Video Games*. Córdoba: UCO Press, 191–213.

Afterword

Translation Studies and related disciplines are growing exponentially. With the rate of technological development and with technology being so closely linked to any type of language mediation (or to any life activity, we might say), various new disciplines and subdisciplines are emerging. As a result, the need for training and accreditation in these disciplines is also rising. Even though most MAs in Translation Studies use a translation commentary as a way of assessment, this is not the case with the other disciplines discussed in this textbook. Some educational and training institutions use reflective reports for interpreting and audiovisual translation assessment. However, this is not a practice that is used particularly widely, and when it is used, it is often not done in a systematic way. In the case of localisation and transcreation training, the use of a reflective report is rare, which is slightly paradoxical when, for instance, transcreators are generally required to write a report for the client.

As we have seen, the benefits of writing a translation commentary or a reflective report are clear. It is not only a way of demonstrating that the learning outcomes have been achieved, but is also a way of acquiring and developing the tools necessary to make informed decisions, so that you can confidently justify them to your clients, teachers, or employers. Writing a translation commentary or reflective report allows you to reflect on your own learning and become and a self-regulated student. Therefore, it is hoped that writing a translation commentary or reflective report will become a common practice used in the learning, teaching, and assessment of most types of language mediation training programmes. Both the translation commentaries and reflective reports may develop into action research papers, PhDs, or research projects, thus helping with the establishment and consolidation of each of these disciplines.

Even though new disciplines are emerging and getting established, the current trend is also crossdisciplinarity. This means that the training provided needs to be focused on acquiring transferrable skills and flexibility. This is particularly important, once again, because of technological development. We might be trained to use a particular software programme, only to find that, ten years along the line, it is obsolete, and an alternative software programme is available on the market. Therefore, the training should be more holistic, by looking at the wider picture and where students and trainees are learning principles and acquiring problem-solving skills. In this way, we would be able to keep up with the technological innovations and easily learn to use a new programme if we need to do so.

Notwithstanding, and despite the fact that much of what has been said in Chapters 1–5 about writing a translation commentary is applicable to the other four disciplines, the next obvious and necessary step to take is to produce other textbooks that focus specifically on the writing of a reflective report in interpreting, audiovisual translation, localisation, transcreation, and any other emerging discipline. This would allow for the necessary space to look at issues relevant to the discipline in question, in a much greater depth than they have been discussed here. Another related area, but much beyond the scope of this textbook, is the writing of reflective reports in work placement modules, where students benefit from experiencing real working conditions and from interacting with people in the industry (Bernal-Merino 2008: 147). In any case, much of what has been said throughout this textbook is also applicable to this type of reflective reports.

List of references

Bernal-Merino, Miguel (2008) 'Training Translators for the Video Game Industry', in Jorge Díaz Cintas (ed) *The Didactics of Audiovisual Translation*. Amsterdam and Philadelphia: John Benjamins Publishing, 141–155.

Appendix 1 – Table for example selection

Category	Examples	Comment
Cultural matrix		
Culture-specific Terminology		
Proper nouns		
Formal matrix		
Phonic/graphic level		
Prosodic level		
Grammatical level: lexis, morphology, and syntax		
Sentential level		
Discourse level		
Semantic matrix		
Denotative and connotative meaning		
Ambiguities		
Collocations		
Neologisms		
Synonyms		
Technical terminology		
Metaphors		
Varietal matrix		
Tenor (writer-reader relationship)		
Language variety		
Social register		
Sociolect		
Dialect		
Temporal dialect		
Diglossia		
Idiolect		
Multilingualism and code switching		

Category	Examples	Comment
Intertextual issues		
Examples of intertextuality		
Other challenges		
Translating sensitive texts		
Translating humour		
Translating (im)politeness		
Translating profanity		
Other		
Examples		

Appendix 2 – Sample assessment rubric for a translation commentary

		Unsatisfactory	Fair	Good	Excellent
Structure, style, and presentation	**Structure**	The commentary lacks coherence. The ideas have not been ordered logically. Most of the issues discussed are not relevant. There is no signposting to guide the reader. There is neither an introduction nor a conclusion. The transition between the sections is abrupt and awkward.	Although loosely coherent, the ideas have not been ordered logically. Only some of the issues discussed are relevant. There is too much focus on a particular point, which is either irrelevant or minor. Too many issues may have been selected for discussion, which is too brief and superficial. Although there is some signposting to guide the reader, it has been done neither effectively nor consistently. The transition between the sections is not fluent.	The commentary is generally coherent and clear, and, despite a few exceptions, the ideas have been ordered logically. However, it might not be totally clear whether it is the source text (ST) or target text (TT) that is being discussed. The space available has generally been divided in a balanced way. The signposting is generally effective despite some exceptions. The introduction and conclusion are generally fine, but they discuss the same issues. The transition between the sections is generally fluent, despite some exceptions.	The commentary is coherent and has a logical structure. It is completely clear whether it is the ST or the TT that is being discussed. The space available has been dedicated to the different issues in a balanced way. There is an effective use of signposting to guide the reader. The conclusion sums up the most important points and makes a link between the techniques used at the microlevel and the translation strategy. The transition between sections is fluent and coherent.
	Use of appropriate terminology	No relevant terminology has been used.	Only some relevant terminology has been used. However, this has often been done inaccurately or in the wrong context. Some of the terminology is eclectic or inconsistent.	The use of the relevant terminology is generally accurate, despite a few exceptions. Some of the terminology is eclectic and, sometimes, inconsistent.	The relevant terminology has been used in an accurate, precise, and consistent manner.

Integration of secondary/ theoretical sources	There is a lack of theoretical engagement.	The theoretical engagement is not effective. The secondary sources have not been effectively integrated into the narrative or they contradict the decisions taken. There are some relevant theories that have not been mentioned. The referencing is inconsistent and some of the sources have not been acknowledged properly.	The commentary is underpinned by theoretical sources, which have generally been effectively integrated into the narrative, despite some exceptions. Most of the relevant theories have been mentioned, although there are a few missing. The referencing is consistent, despite a few errors and all the sources have been acknowledged properly.	The commentary is effectively underpinned by theoretical sources, which have been integrated into the narrative in a coherent manner and have been linked to the examples. The referencing is consistent throughout.
Presentation	There are no titles, headings, or subheadings. The use of punctuation is inconsistent and inaccurate. The examples are presented in an unclear and inconsistent manner, and no back translations have been provided.	The use of headings and subheadings is inconsistent. The use of punctuation is often inaccurate. The examples are presented in an inconsistent manner and sometimes back translations have not been provided.	The use of headings and subheadings is generally clear and consistent, despite a few exceptions. The use of punctuation is generally accurate, despite a few minor errors. The examples have generally been provided in a consistent and clear manner, although some of the back translations have not been provided.	The use of headings and subheadings is clear and consistent. The use of punctuation is accurate, and the examples have been provided in a consistent and effective way, including back translations when necessary.
Macrolevel analysis ST analysis	Only some of the relevant points have been discussed, and they have taken too much of the available space. Some of the issues were not clearly relevant to the discussion.	Many of the relevant points have been discussed. However, some issues have not been mentioned and others have taken too much of the available space. Some of the issues were not clearly relevant to the discussion.	Most of the relevant points have been discussed. The available space has generally been divided in a balanced way. All of the points discussed are relevant.	The commentary includes some relevant background and contextual information about the ST author and the source culture (SC), as well as the ST's genre or text type, its skopos, intended readership, and medium of publication. It also discusses the ST's salient features, such as its particular effect or tone.

(*Continued*)

	Unsatisfactory	Fair	Good	Excellent
Formulation of translation strategy	The commentary only covers one or two of the relevant aspects for the formulation of a translation strategy. Some of the points have been discussed in too much detail at the expense of others.	The commentary covers many of the relevant aspects for the formulation of a translation strategy but not all. Some of the points have been discussed in too much detail at the expense of others.	The commentary covers most of the relevant aspects for the formulation of a translation strategy, although sometimes this has not been done in an explicit manner. The available space has generally been divided in a balanced way.	The commentary mentions explicitly the following: TT genre or text type, its skopos, intended readership, and medium of publication. The available space has been divided in a balanced way.
Setting translation priorities	No translation priorities have been formulated.	The translation priorities that have been explicitly formulated are neither consistent with the translation strategy nor with the salient features identified in the ST analysis. They have also been formulated in a vague and inaccurate manner and they are inconsistent with the translation techniques used.	The translation priorities have been explicitly formulated in a clear and concise manner. They are generally consistent with the translation strategy and with the salient features identified in the ST analysis, despite a few exceptions. They are also consistent with the translation techniques used, despite a few exceptions.	The commentary has explicitly set up the translation priorities in a clear and concise manner, cross-referencing them with the translation strategy and the salient features of the ST identified in the analysis. They are also effectively linked to the translation techniques used.

| Microlevel analysis | Selection, integration, and relevance of illustrative examples | No examples have been provided. | There are either not enough examples or too many. The examples have not been explicitly linked to any part of the commentary. They have been discussed in a descriptive manner without offering a justification for the decisions taken. Only line numbers have been provided, rather than the example. Some of the examples are neither particularly representative nor relevant to the discussion at hand. Other examples have been chosen from inaccurate translation decisions or they are about obligatory rather than optional changes. | The selection of examples is generally adequate to discuss the particular point in question. Most of the examples have been linked to a particular section of the commentary, and they are generally relevant to the point under discussion, despite a few exceptions. The examples have generally been properly referenced. A few of the examples have been chosen from inaccurate translation decisions or they are about obligatory rather than optional changes. | The commentary has a selection of just enough examples to illustrate a particular point. The examples are fully explored and linked to the translation strategy and priorities to justify the techniques used. They are properly referenced to be easily found. They are relevant to the discussion at hand and are important to explore because of either being too controversial and going against the intended TT readers' expectations, or because they contradict other translation techniques used in the same text. |

Appendix 3 – Translation commentary checklist

Structure, style, and presentation

1. Is the structure logical?
2. Is it clear where you are discussing the source text (ST) and the target text (TT)?
3. Is the signposting effective?
4. Is the transition between the sections fluent and coherent?
5. Have you dedicated the allocated word count to the different parts of the commentary in an effective and balanced way?
6. Does the conclusion sum up the most important points?
7. Is the appropriate terminology used accurately and consistently?
8. Are the secondary and theoretical sources relevant to the issues discussed?
9. Are the secondary and theoretical sources linked to examples and are they properly integrated as an essential part of the narrative?
10. Is the referencing consistent?
11. Is the use of punctuation accurate and consistent?

Macrolevel analysis

1. Have you included some relevant background and contextual information about the ST, the ST's author, and the source culture (SC)?
2. Have you included information on the ST's genre or text type, skopos, intended readership, and medium of publication?
3. Have you discussed the ST's salient features?

4. Have you discussed explicitly the TT's genre or text type, skopos, intended readership, and medium of publication?
5. Have you set up your translation priorities in a clear, explicit, and concise manner?
6. Have you linked your translation priorities to your translation strategy and the ST's salient features?

Microlevel analysis

---

1. Do the examples you selected deal with optional rather than obligatory decisions you had to make?
2. Have you selected the appropriate number of examples to discuss a particular point?
3. Do the illustrative examples support the line of argument of the commentary? Are they relevant?
4. Have the translation techniques used in the examples selected been linked to the translation strategy and translation priorities?
5. Is there a clear engagement with both theoretical concepts and illustrative examples to justify the decisions you have taken?

Appendix 4 – Sample assessment rubric for an interpreting reflective report (with a focus on error detection and analysis)

		Unsatisfactory	Fair	Good	Excellent
Error detection	Understanding of the source language (SL) segment	No errors of understanding have been detected.	Some errors of understanding, but not all, have been detected.	Most errors of understanding have been detected, with a few exceptions.	All errors of understanding have been detected.
	Target language (TL) rendering of the SL segment	No TL rendering errors have been detected.	Some TL rendering errors, but not all, have been detected.	Most TL rendering errors have been detected, with some exceptions.	All TL rendering errors have been detected.
	Delivery	No errors of delivery have been detected.	Some errors of delivery, but not all, have been detected.	Most errors of delivery have been detected, with a few exceptions.	All errors of delivery have been detected.
Error analysis	Explanation	No satisfactory explanation for the errors has been provided.	There is some attempt to provide an explanation of the errors made, but no awareness is shown of the reason why the error has occurred.	Good explanation of the errors made, but there is limited awareness of why the error has occurred.	The explanation of the errors is excellent, showing full awareness of why the error has occurred.
	Error categorisation according to the level of seriousness	There is no evidence of categorisation of the errors committed.	There is an attempt to categorise the errors made, but it is often inaccurate.	Good attempt to categorise the errors, despite a few inaccuracies.	Excellent categorisation of errors according to the level of seriousness.
Solutions	Solutions to prevent reoccurrence	No solutions have been proposed.	There is an attempt to propose solutions to prevent error reoccurrence, but most of them are either inaccurate or not feasible.	Good attempt to propose solutions to prevent error reoccurrence, although some solutions are not feasible.	Excellent solutions provided to prevent error reoccurrence supported by the literature.

Appendix 5 – Sample assessment rubric for an interpreting reflective report

	Unsatisfactory	Fair	Good	Excellent
Structure, style, and presentation				
Structure	The reflective report lacks coherence. The ideas have not been ordered logically. Some of the issues have been discussed in too much detail at the expense of others, or too many issues have been selected, so the discussion is very superficial. Most of the issues discussed are not relevant. There is no signposting to guide the reader. There is neither an introduction nor a conclusion. The transition between the sections is abrupt and awkward.	Although loosely coherent, the ideas have not been ordered logically. Only some of the issues discussed are relevant. There is too much focus on a particular point, which is either irrelevant or minor. Too many issues may have been selected, which has rendered the discussion too superficial. Although there is some signposting to guide the reader, it has been done neither effectively nor consistently. The transition between the sections is not fluent.	The reflective report is generally coherent and clear, despite a few exceptions, and the ideas have been ordered logically. The space available has generally been divided in a balanced way. The signposting is generally effective, despite some exceptions. The introduction and conclusion are generally fine, but they discuss the same issues. The transition between the sections is generally fluent, despite some exceptions.	The reflective report is coherent and has a logical structure. It is completely clear whether it is the source text (ST) or the target text (TT) that is being discussed. The space available has been dedicated to the different issues in a balanced way. There is an effective use of signposting to guide the reader. The conclusion sums up the most important points and makes a link between the techniques used at the microlevel and the translation strategy. The transition between sections is fluent and coherent.
Use of appropriate terminology	No relevant terminology has been used.	Only some relevant terminology has been used. However, this has often been done inaccurately or in the wrong context. Some of the terminology is eclectic or inconsistent.	The use of the relevant terminology is generally accurate, despite a few exceptions. Some of the terminology is eclectic and, sometimes, inconsistent.	The relevant terminology has been used in an accurate, precise, and consistent manner.

(*Continued*)

	Unsatisfactory	Fair	Good	Excellent
Integration of secondary/ theoretical sources	There is a lack of theoretical engagement.	The theoretical engagement is not effective. The secondary sources have not been effectively integrated into the narrative or they contradict the decisions taken. There are some relevant theories that have not been mentioned. The referencing is inconsistent and some of the sources have not been acknowledged properly.	The reflective report is underpinned by theoretical sources, which have generally been effectively integrated into the narrative, despite some exceptions. Most of the relevant theories have been mentioned, although there are a few missing. The referencing is consistent, despite a few errors, and all the sources have been acknowledged properly.	The reflective report is effectively underpinned by theoretical sources, which have been integrated into the narrative in a coherent manner and have been linked to the examples. The referencing is consistent throughout.
Presentation	There are no titles, headings, or subheadings. The use of punctuation is inconsistent and inaccurate. The examples are presented in an unclear and inconsistent manner, and no back translations have been provided.	The use of headings and subheadings is inconsistent. The use of punctuation is often inaccurate. The examples are presented in an inconsistent manner and sometimes back translations have not been provided.	The use of headings and subheadings is generally clear and consistent, despite a few exceptions. The use of punctuation is generally accurate, despite a few minor errors. The examples have generally been provided in a consistent and clear manner, although some of the back translations have not been provided.	The use of headings and subheadings is clear and consistent. The use of punctuation is accurate, and the examples have been provided in a consistent and effective way, including back translations when necessary.

Analysis of good renderings	Selection, integration, and relevance of examples	No examples of good renderings have been provided.	There are either not enough examples or too many. The examples have not been explicitly linked to any part of the reflective report. They have not been referenced effectively. Some of the examples are neither particularly representative nor relevant to the overall interpretation approach. Others are actually not good renderings but interpreting errors.	The selection of examples is generally adequate. Most of the examples have been linked to a particular section of the commentary, and they are generally relevant to the point under discussion, despite a few exceptions. The examples have generally been properly referenced. A few of the examples have been chosen from inaccurate target language (TL) renderings.	The reflective report has a selection of just enough examples to illustrate a particular point. The examples are fully explored and properly referenced to be easily found. They are relevant to the discussion at hand and are important to explore because of being particularly good renderings.
	Explanation	There are no explanations of why the examples selected are considered to be good renderings and/or there is no theoretical engagement when explaining these solutions.	There is some attempt to provide an explanation of why the selected examples are considered to be good renderings, however no awareness is shown of the reason why this is so and there is no theoretical engagement.	Good explanation of why the selected examples are considered to be good renderings, but there is limited awareness of why this is so and there is no theoretical engagement.	The explanation of why the examples are considered to be good renderings is excellent, showing full awareness of why this is so by engaging effectively with the relevant theories.
Error analysis	Selection, integration, and relevance of examples	No examples of errors have been provided.	There are either not enough examples or too many. The examples have not been explicitly linked to any part of the reflective report. They have not been referenced effectively. Some of the examples selected are actually not errors. Some serious errors made have not been selected.	The selection of examples is generally adequate. Most of the examples have been linked to a particular section of the commentary, and they are generally relevant to the point under discussion, despite a few exceptions. The examples have generally been properly referenced. A few of the examples are not actually errors. Only a few serious errors have not been selected.	The reflective report has a selection of just enough examples to illustrate a particular point. The examples are fully explored and properly referenced to be easily found. They are relevant to the discussion at hand and are important to explore because of being serious errors. All serious errors have been selected and all the examples selected are errors.

(*Continued*)

	Unsatisfactory	Fair	Good	Excellent
Explanation and categorisation	No satisfactory explanation for the errors has been provided and there is no evidence of categorisation of the errors committed.	There is some attempt to provide an explanation of the errors made, but no awareness is shown of the reason why the error has occurred. There is an attempt to categorise the errors made, but it is often inaccurate.	Good explanation of the errors made, but there is limited awareness of why the error has occurred. Good attempt to categorise the errors, despite a few inaccuracies.	The explanation of the errors is excellent, showing full awareness of why the error has occurred. Excellent categorisation of errors according to the level of seriousness.
Solutions to prevent reoccurrence	No solutions have been proposed.	There is an attempt to propose solutions to prevent error reoccurrence, but most of them are either inaccurate or not feasible.	Good attempt to propose solutions to prevent error reoccurrence, although some solutions are not feasible.	Excellent solutions provided to prevent error reoccurrence supported by the literature.

Appendix 6 – Interpreting reflective report checklist

Structure, style, and presentation

---

1. Is the structure logical and coherent?
2. Have you included an analysis of the complexity of the source language (SL) discourse?
3. Is the signposting effective (including the use of headings and subheadings)?
4. Is the transition between the sections and paragraphs fluent and coherent?
5. Have you dedicated the allocated word count to the different parts of the reflective report in an effective and balanced way?
6. Does the conclusion sum up the most important points?
7. Is the appropriate terminology used accurately and consistently?
8. Are the secondary and theoretical sources relevant to the issues discussed?
9. Are the secondary and theoretical sources linked to examples and are they properly integrated as an essential part of the narrative?
10. Is the referencing consistent?
11. Is the use of punctuation accurate and consistent?

Analysis of good renderings

---

1. Have you selected the appropriate number of examples to discuss a particular point?
2. Do the illustrative examples support the line of argument of the reflective report? Are they relevant?

3. Have you effectively explained why you consider your examples to be particularly good renderings?
4. Is there a clear engagement with both theoretical concepts and illustrative examples to justify the decisions you have taken?

Error analysis

---

1. Have you selected the appropriate number of examples to discuss a particular point?
2. Have you selected all of the serious errors you have detected?
3. Have you categorised the errors according to their level of seriousness?
4. Do the illustrative examples support the line of argument of the reflective report? Are they relevant?
5. Have you effectively explained why you consider your examples to be particularly good renderings?
6. Is there a clear engagement with both theoretical concepts and illustrative examples to justify the decisions you have taken?
7. Have you provided effective plans to prevent error reoccurrence which have a firm underpinning with theoretical sources?

Appendix 7 – Sample assessment rubric for a reflective report for audiovisual translation, localisation, or transcreation

		Unsatisfactory	Fair	Good	Excellent
Structure, style, and presentation	**Structure**	The reflective report lacks coherence. The ideas have not been ordered logically. Most of the issues discussed are not relevant. There is no signposting to guide the reader. There is neither an introduction nor a conclusion. The transition between the sections is abrupt and awkward.	Although loosely coherent, the ideas have not been ordered logically. Only some of the issues discussed are relevant. There is too much focus on a particular point, which is either irrelevant or minor. Too many issues may have been selected for discussion, which is too brief and superficial. Although there is some signposting to guide the reader, it has been done neither effectively nor consistently. The transition between the sections is not fluent.	The reflective report is generally coherent and clear, despite a few exceptions, and the ideas have been ordered logically. However, it might not be totally clear whether it is the source text (ST) or target text (TT) that is being discussed. The space available has generally been divided in a balanced way. The signposting is generally effective, despite some exceptions. The introduction and conclusion are generally fine, but they discuss the same issues. The transition between the sections is generally fluent, despite some exceptions.	The reflective report is coherent and has a logical structure. It is completely clear whether it is the ST or the TT that is being discussed. The space available has been dedicated to the different issues in a balanced way. There is an effective use of signposting to guide the reader. The conclusion sums up the most important points and makes a link between the techniques used at the microlevel and the translation strategy. The transition between sections is fluent and coherent.
	Use of appropriate terminology	No relevant terminology has been used.	Only some relevant terminology has been used. However, this has often been done inaccurately or in the wrong context. Some of the terminology is eclectic or inconsistent.	The use of the relevant terminology is generally accurate, despite a few exceptions. Some of the terminology is eclectic and, sometimes, inconsistent.	The relevant terminology has been used in an accurate, precise, and consistent manner.
	Integration of secondary/theoretical sources	There is a lack of theoretical engagement.	The theoretical engagement is not effective. The secondary sources have not been effectively integrated into the narrative or they contradict the decisions taken. There are some relevant theories that have not been mentioned. The referencing is inconsistent and some of the sources have not been acknowledged properly.	The reflective report is underpinned by theoretical sources, which have generally been effectively integrated into the narrative, despite some exceptions. Most of the relevant theories have been mentioned, although there are a few missing. The referencing is consistent, despite a few errors, and all the sources have been acknowledged properly.	The reflective report is effectively underpinned by theoretical sources, which have been integrated into the narrative in a coherent manner and have been linked to the examples. The referencing is consistent throughout.

Macrolevel analysis	Presentation	There are no titles, headings, or subheadings. The use of punctuation is inconsistent and inaccurate. The examples are presented in an unclear and inconsistent manner, and no back translations have been provided.	The use of headings and subheadings is inconsistent. The use of punctuation is often inaccurate. The examples are presented in an inconsistent manner and sometimes back translations have not been provided.	The use of headings and subheadings is generally clear and consistent, despite a few exceptions. The use of punctuation is generally accurate, despite a few minor errors. The examples have generally been provided in a consistent and clear manner, although some of the back translations have not been provided.	The use of headings and subheadings is clear and consistent. The use of punctuation is accurate, and the examples have been provided in a consistent and effective way, including back translations when necessary.
	ST analysis	Only some of the relevant points have been discussed, and they have taken too much of the available space. Some of the issues were not clearly relevant to the discussion.	Many of the relevant points have been discussed. However, some issues have not been mentioned and others have taken too much of the available space. Some of the issues were not clearly relevant to the discussion.	Most of the relevant points have been discussed. The available space has generally been divided in a balanced way. All of the points discussed are relevant.	The reflective report includes some relevant background and contextual information, and discusses the ST's salient features, such as its effect or tone and, most importantly, its intended reader or user.
	Formulation of translation strategy	The reflective report only covers one or two of the relevant points for the formulation of a translation strategy. Some of the points have been discussed in too much detail at the expense of others.	The reflective report covers many of the relevant aspects for the formulation of a translation strategy but not all. Some of the points have been discussed in too much detail at the expense of others.	The reflective report covers most of the relevant aspects for the formulation of a translation strategy, although sometimes this has not been done in an explicit manner. The available space has generally been divided in a balanced way.	The commentary includes a summary of the brief, when available, and provides further details on the skopos and intended readership or user. The available space has been divided in a balanced way.
	Setting translation priorities	No translation priorities have been formulated.	The translation priorities that have been explicitly formulated are neither consistent with the translation strategy nor with the salient features identified in the ST analysis. They have also been formulated in a vague and inaccurate manner and they are inconsistent with the translation techniques used.	The translation priorities have been explicitly formulated in a clear and concise manner. They are generally consistent with the translation strategy and with the salient features identified in the ST analysis, despite a few exceptions. They are also consistent with the translation techniques used, despite a few exceptions.	The reflective report has explicitly set up the translation priorities in a clear and concise manner, cross-referencing them with the translation strategy and the salient features of the ST identified in the analysis. They are also effectively linked to the translation techniques used.

(Continued)

		Unsatisfactory	Fair	Good	Excellent
Microlevel analysis	**Selection, integration, and relevance of illustrative examples**	No examples have been provided.	There are either not enough examples or too many. The examples have not been explicitly linked to any part of the reflective report. They have been discussed in a descriptive manner without offering a justification for the decisions taken. Only line numbers have been provided, rather than the example. Some of the examples are neither particularly representative nor relevant to the discussion at hand. Other examples have been chosen from inaccurate translation decisions or they are about obligatory rather than optional changes.	The selection of examples is generally adequate to discuss the particular point in question. Most of the examples have been linked to a particular section of the reflective report, and they are generally relevant to the point under discussion, despite a few exceptions. The examples have generally been properly referenced. A few of the examples have been chosen from inaccurate translation decisions or they are about obligatory rather than optional changes.	The reflective report has a selection of just enough examples to illustrate a particular point. The examples are fully explored and linked to the translation strategy and priorities to justify the translation techniques used. They are properly referenced to be easily found. They are relevant to the discussion at hand and are important to explore because of either being too controversial and going against the intended TT readers' expectations, or because they contradict other translation techniques used in the same text.

Appendix 8 – Checklist for a reflective report for audiovisual translation, localisation, or transcreation

---

Structure, style, and presentation

1. Is the structure logical?
2. Is the signposting effective?
3. Is the transition between the sections fluent and coherent?
4. Have you dedicated the allocated wordcount to the different parts of the reflective report in an effective and balanced way?
5. Does the conclusion sum up the most important points?
6. Is the appropriate terminology used accurately and consistently?
7. Are the secondary and theoretical sources relevant to the issues discussed?
8. Are the secondary and theoretical sources linked to examples and are they properly integrated as an essential part of the narrative?
9. Is the referencing consistent?
10. Is the use of punctuation accurate and consistent?

Macrolevel analysis

1. Have you included some relevant background and contextual information?
2. Have you discussed the source text's (ST's) salient features?
3. Have you discussed explicitly the target text's (TT's) skopos and intended readership or user?
4. Have you set up your translation priorities in a clear, explicit, and concise manner?
5. Have you linked your translation priorities to the brief or your translation strategy and the ST's salient features?

Microlevel analysis

1. Have you selected the appropriate number of examples to discuss a particular point?
2. Do the illustrative examples support the line of argument of the commentary? Are they relevant?
3. Have the translation techniques used, in the examples selected, been linked to the brief or your translation strategy and translation priorities?
4. Is there a clear engagement with both theoretical concepts and illustrative examples to justify the decisions you have taken or, in the case of transcreation, to explain the options provided?

Index

action research 159
active languages 150
Adab, Beverly 2
age of audience/readers 18, 41–42
Aibo, Laurence Jay-Rayon Ibrahim 2
Albir, A. Hurtado 180
Albl-Mikasa, Michaela 151, 155
ambiguities 76
Andrews, Edna 30, 65, 70, 85
ante-litteram transcreators 185
appropriate terminology *see* terminology
Arumí Ribas, Marta 160, 161
assessment 3; audiovisual translation
    (AVT) 180; interpreting 151–153;
    interpreting reflective report 163–167;
    localisation 183–184; reflective
    report 192–196; transcreation 186;
    translation commentary 121–126
assignment types 114–118
Association of Visual Language
    Interpreters of Canada 154
audience/readership: source text (ST)
    analysis 17–21; translation strategy
    40–45
audio description: concept 175; skills
    necessary for 179
audiovisual translation (AVT) 174–180;
    assessment 180; skills required
    177–179; teaching and training
    179–180; thematically-structured
    report 188–189; types 173, 174–177;
    writing reflective report for 188–189;
    see also reflective report; *see also*
    localisation

Bartlomiejczyk, Magdalena 152
Benetello, Claudia 184, 185
Bernal-Merino, Miguel 184
bilateral or liaison interpreting 148

Bloom's taxonomy 1, 2
Bored of the Rings (Beard and
    Kenney) 85
Bowker, Lynne 77, 146, 147, 181, 186

Campbell, Stuart 151
Carreres, Ángeles 16–17
Carroll, Lewis 185
Cerezo Merchán, Beatriz 180, 187
Cha, Frances 13
Chartered Institute of Linguists
    (CIOL) 147
Chaume, Frederic 178
China Accreditation Test for Translators
    and Interpreters (CATTI) 151
closed captioning *see* subtitling for the
    D/deaf and the hard of
    hearing (SDH)
code switching 83, 97; *see also*
    multilingualism
Collados Aís, A. 152
collocations 76
community interpreting *see* dialogue
    interpreting
concepts and theories 101–105
consecutive interpreting 148
contextual information 11–14, 46, 48,
    188, 189, 194
courtroom interpreting 148
Cragie, Stella 12, 30, 65, 66, 68, 70, 75,
    76, 79, 82, 85
creative brief 184, 186; *see also*
    transcreation
cultural matrix 65–70; intertextual
    issues 85; proper nouns 66–67;
    taxonomy of techniques 67–68;
    terminology 65–66
cultural sensitivity 182, 185, 190, 192;
    see also transcreation

deaf interpreting *see* signed language
interpreting
degree of specialisation *see* specialisation
of audience/readers
De Higes Andino, Irene 180, 187
denotative and connotative meaning
75–76
desirable features of translation
commentary 63–64
dialect 81–82
dialogue interpreting 148
Díaz Cintas, Jorge 176, 177
Dickins, James 30, 65, 70, 80, 82, 85
diglossia 82
Diploma in Public Service
Interpreting 147
discourse level 72–73
domestication 95–96
dubbing: concept 174–175; skills
necessary for 178
dynamic equivalence 186

educational level of audience/readers
19, 42
effect-producing features 29
Elisa, Calvo 187, 191
El vocabulario de los balcones
(Grandes) 14
error-based approaches to
assessment 183
examples in narrative 105–106
experiential learning 1
extratextual assessment 183

fandubbing 175
fansubbing 175
fan translation of games 175
features of translation commentary:
desirable 63–64; undesirable 63
Foley, Lucy 37
foreignisation 95–96
formal matrix 70–75; discourse level
72–73; grammatical level 71–72;
intertextual issues 85; phonic/graphic
level 70–71; prosodic level 71
formative assessment 152
formative assignments 114–115
Franco Aixelá, Javier 66

Gaballo, Viviana 184–186
Galán-Mañas, A. 180
García-Beyaert, Sofía 151
genres 15–17; translation strategy 39–40

geographical background of audience/
reader 19, 42–43
Gile, Daniel 155
GILT (Globalisation,
Internationalisation, Localisation, and
Translation) 181
grammatical level 71–72
Grandes, Almudena 14
Granell, Ximo 173, 180

Hale, Sandra 151
Hatim, Basil 15, 97, 151
Haywood, Louise M. 30, 36, 49, 64, 65,
68, 70, 72, 75, 79, 81, 85, 94,
97, 174
healthcare interpreting 148
higher order thinking skills (HOTS) 1, 2
holistic evaluation 183
humour 94–95

idiolect 82–83
If I Had Your Face (Cha) 13
I Just Want to be Loved (Watson)
37, 53
immediacy 145, 146
Information and Communications
Technology (ICT) 176
integrating concepts and theories
101–105
intended audience/readership *see*
audience/readership
International Association of Conference
Interpreters (AIIC) 147
interpreting: assessment 151–153;
immediacy 145, 146; as oral
translation 145; overview 145–146;
skills required for 147, 149–150;
teaching and training 150–151; *vs.*
translation 146–148; types 148–149
interpreting reflective report 153–169;
assessment 163–167; error analysis
166–167; good renderings analysis
165–166; as portfolio 156–157;
presentation 165; rationale for
153–154; secondary and theoretical
sources 165; self-assessment
statements 156–157; standalone
report 157–158; structure 164;
terminology 164; thematically
structured 158–159; types 156–159;
writing 159–163
Interpreting Studies 145
intertextual issues 85

intratextual assessment 183
Introducing Interpreting Studies
  (Pöchhacker) 145
ipsative assessment 153
isochrony 178

'The Jabberwocky' (Carroll) 185
Jimenez-Crespo, Miguel 181–183

Kajzer-Wietrzny, Marta 180
Kaur, Jasmin 14, 44
Kelly, Dorothy 180
kinetic synchrony 178
Kolb, David 1
Kruger, Jan-Louis 176

language mediation 173
language variety 80–83
learning 2–3
lip sync/synchrony 178
LISA *see* Localisation Industry
  Standards Association
Liu, Eric 30, 65, 70, 73, 75, 79
localisation 180–184; assessment
  183–184; characteristics 181; as an
  exigent modality of AVT 173; GILT
  181; holistic definition 181; reflective
  report 189–190; skills required for
  182; teaching and training 182–183;
  thematically-structured report 190;
  types 181–182; *see also* audiovisual
  translation (AVT); reflective report
Localisation Industry Standards
  Association (LISA) 183
localisation pack 181
The Lord of the Rings (Tolkien) 85
lower order thinking skills (LOTS) 1, 2

Maksimova, Elena 30, 65, 70, 85
Malcolm, Karen 154
Mason, Ian 15, 97, 151
matrices 92–93; *see also specific
  matrix*
Mazzei, Cristiano 2
medical interpreting *see* healthcare
  interpreting
medium of publication: source text (ST)
  analysis 21–22; translation strategy
  45–46
metaphors 77, 96–97
Ministerio de Cultura (Cuba) 49
Modelos de mujer (Grandes) 14
Morón, Marián 187, 191

multilingualism 83, 97; *see also* code
  switching

neologisms 76
Nida, Eugene A. 35, 94, 100, 101,
  129–130, 134, 186
Nord, Christiane 15, 16, 24, 27, 29, 40
note-taking exercises 150

occupation of audience/readers 19, 43
O'Hagan, Minako 173
ostranenie 29
*The Oxford Dictionary of Critical
  Theory* 29

paratextual devices: source text (ST)
  analysis 23–24; translation strategy
  46–48
The Paris Apartment (Foley) 37
Pattison, Ann 12, 30, 65, 66, 68, 70, 75,
  76, 79, 82
Pellatt, Valerie 30, 65, 70, 73, 75, 79
phonetic synchrony *see* lip sync/
  synchrony
phonic/graphic level 70–71
Plan Your Visit to York 38–39
Pöchhacker, Franz 145, 150–152,
  154–155
politeness 97–98
portfolio-based assessment system 154
prescriptive translation commentaries 116
presentation 123; interpreting reflective
  report 165; reflective report 194
previous knowledge of audience/readers
  19, 43–44
profanity and taboo 99–100
proper nouns 66–67; structuring
  commentary 96
prosodic level 71
public service interpreting *see* dialogue
  interpreting

reflective report 173, 187–196;
  appropriate terminology 193;
  assessment criteria 192–196;
  audiovisual translation 188–189;
  localisation 189–190; macrolevel
  analysis 194–195; microlevel
  analysis 195–196; overview 2–3;
  presentation 194; secondary sources
  193; structure 192, 193; thematically-
  structured 187, 188–189, 190, 192;
  transcreation 190–192

Reiss, Katharina 15, 16
relationship to source text 183
relay interpreting 148
Remael, Aline 177
remote interpreting 148
respeaking *see* speech to text
  interpreting
revised published translation 115–116
role-playing games 182
romhacking 175
Russell, Debra 154

Sawyer, David B. 147, 151, 152, 154,
  159, 187
scanlation 175
secondary and theoretical sources
  122–123; interpreting reflective
  report 165; reflective report 193
self-assessment report 3
self-regulated students 3
self-regulation 3
semantic matrix 75–79; ambiguities
  76; collocations 76; denotative
  and connotative meaning 75–76;
  metaphors 77; neologisms 76;
  synonyms 76–77; technical
  terminology 77
sensitive texts 98–99
service interpreting *see* dialogue
  interpreting
sight translation 149
signed language interpreting 149
simultaneous consecutive
  interpreting 149
simultaneous interpreting 149
simultaneous interpreting with text 149
skopos 15, 39–40
social background of audience/reader
  19, 42–43
social constructivism 1, 3
social interpreting *see* dialogue
  interpreting
social register 81
sociolect 81
source culture (SC) 11
source language (SL) 35
source text (ST) analysis 9–30;
  contextual information 11–14;
  genre and text type 15–17;
  intended audience/readership
  17–21; macrolevel 15–26; medium
  of publication 21–22; microlevel
  26–30; paratextual devices 23–24;

recursiveness 24; skopos 15;
  subject matter 27–28; theme-rheme
  structure 27
space in structuring commentary 92
specialisation of audience/readers 19, 43
speech to text interpreting 149
structure 121–122; interpreting
  reflective report 164; reflective report
  192, 193
structuring commentary 91–100;
  domestication 95–96; foreignisation
  95–96; humour 94–95; matrices
  92–93; metaphors 96–97;
  multilingualism and code switching
  97; politeness 97–98; preserving
  tone and effect of ST 94; profanity
  and taboo 99–100; proper nouns
  96; sensitive texts 98–99; space 92;
  thematic structure 93
Stuart, Douglas 128
subject matter 27–28
subtitling: concept 174; skills necessary
  for 177–178; temporal synchrony 177
subtitling for the D/deaf and the hard
  of hearing (SDH): concept 175; skills
  necessary for 178–179
summative assessment 153
summative assignments 114–115
supervised commentaries 116–117
supervision 118–121; preparation for
  119–120; questions for supervisor
  120–121; time management 118–119
suprasegmental elements 29
surtitling: concept 175; skills necessary
  for 179
synchronisation 178
synonyms 76–77

taboo *see* profanity and taboo
target culture (TC) 12
target language (TL) 35
target text (TT) 10
taxonomy of techniques 67–68
technical terminology 77
temporal dialect 82
tenor (writer-reader relationship) 80
terminology 122; cultural matrix 65–66;
  interpreting reflective report 164;
  reflective report 193
text type *see* genres
thematic structure 93; audiovisual
  translation (AVT) 188–189;
  interpreting reflective report 158–159;

localisation 190; reflective report 187, 188–189, 190, 192; transcreation 192
theme-rheme structure 27
theories *see* concepts and theories
time management 118–119
Tolkien, J.R.R. 85
tone of a text 29, 94
transcreation 173, 184–187; assessment 186; reflective report 190–192; *see also* reflective report; skills required for 185–186; teaching and training 186; thematically-structured report 192; translation *vs.* 184–185; types 185; *see also* audiovisual translation (AVT)
transcreation brief 184
translation brief 33–34
translation commentary 61–87; assessment 121–126; assignment types 114–118; desirable features 63–64; examples in narrative 105–106; illustrative examples 64–86; integrating concepts and theories into 101–105; macrolevel analysis 123–124; microlevel analysis 125–126; overview 1–4; structuring 91–100; supervision 118–121; *vs.* translator's footnotes 62–63; undesirable features 63
translation strategy 33–54; genres 39–40; intended audience/readership 40–45; medium of publication 45–46; paratextual devices 46–48; skopos 39–40; technique *vs.* 35–39; text type 39–40; translation brief 33–34
Translation Studies 145
translation techniques 36
translator's footnotes *vs.* translation commentary 62–63

Turner, Jean 151
Tymczyńska, Maria 180

undesirable features of translation commentary 63

varietal matrix 79–84; dialect 81–82; diglossia 82; idiolect 82–83; language variety 80–83; multilingualism and code switching 83; social register 81; sociolect 81; temporal dialect 82; tenor (writer-reader relationship) 80
Vermeer, Hans J. 15, 16, 38–39, 52, 129
videogame localisation 182
voiceover: concept 175; skills necessary for 178
voiceover synchrony 178

Walliams, David 27–28
Watson, Casey 37, 53
When You Ask Me Where I'm Going (Kaur) 14, 44
whispered interpreting 149
Women and Enlightenment in Eighteenth-Century Britain (O'Brien) 24–26
word creators 185
The World's Worst Pets (Walliams) 27–28
writing interpreting reflective report 159–163; error-focused 160–161; good renderings and errors in 161–162; integrating theories into 162–163

Young Mungo (Stuart) 128–131

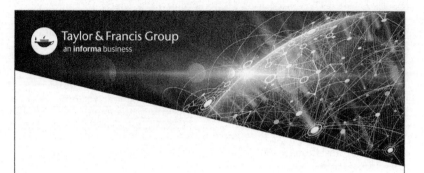

Printed in Great Britain
by Amazon

39387952R00137